Busy

HOW TO THRIVE IN A WORLD OF TOO MUCH

TONY CRABBE

piatkus

PIATKUS

First published in Great Britain in 2014 by Piatkus

A CIP catalogue record for this book
is available from the British Library.

ISBN 978-0-349-40075-4

Typeset in Bembo by M Rules
Printed and bound in Great Britain by
Clays Ltd, St Ives plc

Papers used by Piatkus are from well-managed forests
and other responsible sources.

MIX
Paper from
responsible sources
FSC www.fsc.org   FSC® C104740

Piatkus
An imprint of
Little, Brown Book Group
100 Victoria Embankment
London EC4Y 0DY

An Hachette UK Company
www.hachette.co.uk

www.piatkus.co.uk

Acknowledgements

Dad, thanks for that 'walk around the sheepfold' which saved me from a grey life of numbers and to Mum for being my foundation, my safe place (and my source of the world's best macaroni cheese). I couldn't imagine better parents, or a better childhood.

Paddy, thanks for always being the first to ask; and for endlessly encouraging me. Barry, you're an inspiration, a catalyst for me and so many others. You have both become more like friends than in-laws. Thanks for your amazing support for Dulcie, the children and me; we couldn't have got through last few years without you.

Martin, Pete, Fiona, Doug and Gerry: you're all my favourites! (Pete, by the way, this is the only bit of the book you need to read). I love you all in a rugged, manly way, and look forward to the next annual Crabbe adventure. I'm also hoping this book might create a nickname for me other than Spud!

Dame, thanks for the invite to the conference which triggered all of this; but mostly, thanks for being a good friend and co-conspiritor who really gets what I'm going through. Shiv, how could I have progressed without the chance to debate how hard it is to write with a kindred spirit? Thanks for being such a brilliant pain in the neck to keep me writing.

Dom and Kate, thanks for allowing me to drink all your tea and write the first half of this book in your garden shed/gym: it was the perfect place to write because you always made me feel welcome and at home.

Sue, Justin, Ali and Clair, thanks for selecting your partners so wisely! Dunc and Claire, for continuing to fly the flag for Yorkshire

A big thanks goes to everyone at Little, Brown. My experience of working with you has been one of real partnership. Thanks to Tim Whiting for your faith in me, and for shaping my thinking, transforming my initial ramblings into something much more valuable. To Zoe Bohm, you have been amazing as an editor; patient to the last, it's been a real pleasure working through the book with you. And to Alison Sturgeon, thanks for your copyediting, I have no idea how you did what you did with such speed and clarity; between you and Zoe, you have carved a diamond from the rough.

Jack, thanks for all those great questions and for having the courage to walk your own path: you're very special, I can learn a lot from you. Ben, thanks for skipping down the street, and for your sense of fun: you always make me smile. Seren, thanks for being such a princess, my lovely little girl: full of fire, full of cuddles. Together, the three of you make me happier than any Daddy could hope to be; you fill my life with shafts of pure joy. Thanks for being patient with me and this book. I am hugely proud of all of you: no wonder my favourite number is three!

I owe, by far and away, the biggest debt of thanks to you, Dulcie. You have carried, cajoled and motivated me through this project. Like all our schemes, this was a team effort: a yin and yang pairing of opposites bound by a common purpose. You have given up such a lot to make this book happen; you have taken on so much to make it happen too. This book would not have happened had it not been for you: not only did you make it possible by doing everything else, your smart business guidance over the years has brought me to this place; it helped me to find my own career path. I dedicate this book to you, my best friend, my soul mate, my love, my wife and my life.

Contents

Preface

BUSTING BUSYNESS

*'As the Buddha said two-and-a-half thousand years
ago ... we're all out of our fucking minds'*[1]

Albert Ellis (considered the second most influential
psychotherapist in history, 1913–2007)

How long does it take you to reach for your first shot of email each day? This is followed shortly afterwards by a coffee, and the day starts in a rush. On the way to work you utilise your time wisely, crunching through more email and messages, making the odd call. You hit work at a run, bounce from meeting to meeting, task to task; juggling, responding and executing. It feels like demand after demand; you're drowning but you mustn't show it. So you plough on, faster, head down, doing, doing, doing.

At some point you leave the office, still working you enter your home. Your family are wonderful, but a burden and distraction as well. You spend an evening of split attention, email on tap, you get irritated easily. You know, of course, that in principle you should switch off and enjoy your time with your loved ones, but you are so busy at the moment. Anyway, you're doing it for them.

You try to relax with wine and the TV and go to bed exhausted (with a final check of the phone for email). Your sleep is shallow; your brain is still working and worrying. Tomorrow you'll wake up un-refreshed.

You can't escape the feeling that you're failing as a partner, a parent and a friend; failing to keep up and perform as you'd like; failing to lead the life you'd hoped for. You've become a little hollow, a little brittle and a little helpless.

The alarm sounds and you reach for your first hit of email ...

'Busyness'

Let me start by explaining what I mean by 'busyness' (because this book is no manifesto for laziness). 'Busyness' is that frenetic, always alert, multitasking that propels us through overburdened lives. It involves being always 'on', glancing regularly at our phones and jumping from task to task. It is the juggling, cramming, and rushing that makes up so much of our daily existence. It is urgency, distraction and exhaustion.

Busyness is bad for your health

Stress has a clear biological function: it prepares us for action. In fact, it can be seen as a performance enhancer – to a degree. And stress isn't bad for us, in itself. However, for many of us, our sense of being overwhelmed causes us to push ourselves to superhuman feats of persistence and production. To get through all we have to do, we fuel ourselves with stress (and caffeine). We push, push, push ourselves to stay busy, terrified of dropping the ball; we seldom pause; we seldom recharge. We just keep on driving ourselves. The body isn't designed to be always on; it is not designed for persistent busyness. The body is designed for switching between active and passive states: to fire up into an adrenaline-fuelled, alert state; and then cool down to a calmer one. Yet the rush of busy isn't occasional, interspersed with periods of calm and quiet; busy is constant. We are flat-lining at full-speed ahead. When we don't allow this pulsing between on and off, we fail to allow ourselves to recover. This causes an 'allostatic load' – best described as accelerated wear and tear on the body and brain.

In Japan there is a word for the consequences of extreme busyness: *karoshi*, which means 'death from overwork'. *Karoshi* happens when chronic fatigue, stemming from long hours and persistent stress, leads to stroke and heart disease. For most of us, the results of a busyness-induced allostatic load are much less dramatic, but still pretty bad: being 'always on' has been linked to reductions in performance, reduced memory, and increased health risks of all kinds: cardiovascular disease, reduced immune system performance and an earlier death. One expert in the US approximated that 60-90 per cent of all visits to the doctor were stress related[2].

Yet, in our frenzy, persistent stress is on the increase globally, with 75 per cent of people in China feeling their stress has increased over the last few years and across the globe nearly half of all workers feel their stress has increased over the last year[3]. In Mexico, Russia and Brazil around 70 per cent of women claim to be stressed most of the time[4].

Busyness is bad for relationships

The first victims of busyness are those nearest and dearest to us. We assume that they will understand, so we steal our time, our attention and even our affection from them. In most cases, this theft doesn't kill our relationships with those closest to us, but it does hollow them, eating away at them from the inside. For example, in the US, 69 per cent of parents believe their stressful, busy lives have no impact on their children; yet 91 per cent of those children disagree, because they experience the yelling, absence and distraction[5]. South Koreans, who work longer hours than in any other country, are becoming too busy to have children; they have the lowest childbirth rate of all OECD countries. 'Raising children when you lead a compulsive, nervous and empty life is a problem', wrote columnist Kim Young-hwan[6]. South Koreans also lead the world in suicide rates. In India, busy parents struggle to find time with their children, with one study finding that fathers spend an average of only seven minutes a day talking to their children, mothers only 11 minutes[7].

Busyness is bad for your happiness

Underlying the drive for success through busyness is often an assumption that more money, more stuff and more status will make our lives better; that it is worth putting our values, our relationships and our health on hold while we strive to make our lives better. But this is a really dumb idea. Firstly, research has shown that achieving these goals will have very little impact on our wellbeing[8]. Secondly, the things we sacrifice – relationships, meaning and health – are the only things that can make us feel truly happy and that our lives are worthwhile. Thirdly, people who focus on external values – money, stuff and status – are less happy and less healthy than people who focus on the things that busyness kills: relationships, personal growth or contribution to your community[9].

Busyness is bad for your career

The Industrial Age was all about productivity; it was about doing things more efficiently and quicker and (ideally) better. What mattered was activity. Those that worked the hardest and most efficiently succeeded. As the amount of information, communication and therefore work has increased, so have our tools for increasing our efficiency. For the first time in history we can work whenever we want, wherever we want – and so we do. In doing so, we have become drudges, too busy to lift our heads and do the things we know will make a real difference for ourselves or our businesses. We have become commodities producing as much stuff as we can. But in a world of 'too much', it's not quantity that counts; it's probably not even quality. The thing that matters is attention and differentiation: people who are able to cut through the frenzy of activity and get noticed. This won't happen if you have your head down.

Busyness is bad for business

A recent survey of more than 1,500 CEOs across the world by IBM[10] identified that the biggest single challenge facing businesses in the coming decade is complexity, which is driven by the increasing interconnectedness of global markets. This is not the world these businesses were originally built for, where problems are dissected and analysed; where experts provide answers; where diligent workers execute long-term strategic plans; where we all know what we're doing. CEOs worry that their businesses aren't equipped to deal with a world of constant flux and interconnectivity. These are new problems that cannot be addressed by simply refining or adapting old solutions.

When the CEOs were asked what capability was most needed in order to thrive in the new market conditions, they chose a strange word – a word which has had little place in the lexicon of business: 'creativity'.

In the coming decade, the ability to respond to new challenges with genuinely novel and useful solutions will be crucial. Businesses need people to step back, imagine fresh possibilities for their business and create entirely new solutions. In short, they need people to *think*. Businesses will need people to look up from their to-do lists, to identify and solve new problems, to create disruptive solutions. The problem is, taking the time to think and imagine is the last thing that's likely to happen among a frantically busy workforce. People have too many emails to respond to, too many meetings to attend and too many objectives to deliver.

Why we think we're busy

We feel we are busy because of the demands on our time: our inbox and our to-do list are bulging, a huge amount of people expect things from us, and our organisations are trying to do more with fewer people. We tell ourselves that 'next year will be better' – more in hope than in expectation. The pressure doesn't stop when we get home, with a seemingly endless list of tasks and responsibilities awaiting us there.

Why we're really busy

- **Lack of control:** we give up our sense of control and feel helpless in the face of so many demands.
- **Lack of choice:** we are too lazy to think of alternatives; busyness seems the easiest option.
- **Lack of boundaries:** the boundaries of time and space which separated work from life are gone; we won't achieve mastery over our lives unless we learn to draw the line.
- **Lack of focus:** we focus on busyness as a success strategy, rather than on what will make an impact; because of this we fade into the background.
- **Lack of meaning:** when we become busy, we disconnect from what really matters to us; we feel empty, and we fill this emptiness with more busyness.

- **Lack of confidence:** we are anxious, so we take a defensive, busy approach rather than a more positive and individual one.
- **Lack of momentum:** we know we should live and work differently; yet days, weeks, months and years pass and we fail to make the required changes. Our lives pass us by, our relationships wither and our careers stall – not because we don't know what we need to do, but because we don't do it.

Busyness isn't essential. Yes, there is a lot to do, but believing you're always busy because you have so much to do is both false and unhelpful. Busyness is a normal response to a world of too much, but it isn't the only response.

Too much

We live in a world of too much: too much to do, too much information and too much insecurity. In the time it has taken you to read the first few paragraphs of this book, 200 million emails have been sent. In the last minute, three days' worth of content has been uploaded to YouTube. In the last second, 10 people have discovered the internet and email for the first time and are now adding to the noise. We live in an age where computing power and internet connection speeds are increasing exponentially along with sheer quantity of information, and entertainment. David Foster Wallace, the award-winning novelist and chronicler of modern life, described our environment as one of 'Total Noise'[11], in which we are constantly bombarded with the 'seething static' of limitless information, communication and choice. In this world of too much we are simultaneously overstimulated and bored; enriched and empty; connected yet isolated and alone.

For information workers, the last 20 years have felt like drinking from a water fountain that has become a fire hose. The simple fact is that, as our tools for productivity improve, we produce more. As it becomes easier to communicate, we communicate more. As the world becomes more international, more people join the global conversation. As technology increases efficiency, so organisations expect more from fewer people. As we feel more insecure, we hide behind the protective force field of our busyness. Every action we take, every email we send, has a consequence for someone else. So as we are all able to do more; we create more work for others; who in turn are doing more; which means we all have more and more demands on us.

You can't change the fact of 'too much'

The simple fact is that 'too much' is here to stay, and will worsen each year. There is an inevitability to the increase of this overload. Year on year you will receive more electronic communication, be exposed to more information and be expected to be on top of more stuff. You *will* receive even more emails next year. None of us is going to turn the technological clock back 30 years, and our organisations are unlikely to start saying 'Relax! Don't do as much work!'. We need to figure out a different response.

For the whole of human history we've been living in a world of scarcity. When there is too little, we constantly strive for more. Whether food, stuff or information, we try and get as much as we can. This applies in the workplace too. The basic principle of agriculture, manufacture and even office life has been productivity. So we play the 'More' game. At work, we assume we'll succeed by communicating more, producing more and working more. In our personal lives we feel we'll be happier by acquiring more, earning more or having more status. We're dead wrong on both counts. In a world of too much, 'More' no longer works as a strategy professionally or personally.

Beyond 'busy'

I guess it is clear by now that I want to reframe the way we talk about being 'busy'; I want to marginalise it; I want to kill 'busy' as a brand. However, I am even more interested in the positive. What does moving beyond 'busy' mean?

The opposite of being 'busy' is not relaxation, since even in much of our non-work time we skim and skip between family commitments, social media and digital consumption. The opposite of busyness in today's world is sustained, focused attention: deep engagement in conversations and activities that really matter to us.

It is taking the time to think, to amble and to plunge into the moment.

There are four essential elements to moving beyond busyness, which I explore in the four main sections of this book. They are strategies to combat split-attention busyness as well as a goal in themselves.

Mastery

Learned helplessness happens when people are continually subjected to unpleasant things over which they feel they have no control. After a while they give up trying to change or escape from the unpleasantness (even if they have the chance); all they try to do is cope, stoically. A lot of busyness is driven by a sense of helplessness; a feeling that we have no control; that everyone's doing it . . . so we just have to keep pushing on.

To move beyond busyness we have to start by regaining a sense of mastery over our lives. To do this we need to address the two main underlying causes of busy: lack of control and lack of choice. My view is that these are foundational; unless they are addressed, it is hard to move forward. This section will show you how to build a sense of control back into your life; take responsibility for making choices about how you live and what you do; and will show you how to set boundaries to protect you from the flood of demands and information.

Focus

One of the drivers of busyness stems directly from applying an Industrial-Age work ethic to a world of too much: a constant striving to increase personal productivity through more activity and efficiency. In so doing, we inadvertently prioritise doing 'stuff' ahead of focusing on the core things that will make a real difference. In a world of too much, success is not about producing more, but making an impact. As long as we play the 'More' game, we are playing the wrong game.

Thriving is more than just having a good work–life balance and not being overwhelmed. Thriving is also about succeeding in your career. This section will focus in-depth on how to succeed and will propose an alternative to busyness as a brand. It will outline three key areas of focus to move to a career strategy that doesn't rely simply on building a brand around busyness. Specifically it will address apply-ing a business strategy to your career; on using what we know about the brain to think (and focus) better; and to make more of an impact in your organisation, and so differentiate yourself.

Engagement

Busyness can cause us to disengage from the people, values and activities that are important to us. Disengagement doesn't happen suddenly. It happens as a result of a persistent lack of attention to the things that really matter to us, whether that is loved ones, values or pastimes. As we disengage, our ability to re-energise ourselves, our ability to stay positive is diminished. Disengagement is also not just an effect of busyness; it's also a cause: busyness makes us disengage, which, in turn, creates emptiness in us – which we fill with further busyness.

This section will address three key ways to re-engage with your work and life; ways to banish the greyness and bring back the colour. First it will talk about redefining success in a way that is more closely connected to your core values – what really matters to you. Then it will explain how to replace the transient buzz of busyness with the more nourishing, sustaining joy of deep engagement. Finally, in a world where we're connected to thousands of people, it will discuss which relationships really matter and how to deepen them.

Momentum

Part of the challenge in moving beyond busy is that, even if you totally agree that you should make the change, you're too busy to find the time and energy to do anything about it! In addition, change is hard; moving from good intention to sustained habit is far from automatic.

This section is dedicated to helping you get momentum work-ing for you, to make this change, creating the impetus, energy and clarity to move to a life less busy; a more focused and engaged life, where you feel the master of your own destiny.

The first step is to move beyond the fear-induced defensive busy-ness to a more progressive, positive approach where you can start to create forward momentum, with confidence. The final chapter will then share what we know from psychology about how to change behaviour: the tricks of the trade for turning good intentions into sustainable habits. It will share some concrete ideas to make lasting shifts and to get more from your willpower, so you can become less busy and more fulfilled.

It's not easy

I wrote this book because I struggle with busyness. Yes, I thought I had some ideas on the subject; I also believed there was some great research that hadn't yet been pulled together to address what is, for me, one of the biggest blights on modern life. But I really wrote the book to help myself. It is a true 'self-help' book. Busyness for me is a constant lure, a constant challenge. I have to fight to regain mastery, to focus and to engage. I persistently need to remind myself to step away from the herd and follow the subtle call of my individuality. I can't pretend to have always won the battle this year. The irony for me is that the year I wrote a book called 'Busy' has been, by far and away, my 'busiest' consulting year ever. I have been pushed to make hard choices and to really focus my time and attention. I haven't always got it right. A bit like an alcoholic who gives up drink yet remains a lifelong alcoholic, I suspect, for as long as I work, I will battle with busyness.

That may sound wearisome, but the busyness battle is a great one – and this is one of the big insights I've gained while researching and writing this book: beating busyness isn't about quick tips, or time management techniques. Most of the tips I had initially lined up to be in the book were discarded after I found they didn't help me. Beating busyness is incredibly simple, but not always easy. It is about focusing on the things that matter; on being present in the moment or with people you care for. It's about being uniquely you. To help you to make that shift, I have drawn on great research and thinking in psychology. Some of this research is directly applicable to the topic. Most of it isn't. In some cases, it is better to see the research stories as metaphors as much as evidence: I have used the research to highlight underlying psychological processes that I feel are relevant in the fight against busy, to tell stories that illustrate why we do things, and how we can respond differently. Mostly, I have used research where I think it helps generate real insight into a better way of responding in the face of too much.

Beating busyness isn't easy, but it's a fight worth having. The harder you struggle against the broiling froth of demand, the harder you resist the lure of the immediate, or the call of the ping or ring, the clearer you become about what really matters to you. Active resistance against the norm of mediocrity builds your commitment to your cause.

GETTING STARTED

Too busy to read this book?

The fact that you bought this book implies that you're busy. You're possibly also feeling overwhelmed, like a pressure cooker about to explode. If that is the case, how on earth do you make time to read this book, let alone apply the principles I discuss? So here are 12 simple suggestions to let off some of that steam. They will help you to do less, do things quicker, or feel more in control. These suggestions will not solve the underlying problem, but they should help you to create enough space and time to read, digest and apply the deeper strategies that will make a real difference to your life.

1. Use the word 'because'

There is a magic to the word 'because'. Research by Ellen Langer, Professor of Psychology at Harvard University, found that simply using the word 'because' in a request doubles the likelihood that you will get what you want[1]. In this study, the word 'because' didn't need to be followed by anything meaningful; just including the word 'because' makes the listener respond as though there must be a good reason.

Doing less work often starts with influencing people around us. Whether you are saying 'no' to a request, or explaining why you will be leaving work on time (rather than at 8.00pm), or asking permission to delay the deadline for a piece of work, if you include 'because' your argument will be seen as more rational and acceptable.

2. Switch off

The brain is not built for constant busyness. One very small, but interesting study into the impact of being 'always on' (via phone and email) at the University of London suggested that it can reduce IQ as much as smoking cannabis or losing a night's sleep[2]. While we can't draw too many conclusions from the above study, we do know the brain needs its down time. Gary Small, Professor of Psychiatry at UCLA, comments that, while there can be a short-term buzz from being hyper-connected, long-term it can lead to depression and impaired cognition.

Give your brain a break; be deliberate and intentional when you 'check in' on mail and messages. Set specific times aside to do it in a focused way, rather than constantly grazing . . . and certainly don't check email just before bed (the world will survive without you for a few hours!).

3. Turn off the notifier

Research into office workers has found that they hopscotch between tasks, changing activity on average every three minutes[3]. Whenever we switch tasks the brain needs to re-orientate itself to the new rules of the game. David Meyer, Professor of Psychology at the University of Michigan, suggests that jumping backwards and forwards between even just two tasks increases the time taken for overall completion by up to 40 per cent.

One of the biggest culprits for gratuitous task-switching is the email or IM notifier. How many of us can resist the allure of the 'ping' that announces a new message from the world out there? Yet in taking a peek, we distract ourselves and reduce our efficiency. In recognition of this phenomenon, Microsoft have built an internal app called 'Thinking time', which allows staff to turn off all their email, IMs and VOIP (online calls) for a specified amount of time to allow them to think.

4. Kill a meeting

Meetings are a major source of busyness. They are on the increase, and have been increasing steadily in frequency and duration since the 1960s. Some surveys show that middle managers can spend up to 50 per cent of their time in meetings[4]. Yet, the value of many of these meetings is questionable. One study performed a careful value analysis of 7,000 managers in a major company and found that poor planning and management of meetings was costing the business $54 million annually[5]. American multinational, 3M, estimated the inefficiency of their middle-manager meetings was costing them $79 million annually[6]. Interestingly, there may be additional *indirect* costs: Michael Doyle and David Straus, authors of the bestselling book *How to Make Meetings Work*[7], have identified something they call 'meeting recovery syndrome' – the time it takes to regain our focus and composure following a (rubbish) meeting.

So, do yourself and your organisation a favour: kill a meeting this week. Identify at least one meeting that you can either cancel or simply not attend.

5. Think of the time … and double it

How do you establish whether you will be able to do something? We think about how long it will take, about all the things we already have on our plate, and we make a judgement; and we get it wrong, persistently. To show this, one study asked college seniors students to estimate when they would finish their thesis[8]. They were also asked to estimate when fellow students would finish, many of whom they didn't know too well. Students massively underestimated when they would finish their own work, but pretty accurately judged the completion date for colleagues. This is something known in psychology as the Planning Fallacy. We overestimate how much we can do; endowing ourselves with greater intellectual and focusing capabilities than we really have, and ignore all the contextual factors that could get in our way.

So, next time you are asked to do something, assess how much 'spare time' you have for this task given all your other commitments; then halve it. Next assess how long you think this new task will take; then double it. Now you can make a better-informed judgement over whether to take it on.

6. Watch the clock

How much work do you get through on the day before you go on holiday? Loads, I imagine. Research shows that when we are more aware of time, such as just before a holiday, we are significantly more productive[9]. So the suggestion is simple, if you want to crunch through a lot of stuff in a short amount of time, make yourself more aware of time. For example, get a very big clock and put it where you can see it easily, or set little alarms for every 30 minutes: it will feel like time is expanding!

7. Finish on time

Do you have a spare room? Is it empty? The fact is, there is something inherent in human nature that, when given space, we fill it[10]. Giving yourself a clear time to finish (whether a deadline for a project, or a time to leave work) helps in two ways. Firstly, as suggested above, it raises our time awareness, creating a goal. Secondly, it stops us creating space and time in our diaries, because things will always fill up that time.

8. Start quicker

In 1927, a Gestalt psychologist called Bluma Zeigarnik was sitting in a Vienna coffee house with a group of friends. They ordered a few rounds of drinks, yet the waiter never wrote down their order. Zeigarnik was intrigued by this, and, after the bill was paid and the group had left the coffee house, she returned. On questioning the waiter, she found that he could no longer recall what drinks had been ordered by her group. One way of interpreting this is that the brain works with open and closed 'files'. Once the bill had been paid, the waiter closed the file and forgot it. This has become known as the Zeigarnik effect (and people tend to be twice as likely to remember things in open files than in closed ones).

You can use the Zeigarnik effect to get started more quickly (and procrastinate less) by 'opening your file' on a subject early. The things we normally procrastinate over are the big, difficult or creative tasks, but you can overcome this tendency by opening the file on a job a few days before you actually need to begin the work. In practice, this simply involves starting work on the problem for about 20 minutes, possibly in the form of a mind map. Then leave your subconscious to work its magic; when you finally begin the task in earnest, your thinking and ideas will really flow.

9. Clear your head

I recently changed my life – well, the performance of my computer anyway! It drives me crazy when my laptop starts to get slower and slower, freezing and crashing. So I wiped the hard drive and re-installed everything. In essence I cleansed the system of all the unwanted software and cookies. In doing this, I freed up the processor to focus all its power on what I actually want it to do. It's now working perfectly again.

The brain works very similarly. We have a very limited processing power at any time. Any thoughts, worries or ideas that you're holding onto are reducing your processing speed. So don't. I read David Allen's book *Getting Things Done*[11] and the thing that made a real difference for me was this: create a brain dump. Find a way of getting things out of your head, of cleansing your system. For most people this means capturing things in either a notebook or their smartphone. There are three crucial elements to this. First, whatever you use to record ideas should always be with you. Second, don't try to analyse or sort things as you capture them (because that's distracting you from your current task) – simply write them down. Third, make a habit of going through your brain-dump list regularly (for me this is once a day). It's amazing how liberating it is to be able to get stuff out of your head, with the confidence it will be dealt with.

10. Hold on a minute

Imagine every time you put your shoes on, you had to work out how to tie your laces, as if for the first time. You wouldn't achieve much. Fortunately, with most things, once we have learned how to do them, the process is submitted to memory and it becomes a simple ritual. This automation is one of the core capabilities of the brain. However, it can sometime leave us doing things ineffectively. Mental processing has been split into System One (automatic, fast, intuitive, easy) and System Two (conscious, slow, rational and hard). When we are busy, we rely more strongly on System One automation, racing into the task following the normal pattern of activity.

How often have we wasted hours or weeks of work because we didn't think things through before we started? It isn't simply a question of planning; it's also about re-creating. It's about taking a moment to challenge the process, the purpose or the outcome before diving in. As an incredibly simple example of this, I recently realised I was spending hours a week writing proposals and reports for clients. I steadfastly refuse to write 'standard' reports because that goes against my business principles. So I took a minute to ask myself, 'Is there another way?' The solution was obvious – once I took the time to look for it: I changed my reports from Word documents to PowerPoint presentations; increased the visuals, and decreased the word count by about 80 per cent. Clients loved them, and I have saved hours a week.

How could you take a minute to save hours?

11. Take a (good) break

We all know we should take a break every now and then, but do some breaks make more of a difference than others?

There is an old saying, 'a change is as good as a rest'; but research suggests 'a change *is* a rest'[12]. Breaks are costly if you are incredibly busy; they rob us of time when we have precious little to give. So, if you are going to take a break (and I, of course, suggest you do), make sure it's a valuable one. Make it different to what you've been doing: scatter when you have been focused; be physical if you've been stuck in your head; have a rambling chat if you've been silently producing; and be careful about more coffee if you're already revved up!

12. . . . and smile

Busy is not just a fact, it's also an experience. We get into spirals of activity; we feel under pressure, so we rush, which makes us feel under pressure . . . The final quick fix is simple: don't take it all too seriously! Wear your life more lightly. There is a ridiculousness to much in ourselves and our lives; we notice this with startling clarity at times of major crisis, but are blind to it for most of our lives. We see only the calamitous consequences of non-delivery in our immediate lives, and, as Harvard psychologist Daniel Gilbert has found, we see our possible future through the rosiest possible glasses. So, caught between immediate fear and future hope, we get deadly serious (and a little dull).

Why don't you smile instead? Smiling is good for you: it reduces stress, lowers blood pressure and releases endorphins. As Ron Gutman, founder and CEO of HealthTap, announced in his TED (Technology, Entertainment, Design) talk[13], a single smile stimulates the brain as much as 2,000 chocolate bars, or as much as receiving £16,000. People think you are more competent and remember you better when you smile. You may even live longer if you smile more: in one of my favourite studies, those players on old baseball cards who weren't smiling in their profile photo lived, on average, 72.9 years; those with a little smile lived 75 years; but those who were beaming lived 79.9 years[14]!

Yet only a third of adults smile more than 20 times a day (20 times less than children). No matter how much stuff you have to do, you may feel less busy if you smile ☺.

Section One

MASTERY

You are not busy because there is too much to do. It is true, there is too much to do. It is also true that this will never change, and in fact, in the exponential world we live in, it is certain that next year you will have more coming at you than this year. If we start from the assumption, as I do, that we can't get it all done, then we have to ask ourselves what makes us keep trying to achieve the impossible.'

My answer is that we don't have mastery over our lives. I don't say we have 'relinquished mastery' because I'm not sure we ever had it. Before 'too much' we could allow our environment to dictate our activity and attention, because our environment was limited, and had natural boundaries between work and non-work. Now we have handed mastery of our lives to the world of too much, via our smartphones and other screens; and it's a merciless dictator.

Every generation has challenges it must resolve. The challenge facing us all today is how we learn to gain mastery over the infinite, the endless and the ceaseless. How do we regain a sense of control when we can no longer control our environment? How do we make choices in the face of limitless possibilities? These are the questions we must wrestle with to gain mastery. These are the questions addressed in the section.

Learned helplessness

In a University of Pennsylvania laboratory back in 1967 some unfortunate dogs were being trained using electric shocks. While observing them, Martin Seligman, now Professor of Psychology and the founder of the field of positive psychology, noticed something unexpected[1]. Typically you would expect any sensible dog to seek to avoid the pain of an electric cattle prodder if possible. Yet, after repeated shocks, the dogs appeared to give up trying to escape from the pain, even when they had the opportunity: they simply lay down and whined. Why would they do that?

This observation led Seligman to develop the concept of *learned helplessness*. At times, humans, as well as animals, seem to give up any attempt to change their situation. They accept their role as victims and their total inability to do anything about it. Their only coping strategy is to be stoical, putting up with the pain or unpleasantness with the minimum fuss possible.

I see this attitude in many people I work with today. They recognise they are too busy, yet they don't feel they can do anything about it. They may feel they have little control over their lives; they may not feel they have a choice; or they may be crippled by fear and anxiety. Whatever the cause, they become helpless and give up any hope of making a change. Any energy they exert is to help cope with – not change – their situation: revving up with caffeine, cooling down with alcohol; 'vegging' in front of the TV with a pizza or chocolate; hot baths and candle ... Silently they anaesthetise themselves into inactivity, explaining to anyone who will listen (and most of all themselves) that there is no other way.

Embrace opportunity

The sense of being overwhelmed can paralyse us from making tough choices. When we are stretched and exhausted, we don't have the energy to risk doing things differently. Busy becomes the natural response when we have a lot to do; it is the choice-free option, since it is the social norm; and it appears to be a low-risk choice.

However, we lose a lot when we opt for the 'safe' option of busy. The world of 'too much' is also one of amazing opportunity; we live at a time in history where we have more options open to us than at any other time in history. When we are hunkered down in our protective shell of busyness it's hard to grasp these chances. As we allow ourselves to feel victims in the face of exponentially increasing demands, we take the obvious, busy path of greyness and close our eyes to more exciting, more rewarding and more important options. When we achieve mastery over our lives again, we will be able to chart our own course despite being busy. Mastery is about taking a positive approach to a world of abundant opportunity; not helplessly coping with a world of too much.

Chapter 1

Feel more in control

On August 17, 2000, Darrick Doerner was riding his Jet Ski in some of the roughest, most dangerous waves in the world: Tahiti's Teahupo'o break. Described as a freak of hydro-dynamics, Teahupo'o creates waves of almost unimaginable power and ferocity – pummelling tubes of water which crash onto a shallow, razor sharp reef. You might think Doerner was nuts, but what about the man he was towing behind him! Laird Hamilton, his feet strapped to a surfboard, was being accelerated onto a wave that was too big and too fast to catch without a tow, a wave that even to a veteran of big wave surfing was a once in a lifetime phenomenon. Doerner realised the wave was deadly and turned to shout, 'Don't let go of the rope,' only to see that Hamilton had already released it.

Hamilton raced down the face of the wave, keeping just ahead of the collapsing barrel. The wave was so potent, he started to get sucked up the wave. Surfers often drag their forward hand in the water for balance; in this case, balance wasn't what he needed, he needed to avoid climbing to the treacherous, collapsing crest. In the moment, Hamilton improvised, sticking his trailing hand in the water to slow his rise, and safely rode out the monster. As the wave collapsed Hamilton disappeared, seemingly caught in the explosion, only to emerge, after agonising moments, still standing.

When a photo of Hamilton on this wave appeared on the cover of *Surfer* magazine, it ran with the simple caption 'oh my god … '.

Hamilton had just surfed the heaviest wave ever ridden. It is commonly accepted that this ride affected the course of surfing history. It changed the collective perception of what is possible in surfing and secured Laird Hamilton's reputation as the greatest big-wave rider of all time.

Like the waves at Teahupo'o, the information tsunami leaves us feeling insignificantly small and powerless. There was a time, in the not so distant past, when 'being on top of things' was not only realistic, but expected. Those days are gone. We have to let go of our fantasy of getting back in control through better organisation; there is just too much information and too many demands on us. Buffeted by wave after wave of demands, we become overwhelmed, defeated and even begin to feel guilty. Accept it; you will never, ever be in control of everything again.

However, you could *feel* a greater sense of control by adopting a different mental model – a new way of thinking about control that's more suited to a world of too much. The control that I'm talking about is less like that of the meticulous wedding planner, managing everything like clockwork, and more like Laird Hamilton, skilfully and joyfully carving out a great ride in the face of Poseidon's might. Facing the full force of the ocean's power, Hamilton was never going to control that wave, but neither was he overwhelmed by it.

Control is important. In one study, elderly residents of a care home were given some influence over their environment: they could make three choices about their furniture or what was in their bedroom. In the group with this extra level of control, the number of deaths was halved! The link between control and demands was shown by Robert Karasek, (now Professor of Work Environment at the University of Massachusetts, Lowell) back in 1979[1]. Simply put, if we feel in control when we have a lot of demands on us, we experience a lot less stress than if we feel we have little control. Control is also linked to optimism and the feeling that we will be able to manage, and thrive.

This chapter explores how to meet 'too much' with a different response to that suited for previous generations. It will help you to identify where control can come from, and explain how to rebuild a sense of control over your life, so you can take the first step back towards mastery. It will walk through three strategies for changing your response so that you feel more in control: how to let go of your desire to control the uncontrollable; how to move from a sense of drowning to deep immersion; and how to feel more control in the face of chaos. Collectively, these strategies can help you to start to enjoy the ride again.

Letting go

'By letting it go it all gets done. The world is won by those who let it go. But when you try and try, the world is beyond the winning. When I let go of what I am, I become what I might be.' Lao Tzu

In the case of busy people, learned helplessness creeps in when everything we try seems to leave us in the same place: overwhelmed and struggling to keep our heads above water. How many different time-management techniques, new systems or pieces of technology have you adopted in order to get back in control? How many nights have you worked late to try to catch up? Yet nothing we do seems to bring our work and our lives back into control for anything more than a short period. Disillusioned that our responses are not changing the outcome, we go into coping mode: we put our heads down and struggle on; victims of 'too much', we become controlled by our environment. It's time to let go of your dependence on inputs. Let them wash by you, and instead focus on your outputs.

Inputs and outputs

I like to keep things simple by viewing the demands of modern life in terms of 'inputs' and 'outputs'. To describe the stuff that comes your way in the form of tasks, information and expectations, I'll use the word 'inputs'. These include emails, meeting invites and delegated tasks. 'Outputs', on the other hand, are the things you do. Many of us find our outputs are driven by our inputs. Think how much of your daily activity at work is driven by inputs: you respond to emails because they have been sent to you; you attend meetings because you have been invited; you join a project because you were asked. Time and again I hear clients describe the causes of their actions from an external perspective. Their outputs are primarily an attempt to get on top of their inputs. This is the wrong approach for three reasons:

1 We have absolutely no control over the demands that hit us. Since we have no control over these, and can never control them, why should we feel held to ransom by them?
2 In an exponential world, the inputs will continue to increase, but your ability to do it all will not. So at some point you will fail or collapse. Like the surfer, we might watch in wonder as the waves roll by us, but the quantity or frequency of the waves shouldn't worry us. We should simply consider which ones we want to catch.
3 Your inputs are relatively random; unprioritised, they have little or no connection to what you hope to achieve. We have to lose the direct connection between the quantity of demands thrown at us and the quantity of our response; we have to let go of our input dominance.

Laird Hamilton's ride didn't start, it couldn't start, until he let go. It was the simplest thing to do: all he did was open his fingers. Yet, it wasn't a natural act to let go of the relative safety of a motorised tow to drop into the abyss. Letting go in a world of too much is essential and it is simple; but it takes optimism.

Staying optimistic

In the shock experiment about a third of the dogs who had no control did not develop learned helplessness[2]. Apparently they didn't lose hope because they had what in psychological literature is called a different 'explanatory style' (though don't ask me how they tested that in dogs!). In simple language, our explanatory style determines how we explain events to ourselves. Those dogs with a different explanation had a different response.

Building on his work around learned helplessness, Martin Seligman started to look on the bright side and began exploring subjects such as optimism. This gave birth to the field of positive psychology. The essential difference between optimists and pessimists, he found, was the way they explained experiences and events. The optimist would explain good things as being due to themselves and their actions; bad things they would see as caused by external factors such as chance or other people. Pessimists, on the other hand, would blame bad things on their personal failings, and good things would be seen as down to chance or because of other people[3].

When you can't do everything, you might feel you are to blame in some way. You might explain the cause of this failure as being you: your lack of time-management skills, effort or ability. Our organisations help us to reinforce these beliefs (subtly and often not explicitly); it's our fault, we should be more efficient and better organised. I don't agree.

A healthier, more optimistic explanation of this would be to recognise the reality of the situation: the quantity of inputs is entirely beyond your control; you can do nothing about it. There is an external cause of our inability to get on top: we can't do everything because there is simply too much to do. Full stop.

You are not to blame for too much, so you should let go of your guilt for not doing it all. It's not your fault.

Acting 'as if'

If you recognise a tendency to allow too much of your activity, time and attention to be dominated by inputs rather than outputs, what can you do? No matter how convincingly I've argued my case about the way you should respond to inputs, and even if you agree intellectually, I am unlikely to have shifted your deep-seated beliefs or fears, formed and reinforced over a lifetime. These underlying beliefs are not always conscious, and they are pretty resistant to change. Yet these beliefs drive your choices and actions. To change behaviour, we often need to go beyond compelling arguments: we have to shift the deeper beliefs; to shift these beliefs, it helps to change behaviour!

People often think the way to change behaviour is to alter beliefs first, but I find that often the best way to shift behaviour in the longer term is to act 'as if' your deep beliefs were already aligned with the shift you want to make.

There is a concept in social psychology called cognitive dissonance, which describes our desire for consistency between our various beliefs, or between our beliefs and actions. So, if we consistently act in a particular way, it is cognitive dissonance which shifts our beliefs to align with our actions. Let's imagine you were trying to choose between a Ford Focus and a Seat Ibiza. You carefully weigh up the pros and cons of both choices. In the end, you still believe that both cars are equally suited to you. Even though you have no clear preference, you pick one. Over the coming months, you get into your Seat Ibiza every day; this behaviour tells your brain that you have a strong preference for the Seat, so your brain responds: in a short while you find it hard to imagine you ever even considered a Focus! Our beliefs fall in line with our behaviour. The brain reasons thus: if I really believe that the Focus is as good as the Ibiza, why am I getting into an Ibiza every day? Since the action seems inconsistent (to the brain at least) with a belief that both cars are equally good options, a tension is created. It's at this point that cognitive dissonance kicks in; it shifts your belief to resolve the tension between your actions and your beliefs. Hey presto – in no time you think the Focus is rubbish.

Following this reasoning, if we want to change behaviour sustainably, behaviour that is driven by underlying beliefs, we might do worse than to start acting 'as if' we currently held the desired beliefs. So what might you do if you were acting 'as if' inputs should not drive your daily activity? What would you do differently if you accepted that you couldn't do it all, and that doing it all is counterproductive for your career and your happiness? What would you do differently if you genuinely believed that you would add most value by focusing on what you wanted to achieve, what you thought was most important?

When I ask these questions of clients I get some common (and obvious) responses such as:

- I would only turn on my email twice a day.
- I would not turn my email on, or listen to voicemails, for the first few hours every day.
- I would work from home once a week to avoid distraction.
- I would reduce the number of meetings I go to.

What would your answer be?

What matters is not the originality of the ideas, but that whatever you identify is simple and that you *do* it; repeatedly. The importance of this might not be obvious straight away, but by making a commitment you are slowly retraining your prioritisation system away from input dominance; you're slowly extracting yourself from the hypnotic pull of reactivity.

Moving from drowning to immersion

When Laird Hamilton let go of the rope and dropped onto that wave, he wasn't worrying about his inbox, or his board-shaping business, or what he would buy for dinner that night. He was focused, 100 per cent, on the moment, on the task at hand; he wasn't drowning, he was completely immersed in his surfing. By contrast, when we are busy, we are drowning in the endless stuff that makes up our complex reality. We are lost in the multitude of tasks and demands hitting us; dominated by inputs. We are scattered, our attention jumping from one thing to the next as we try to stop ourselves from drowning in the hurly burly of modern life.

If we stop and reflect on what causes us to feel out of control, in most cases it isn't that we can't get on top of our inbox. It is that all the activity we undertake to get on top of our inbox drives out the time to do the things that matter to us. Busyness is bad, but that doesn't mean incredibly full and active lives are bad. Many of us have a lot of things we want to achieve, and which will only be delivered with hard work. However, there is a huge difference between a deep focus on an important activity, and hopscotching busyness. It's not a quantity thing, it's a quality thing; scattered attention, doing trivial stuff rather than things that really matter is bad. Days and lives crammed with deep immersion in projects, interactions and experiences that are truly meaningful to you are what life's about.

From input-dominated to output-focused

Control is found in what we choose to do – our outputs – not from our inputs. How many times have you arrived at work, full of ideas and of good intentions to get your teeth into work that will make a real difference? How many times has your focus been dissipated, your intention battered into submission, through the simple act of opening your email? The contents of your inbox are setting the agenda, not because they're the right thing to focus on, but because they're in your inbox.

In the previous section I suggested we learn to let go of input dominance. Clearly we shouldn't ignore all demands for activity driven by external causes; I am just suggesting a rebalancing. The starting point, and primary driver for activity, should be internal: 'what do I want to achieve?'

I have said that we learn to become optimistic in the face of too much by accepting that we are not to blame when we can't do it all. We *should*, however, blame ourselves if we allow our outputs to be externally driven. The inputs are not your choice; what you do, your outputs, *are* your choice. We are right to feel guilty when we get to the end of a day and have failed to work on what is important. We should feel responsible for an unremitting proactive focus on what we want to achieve. As for the endless demands thrown at us by the world, we should respond to these, at specific times of our choosing; but, if you want to feel in control, it should be you who sets the agenda, not them.

Getting in the zone

The single biggest concern of sports psychology is helping athletes get into that state of peak performance in which they feel totally focused: 'the zone'. When athletes are 'in the zone' they are operating at their best because they are entirely wrapped up in the activity. However, this is not always easy to achieve: athletes can get distracted by the excitement of an event, by the spectators or by personal performance anxieties. In the same way we, in our daily lives, are routinely dragged out of an optimal state by a multitude of distractions: the ping of a text, the lure of the inbox, the conversation at the nearby desk.

So how do we get more immersed more frequently? How do we get into the zone? Dr Daniel Gucciardi and Associate Professor James Dimmock from the University of Western Australia, experts in mental toughness in sport, have studied performance under pressure in professional golfers. They asked one group of golfers to focus on three specific aspects of their swing such as 'head', 'shoulders', 'knees' (. . . and 'toes'?); another they got to focus on a single, all-encompassing aspect of their performance that they wanted to achieve, such as 'smooth' or 'effortless'. When not under pressure, both groups performed strongly (they were professionals after all!). However, performance differed strongly when pressure was applied in the form of cash prizes. The pros who were concentrating on three aspects of their swing started faltering; those with a simpler focus continued to perform well[4].

The enemy of 'the zone' is the breaking of our concentration by pressure, thoughts or external influences. Focusing on specific aspects of the swing, we might think, would help this by keeping our attention on the activity. However, when we are under pressure, this requires too much cognitive effort, and we stall. We get lost in the mental jump between 'head' and 'shoulders'. We think of too much, we start drowning and we lose immersion.

To remain fully immersed in what you're doing, you need to maintain a simple focus. This can take a number of forms. Most obviously, it's about focusing on one thing at a time. This might sound obvious and easy, but I come across few enough people in work today who do only one thing at a time. However, it's also about maintaining a focus on the 'how'. Thinking about a single aspect of your performance within a task, one that stretches you, appears to be just enough cognitive demand to accelerate you into the zone. For example, focus on making the next presentation you put together 'beautiful', or focus on making a report 'surprising'. Focus simply and immerse yourself in the task you're facing.

Limit your focus

I once had a tennis lesson with an unusually wise coach. He told me he would fix my serve in 10 minutes. Of course I didn't believe him. He got me standing in position ready to serve, and showed me how and where to throw the ball. He had me practise this for a few minutes. Then he got me to move to the position my body should be in at the end of the service motion. He got me to move repeatedly from the starting position to the ending position. He didn't want me to go through the full motion: I didn't have to swing my racket at all. Just starting position and ending position. He told me my job was simply to focus on throwing well and getting to the end position. I should consider everything else in the serve to be what the I Ching refers to as the Ten Thousand Things: they'll take care of themselves. He went on to explain, the biggest reason people struggle with technique is they focus on too many things. His lesson worked; unbelievably. Following his five minutes of bizarre coaching, my serve was better than it had ever been.

I have learned that I can immerse myself best when I bookend activities. I think very hard about how I'll start, and where I want to get to. Once I am clear of my end point, the rest seems to take care of itself.

When you think about the next chunky task you want to address, ask yourself:

- How will I start?
- And where do I want to get to/what do I want to achieve?

The rest will take care of itself in a blur of focused immersion.

Play to your strengths

What gives surfers a sense of control on a wave? It's their skill. What helps them to stay totally immersed and focused? It's that they are practising that skill. Ask yourself, which subjects did you enjoy most at school? If you were good at sports, you'd probably say PE; if you were always the last person to be picked for a team, you probably hated it. The point I'm making here is that when we use our strongest skills, we enjoy ourselves, become immersed in what we're doing and feel more in control.

In a famous study by Gallup (the data-driven news website), researchers found that employees in large corporations use their key strengths less than 20 per cent of their time at work. I meet people all the time whose primary focus and concern seems to be organisation or time management. These are talented people, with great capability, crippled by a desire to execute in order to get it all done. They judge themselves, and feel they are judged by others, only on their efficiency and productivity – on how much they do and how fast they do it. It feels like judging a Ferrari on the basis of its fuel consumption.

What are you great at? It might sound odd, but you're unlikely to regain a sense of control by getting quicker and slicker. You'll get it from immersing yourself in activities that allow you to make the greatest contribution – to your organisation, to your family, to the world – that you are capable of.

Look at your life and work, at the pockets of time when you are doing something you really excel at. If you want more immersion, if you want more control, your task is not to organise yourself better so that you create more time to do what you are good at; it is simply to use your strengths and skills more, to choose activities that allow this. Do what you're best at and the rest will take care of itself.

Clear your mind

Working life today can be a little like walking across a paintball zone (only a little less painful). Inputs hit you, splat! The file bursts open, and because you don't have time to do everything immediately, your brain starts churning over loads of pieces of unfinished business, skittering from task to task, worrying over forgetting any of the open files. This happens because of something I've already touched on: the Zeigarnik effect (see p. 6). When a file is open, it is in active use; when it's closed it's out of your consciousness. Carrying open files creates a burden; it makes you feel like you're out of control. But how to avoid it when those paintball pellets are hitting you from every direction? Surely the only way to stop the churning is to close all the files by completing all the work?

One of the characteristics of feeling out of control is the 'churn': the relentless washing-machine spin of thoughts, mental checklists and fears. It feels terrible, it's exhausting, and it won't surprise you to know it reduces your thinking power and ability to fully immerse yourself in important tasks. It's easy to mistake this churn as a natural consequence of having too much on – one that won't go away until we're back on top, having done it all. In fact, that's not why we churn. More importantly, there is a simple cure for churning.

A graduate student from Florida State University, working with psychologist Roy Baumeister, came up with an interesting little study[5]. He asked some students to think about their final exams and others, the control group, to think about an important party at the end of term. Among those who thought about the exam, half were also told to make specific plans for their study regime. Nobody was given any time to actually study.

He then tested the students to see what open files they were carrying. He gave each person word fragments to complete. For example, subjects were asked to complete 'ex**' and 're**' into four letter words. Each of these could be completed to form a study-relevant word (exam, read), but could also be completed to form a totally different word (exit, real). We would expect more study-relevant words from those people who had begun churning over their exams, because a relevant file had been opened. This was very much the case: those with exams on their minds identified a lot more exam-related words than those who had been tasked with thinking about a party. However, those who had thought about the exam, but subsequently made a study plan, showed no evidence of open files, the words they identified were no more exam-related than those who were thinking about the party. They had stopped churning.

This experiment, and subsequent similar studies, shows us that we've been interpreting the Zeigarnik effect incorrectly. We thought that files would remain mentally 'open' until the work had been completed. It turns out we don't need to do the work; we just need a plan.

The starting point to massively reducing your churning is to catch yourself doing it – and stop. Take a few minutes to write down a plan of action. Additionally, rather than waiting for the churn to hit, many people I work with develop a discipline to write a plan at certain times of the day, the most common being when they arrive at work or just before they leave. Writing a simple plan doesn't take long, but it's the most powerful technique we know for closing those files and freeing your mind to focus on more pro-ductive matters.

Successful surfers immerse themselves 100 per cent in the moment; this allows them to control and enjoy the ride. Simple plans can free your mind of the intellectual flotsam and jetsam that fractures attention, dissipates energy and prohibits immersion. Free your mind and you'll regain a feeling of control.

Immersion needs recovery

What causes the rhythm of your pulse? The heart muscle contracts, sending blood all around the body, then relaxes. All muscles work this way, they are designed for bursts of activity followed by a period of rest. You will realise how rubbish muscles are at sustained, continuous effort if you have ever tried that exercise where you have to hold your arms outstretched and unmoving for as long as you can. It gets pretty uncomfortable pretty quickly. Muscles come into their own when we put them through periods of intense stress, followed by a period of recovery. This is what we do when we go to the gym; we rip up then repair. Using muscles all the time, without recovery, is as bad for them as not using them at all.

The same is true of our brain: it works best under periods of stress followed by recovery time. For an image of the most optimal way to use your brain (or body, for that matter), picture a heart-beat monitor that shows the peaks and troughs, activity and recovery, ebb and flow of the human heart. Yet our busy lives these days are anything other than pulses of activity. For many of us, our experience from the moment we rise to the moment we sleep, is one, long, steady state of busyness – like a flat line on a heart monitor. We tell ourselves we have too much to do to allow ourselves any pause, or any change of gear. It's easier to plough on, flat-lining our way to exhaustion.

However, if flat-lining simply led to exhaustion, it wouldn't be so bad. I explained in the introduction how being 'always on' makes you more stupid, it reduces your creativity and your ability to solve problems. It also builds an allostatic load. 'Allostasis' is the process by which the body activates its neural and chemical systems for threatening and stressful situations. Allostasis is a necessary and beneficial thing to help us escape predators and fight our enemies. It increases heart rate and the body generates stress hormones, which have a host of effects including an increased alertness. This is all good in small doses but not as the steady-state response to too much. When we remain in a heightened state of alertness and arousal fed by demand and stimulation, when we don't allow our systems and organs to fire up, then cool down, we wear our body and our brains down. We place an allostatic load on our systems which damages our health, happiness and intellect.

To gain a sense of control, the last thing you need to do is stay alert and immersed 100 per cent of the time. If you try to maintain a pulse-free busyness, you will be less able to immerse yourself, you will perform less well and feel less well. Instead you need to think of your days as being intense pulses of focus and stress, followed by recovery. These pulses of activity can be 90 minutes. The recovery periods allow your body to relax and your attentional systems to regroup. These breaks can provide a rhythm, a beat to your day; bouncing you along, energised and immersed (and maybe even whistling). Regaining a sense of control can be less about adjusting the quantity of activity, and more about altering the shape of your graph from a flat line to a pulse. Creating pulses not only makes you feel better, it will help you immerse yourself more deeply and increase your sense of control.

Four things to change

There are four things you should do to optimise your recovery periods ready for the next burst of activity.

Movement	Attention
If you have been physically passive during your period of activity, the first thing to do is to move. Change your actual pulse; get out of your head and into your body for a few minutes. Walk, do some stretches, climb some stairs. Anything that put your body into motion.	For simplicity, think of attention as being of two types: focused, intentional attention and meandering, mind-wandering attention. If you have been focused during your period of activity, you should de-focus during your breaks (more on this in Chapter 5). If you have been staring at your screen, turn away (switching to Google searches or Facebook during your breaks gives the brain little opportunity to recover).
Emotion	**Fuel**
A great way to recover quickly is to change your emotional tone. Use music, conversation or activity to change your vibe. (More of this later in the chapter)	Boost your energy with water and food. About half the population walk around with mild to chronic levels of dehydration so make sure you drink some water. You should also try to eat low glycemic foods, such as nuts and beans, which release energy more slowly.

Rituals

Have you ever noticed that some tennis players perform elaborate rituals between points; getting a towel, adjusting their strings, bouncing the ball three times, etc., etc.? Jim Loehr and Tony Schwartz[6] explored these rituals and found that the very best players used these rituals to serve a powerful purpose. By performing a repeated ritual in those 15-20 seconds between points, they were able to reduce their heart rate by 15–20 beats per minute. Imagine the performance benefit of being able to do that every point!

Recovery is important, but it doesn't need to take a long time if we develop rituals. Like in the example above, rituals are a way of switching off quickly. The best way to describe this is the advice that people are given if they have trouble sleeping: develop a routine before bed. The best sleepers, without thinking, have a ritual they perform at bedtime, which might involve what they do before getting into bed, or the side of the bed they lie on. Each step of that ritual signals to the brain that it's sleep time, so they fall asleep more quickly. When we take breaks from work, we feel the benefits more quickly and more powerfully if we identify activities which help us to disconnect from what we were doing and perform those activities in a ritualised or repeatable way. The ritual nature of the activity trains the brain to recognise its switch off time and so it switches off quicker.

Another useful dimension to rituals is their predictability which makes them easier to stick to. In some work with the Boston Consulting Group, hard-working consultants were practically forced to take planned breaks[7]. Typically they took one night off a week, no matter how busy they were. Even this small step caused alarm in the consultants, they were afraid that they would disappoint clients, that their work would pile up (most would work hard during mid-week evenings while in hotels in order to have more free time at the weekend) or that it would have an adverse effect on their careers. Instead, the results showed increases in satisfaction, in career success, in development and in the value they felt they were contributing to their clients. The trick was making these breaks predictable, so they were more likely to be taken.

Create a sense of control

Implicit in most of our attempts to feel more in control is an assumption that certain actions will result in greater control over our work and life. We assume that by gaining more control through our actions, we will then *feel* more in control. As we've seen so far in this chapter, it is possible to feel more in control of busyness through actions, but in a world of too much this is not always the case. This next strategy puts aside action and asks how we can directly influence our emotional response to our environment so we *feel* more in control (irrespective of how in control we actually *are*).

Breaking the stimulus-response cycle

We respond rapidly and emotionally to our environment. Someone does something annoying, you get angry; your task list is longer when you leave work than when you came in, you feel overwhelmed; you bounce from meeting to meeting, unable to address the torrent of email, let alone do any work, so you feel helpless. Emotions are natural, but with regard to helplessness, not very useful. Helpless people, like the laboratory dogs, focus any energy they have on coping, not taking control; they shrug their shoulders, tell everyone how busy they are ('poor me') and, like a martyr, they struggle on.

There is another way: it's all about how we feel. For example, Amy Arnsten, the neuroscientist, showed that when we feel out of control, the limbic system fires up and we don't think very well: more specifically, our prefrontal cortex – the most important part of the brain for conscious thinking – is impaired[8]. However, when we *feel* in control, irrespective of the demands, she found the prefrontal cortex continues to function as normal.

Our reactions to circumstances don't have to be automatic; we can change our emotions. Or, more accurately, we can rationally choose an alternative response to the immediate emotional one; and therefore feel more in control. This may sound theoretical or academic, but it works in even the most extreme situations.

> *'Everything can be taken from a man but one thing: the last of the human freedoms – to choose one's attitude in any given set of circumstances, to choose one's own way'*[9].

These aren't the words of some modern-day, pampered, so-called guru. They are the words of Viktor Frankl, a psychiatrist and a survivor of some of the worst brutality ever inflicted by the human species: the Holocaust. Frankl made this comment while reflecting on his experience as a prisoner of war at Auschwitz and Dachau (amongst others). He observed and experienced unimaginable horrors in the death camps. He also noticed that different people responded differently to their situation. Some gave up hope and 'ran into the wire' (the camp term for committing suicide by running into the electric barbed wire fence). Others became aggressive and animalistic; he tells of how many of the most brutal people in camp were the 'Capos', prisoners who assisted the guards in maintaining order in the camps. Yet many prisoners took a different path: they seemed to go inside themselves, to a heightened inner life. He tells of how on a march to a day of relentless manual labour, frozen to the core, swollen feet bursting out of his boots and half-starving, his friend brought up the topic of their wives. For the rest of that day he actively maintained his wife's image in his head, imagining talking to her, hearing her laugh. He escaped from the horror of the moment into the joy of the past and the hope for the future. He tells of how, in the depths of their horror, they would rush out of their huts just to see a lovely sunset, gazing in wonder at the skies, drinking in the beauty. Even in a situation where death was likely, life was horrible and the future seemingly hopeless, the prisoners still retained one area of their life where they could feel some control: their thoughts and feelings. He came to the conclusion that, no matter the scenario, we never lose the ability and the freedom to choose our response.

Choose your response

Your emotions ebb and flow throughout the day, even when you are extremely busy. While they may seem ever-present, your feelings of being overwhelmed or of impotence are not constant, but in reality spike at some times, fading into the background at others. The key to gaining control over our emotions is to spot the triggers for these spikes. The very act of noticing extreme emotions can start to give us distance from them and we can start to move beyond the automatic stimulus-response cycle; we can begin to insert control into the process.

Buddhists have been making this work for 2,500 years through a practice called mindfulness. The practice of mindfulness aims to enhance awareness of the present: the person observes their own thoughts and emotions without judgement. This technique has been getting a lot of attention in psychology and neuroscience because it produces a lot of intellectual and emotional benefits. In the context of managing feelings of helplessness, the first step is simply to observe your emotional response as if you were seeing it from a third person perspective. Give the emotion a name, if that helps (in fact this technique of labelling emotions has been shown to work quite well)[10]. It's not right or wrong that you have that emotion, but it *is* important to recognise that it isn't your only option. When you have done this you can move on to the second step: generating an alternative response.

Take the story of a friend of mine, Simon, who was struggling with persistent traffic on his commute. Day after day his car would come to a standstill on the congested roads. Each time he came to a stop, he could feel his tension rise, and his blood begin to boil. For him, these weren't simply moments of irritation: they were emblematic of a life that wasn't living up to his expectations; they were the emotional epicentres of his feeling of despair.

He decided to take control again. Clearly he could do nothing about the traffic jam; nor did he want to change his job, and, for family reasons, he didn't want to change his home. This all left him with one option: he had to change his response to the inevitable. Following a number of conversations and a few experiments, Simon ultimately came up with a solution that worked for him: he would use his traffic-jam time as a chance to do two of the things that had been hanging around in his 'should' list for years: learning Spanish and practising the harmonica. During his morning journeys listening to Spanish lessons, a little extra time in the car due to traffic jams improved the conjugation of his verbs; on his return home, each time he ground to a halt he'd snatch up his mouth organ and play the blues (appropriately!). Trivial though this may sound, he'd chosen a different response to an unavoidable situation which, through practice, gave him a feeling of control again (as well as some new talents).

Reversing your motivation

Have you ever noticed that you can have completely different reactions to the same experience from one occasion to the next? An invitation to dinner at a friend's house can be relished one day and dreaded the next; a looming deadline can trigger energy or fear.

Reversal Theory[11], developed by the British psychologist Michael J. Apter explains that these differing reactions to identical scenarios are a result of changing motivational states, which drive how we respond to situations and experiences. Reversal Theory is organised around four domains, each of which comprises two opposing states. We fluctuate between these two states within each domain, changing our response to situations depending on what we are motivated to achieve at that moment. The interesting thing about Reversal Theory is how easy it is to flip from one motivational state to another once you recognise what is going on.

One of the four domains within Reversal Theory is the 'Means-end' domain, which has two motivational states: 'serious' and 'playful'. When we are operating with serious motives, we are focused on goal achievement and working towards longer-term ends. When things are going our way in this state, we feel calm and relaxed. When they are not, we feel anxious or even fearful. By contrast, when we adopt a playful state, we look for in-the-moment fun and arousal and we will either feel excited and energised, or bored, depending on whether our motives are being met or frustrated.

Busyness comes from approaching life with serious motives. We only feel too busy when we're taking it all too seriously and are too heavily focused on the longer term. Reversal Theory demonstrates that in every serious situation there is an alternative response – if we recognise that we are operating with serious motives, we can flip our motivations and see the ridiculousness in situations, the lightness of the moment; we can aim to have fun.

A number of years ago I was asked to run a big event for Microsoft. It was possibly the biggest event of my career at that point. It was in Seattle, with 120 senior, high-potential leaders. I was also leading a team of 20 experienced external facilitators. In the run-up to the event I put in months of preparation; I had designed and redesigned the event scores of times. No stone was left unturned; every eventuality was thought through. I was taking the whole event very, very seriously. I was working very, very hard. Halfway through the event, a wise colleague and friend, Bobbi Riemenschneider, took me to one side and gave me some feedback. She told me I hadn't smiled once through the entire event; she told me I was taking it all too seriously and that I should 'play' a little more. What I hadn't realised was that my very determination to get it right, my work ethic and earnestness, was making me less present with the group, less fun and less flexible. In my seriousness I was a less effective facilitator.

Over the years I have identified my tendency to take it all too seriously. I have also learned that I am at my most impactful, creative and engaging when I am in a playful mood. The ability to flip into a playful motivational state has become an essential tool in helping me to think and perform better; it also helps me enjoy the ride more. I'll often ask myself how I could go about what I'm doing in a more playful, mischievous way. As a facilitator, what is interesting is that the ideas that emerge for me in a playful state make me really nervous when I'm about to start an event and am tipping into a serious state. Yet I have learned that while these ideas are nearly always more risky, they are also more striking and innovative.

It isn't hard to change your state. Three things help me to trigger a change in state: music, movement and the word 'playful'. There is nothing like a blast of music to move me into a more present-oriented, less serious state. To encourage movement, I put a massive great whiteboard on the wall of my office; I find that I can break out of my seriousness by jumping up to my whiteboard and starting to kick around my ideas with multi-coloured pens and images. Finally, simply thinking of the word 'playful' triggers a change, as I remember the feedback from Bobbi.

We can all exercise more control over how we feel by spotting seriousness and, when appropriate, triggering a reversal into a more present, playful state.

When are you most unhelpfully inclined towards the serious, future-focused state? What could you do to trigger a reversal?

The big messages in 'Feel more in control'

Think of yourself as a skilled **surfer**, carving a great ride across the face of too much. Your job is not to control the demands made on you; it is to **feel in control of your response** to it.

LETTING GO

- You **can't control the inputs, but you can** control your **outputs**. Let the inputs wash by you and focus on the outputs you choose to make.
- **It's not your fault** you can't do it all – there is simply too much to do. **Let go of your desire to do it all.**

MOVING FROM DROWNING TO IMMERSION

- When we are **fully engaged** the **sense of being out of control dissipates**. Feeling out of control springs from scattered attention and never becoming immersed in anything.
- **Control is found in what you choose to do** – the outputs you deliver, not the inputs you react to.
- **Immersion** happens when you bring **simple focus** to what you do – a single broad aim, like the golfer who simply thinks 'smooth'.
- **Control comes when we do what we're best at**. Don't judge your control by your efficiency or productivity, but by the degree to which you use your greatest skills to solve important problems.
- **Create a rhythm to your day.** Build in breaks and recovery time to reduce your allostatic load and to increase your ability to immerse yourself in the things that are important.

CREATE A SENSE OF CONTROL

- **You can choose to feel in control** – you can choose how to respond and how to feel in almost any set of circumstances.
- Replace stimulus-response with **stimulus-choice-response**.

- **Flip seriousness into playfulness** – a state of busyness comes from being too serious; change your motivational state to have more fun, be more creative and engage people better.

Go-Do

ACT 'AS IF'

Sit down and identify one thing you would do differently if you genuinely believed your outputs are more important than your inputs. Then do that thing, daily.

RECOVERY

Be strategic about recovery. Build breaks into your days at 90-minute intervals. They don't have to be long, but move, change the mood and nourish yourself.

Experiment

CHURNING

Next time you're churning, grab a pen and a piece of paper and devise a cunning plan. Not only is this helpful, it also gets the churning thoughts out of your head.

REVERSE YOUR MOOD

Identify what will trigger a switch in mood from a serious to a playful mood. This might be music, environment or trigger words. Experiment with it and get good at the flip.

Chapter 2

It's your choice

The Siamese fighting fish (known as the betta fish in the US) originates from the paddy fields of Malaysia and Thailand. In the early 19th century the King of Siam collected them for their aggression, wagering large amounts of money on male versus male conflicts. Today, they have become popular with aquarium owners because of their beautiful colours and large, flowing fins. What I find interesting about these fish is their appetite. Owners have to limit their food because, given the chance, they will quite literally eat themselves to death. Unlike most living species, they just mindlessly consume what's in front of them, not seeming to recognise when enough is enough (or maybe it's just that they can't help themselves).

There seems to be a parallel to busyness here. For the whole of history and beyond, we have inhabited a world of scarcity. The resources and opportunities open to us were limited by our environment. These limits restricted our lives; but they also protected us. Now, in our world of too much, the limits have been removed. We are now exposed to almost limitless knowledge, communication and stimulation, and with this explosion of information has come opportunity, but also increased expectation and work.

To put the speed of the switch from informational scarcity to excess in context, think of it in evolutionary terms. The first of the homo genus, our ancestors, appeared in Africa about 2.3 million years ago. Informational excess has only been with us for the last 20 years. If we view our evolution as a single calendar year, excess didn't arrive until 11.55pm on New Year's Eve. We can't hope to have adjusted to this new world of limitless abundance yet, so we're still operating as if we lived in scarcity: we're consuming what we can. The Siamese fighting fish see food and eat it, not stopping to consider how it will affect them. We too are getting dangerously close to a terminal case of consumption. We see email or texts or voicemails; we consume them. We don't seem to realise when enough is enough.

Did you ever actually *decide* to be really busy – to race from task to task? Is this the life you planned and hoped for? Without choices, we feel helpless and overwhelmed. We may also feel slightly heroic victims, stoically facing a universe of demands. Yet, from a psychological point of view, busyness could also be seen as laziness, intellectual apathy or timidity. There is nothing marvellous about going along with the herd. There *is* too much to do; but that's not why you're busy. You're busy because you haven't made tough choices and asserted your will on your environment.

Mastering a world of too much involves the ability to make deliberate and intentional choices; to choose one course of action, and un-choose another. Choosing is often easy, but un-choosing is much harder. This capability hasn't been so essential in the past, but we cannot thrive today unless we stop trying to do and have everything; that involves choice. This chapter aims to insert a great big question mark into your working patterns, into your lifestyle. I want to show you three things: how you drift into busyness, how to raise your awareness of why busyness results from a failure to make choices, and how to recognise this failure in your life. Then I will suggest practical ways you can help yourself to start making choices when dealing with excessive demands.

As I said before, this book is no manifesto for the easy life; in many ways, being busy is the easy option. Not being busy is hard work; but it is, in every way, better. In short, I will outline how to thrive by bettering the betta (fish): recognising when enough is enough, and, when you know what's good for you, being able to help yourself.

How we make decisions

You're busy due to a failure to make choices. To understand why you aren't making choices, it's helpful to understand *how* you make choices. Economists assumed for many years that more choice is a good thing, that we will rationally decide what's best for us. We now realise this is not the case[1]. Our choices are driven to a surprising level by our environment, without our rational awareness, and even if we are aware of what would be good for us, we often fail to make the critical decisions.

The reason for this is that the brain has developed a smart way of managing the energy required for decision-making. It has to do this because, although it only accounts for about two per cent of your body weight, it uses about 20 per cent of all the energy you consume. It's the 4x4 of your organs. The worst offender of all is the part responsible for decision-making, the most recent part of the brain to evolve: the prefrontal cortex. This isn't just any old 4x4, it's a 6.6-litre Hummer! This means that making choices and analysing every aspect of your life is hard work, so the brain does all it can to avoid the effort. It's not that the brain is lazy; it's just on a budget. It hasn't got that much energy to go around, so it has to be sensible.

Psychologists, such as the Nobel Prize-winning Daniel Kahneman, have split our thinking into two forms: System One and System Two[2]. System One is fast, automatic and unconscious; System Two is slow, effortful and conscious. Both systems are always on while you are awake. System One automatically responds to experiences, generating immediate impressions, intentions and feelings. System Two prefers to take things easy when it can, spending most of its time coasting along, vaguely scanning what is generated by System One. On the whole, System Two accepts System One's impressions, which become beliefs; it accepts intentions, which become actions. This works well, most of the time. By doing this, humans have evolved an incredibly energy-efficient thinking machine: only about two per cent of all mental activity is effortful and conscious. It's like having a hybrid car that runs silently and cheaply on battery power for 98 per cent of the time!

Smart energy efficiency doesn't result in intelligent thinking, though: automating such a lot of our thinking means that a huge proportion of our perceptions, preferences and decisions occur below the radar of awareness. At times, the lazy System Two is jerked out of its languor by something unexpected; but mostly it just rubber stamps System One. The first risk is that when we don't take the time and effort to arrive at quality, informed (System Two) decisions, we can make flaky, irrational (System One) choices or fail to make choices altogether and just 'go with the flow'. The second risk is that System One helps us leap to conclusions, intuitively. If challenged or asked about why we took a particular decision, we would very comfortably give a rational explanation: we jump to conclusions first and work out the rationale second. Providing a rational explanation retrospectively means we have no awareness of how bad our decision-making process was.

An example of this comes from the world of education: one of the biggest predictors of school grades is the physical attractiveness of the student. This phenomenon is so widely evidenced it has gained a name: the attractiveness halo effect. In one study, five professors rated the attractiveness of 885 economics students (with an even gender split) on a scale of one to five (five being most attractive). Those who were rated a four achieved a 36 per cent better mark than those rated a two[3]. Now imagine asking their professors why they gave the 'twos' such low grades. They will point to flaws in the students' work, they will give a strong rationale; and they will remain oblivious to the effect attractiveness had on their marking.

So we don't realise how much of our choices are based on shaky System One foundations, rather than well-thought-through principles. We don't realise how biased we are. We don't realise that most of our lives are spent on autopilot.

The power of default decisions

Defaults exert a powerful (if invisible) influence on our behaviour and in a world of too much, busy is the default, standard condition. Imagine you have just started in a new job. One of the attractive benefits being offered is an employee contributory-pension plan. It is universally accepted to be a good deal, with your firm matching your contributions and tax benefits: it's virtually free money. Would you join? You probably think your answer to this question would be most influenced by the details of the plan, the quantity of money at stake or your current financial situation. However, it is likely that the biggest factor in your decision-making on this important financial question is whether you had to fill out a form or not. In one study, economists Brigitte Madrian and Dennis Shea found that when employees had to opt into the scheme, only 20 per cent joined in the first three months, rising to 65 per cent after three years. In contrast, when membership was automatic – the default condition – initial enrolment was 90 per cent, rising to 98 per cent after three years[4].

The default for all communication is to ingest (read or listen) and respond to. Let me ask a few questions about emails, for instance. How many emails do you get a day? How many did you get a day three years ago? Let's say you currently receive 200 emails a day, a figure which has doubled in the last three years. At what point do you need to fundamentally question the value of reading and responding to all these: when they get to 400, 1600, 12,800? At some point we need to make a stand for thinking, for proactivity and for creativity.

I find few people who don't moan about the number of meetings they 'have to' attend, how time-poor they are, and how disruptive meetings are to their day. Yet I find very few people with a solution – only good intentions. I cannot tell you how many times I have run leadership seminars/workshops where this topic comes up and the group decides to slash the number of internal meetings, or agree that all meetings should last a maximum of 45 minutes. But when I meet these teams months later, little has changed. One of the issues is that it is so easy to invite people using Outlook or Gmail. Given the inviter can see your calendar, can see you are free, there becomes something of a default expectation that you will accept. Acceptance is a click, opting out requires an explanation. This is especially evident in the curse of all office life: weekly meetings. These meetings happen whether there is a purpose or not, but since they are regular, by default, you are expected to attend and another hour is lost.

How are defaults shaping your life at present? What are the unspoken assumptions and expectations that are driving a large amount of activity for you? Some of these defaults may serve you well, some will not. Collectively they are strangling you.

If you were to redesign your working life from scratch, in order to maximise your capability to contribute more meaningfully to the business, to love your work and harmonise it with your personal life, what would it look like? You probably imagined a working life free of a lot of the unhelpful defaults. Choose one default and redesign how you respond. Choose to be less mindless.

The lure of social norms

How would you persuade people to recycle towels in hotels? A famous study by Robert Cialdini into social norms revealed that the standard environmental plea persuaded about 30 per cent of people to recycle[5]. When the wording was changed slightly to state that most guests choose to recycle at some point in their stay, 26 per cent more people recycled. When the wording was made even more specific, stating that most guests staying in that particular room had chosen to recycle, the percentage increased by 33 per cent. Again, this influence doesn't happen at a conscious level. None of those additional 33 per cent of recyclers would have explained their choice in terms of other people's behaviour, but it is a powerful example of how our behaviour is influenced by other people – we are affected by the social norm – what other people around us do. The reason the more specific hotel card worked even better, is that the more similar people are to us, the more their behaviour influences us.

In another example, a classic study in the 1950s by Solomon Asch[6], an American pioneer in social psychology, gave students a simple perceptual task. He showed them two cards. On one card, there were three lines, marked A, B and C. Lines A, B and C were clearly different lengths. On a second card there was a single line that was the same length as one of the lines from the first card. Asch asked the students which line on the first card matched that on the second, A, B or C. It was an easy task, and in all those who completed the activity, only one per cent of all responses were wrong.

He then ran the experiment in groups. Each group got 18 trials of this type; the two comparison cards were different each time; each time subjects had to choose which line, A, B or C was the same length. What was different this time was that all but one of the students involved had been briefed before the experiment to give the wrong answer to 12 of the trials. On those 12 trials, all the confederates gave the same, but wrong, answer. The other student had no knowledge that they were the only one giving their real opinion.

Would the unwitting student give the wrong answer? Remember, the right answer was very clear and easy to see. This time, the error rate was 33 times higher. In fact, 75 per cent of all subjects gave at least one wrong answer out of 12. Only 25 per cent gave the obviously right answer each time. In the face of clear and visible evidence, these students changed their answer to comply with the group.

It's hard to go against the social norm, even if it's the self-evidently correct thing to do, so we conform. You might believe that the reason you work like you do is because of the demands upon you. I would argue that this is only a small part of the picture. The quantity of work you do, and your perpetual busyness, develops because that's what everyone else is doing.

The effects of social norms are even more powerful when we compare ourselves to people we actually know. Everyone we come into contact with is incredibly busy, so we become busy. The fact that our social peers and work colleagues are frantically juggling too many things powerfully shapes our expectations and behaviour and makes it difficult for us to assess how busy we should actually be.

When was the last time you met someone who explained how un-busy they are? When was the last time you travelled to work on a train not filled with people tapping away on laptops, phones or tablets? Think about how their behaviour might be affecting your own feelings of busyness.

When you compare your busy behaviour to those around you – your peers at work, network contacts, fellow commuters, friends and family – how much of what you do is just the norm? Remember, 'the norm' isn't the degree to which you have an intellectual rationale for your behaviour; you always will. It is the degree of similarity to those around you. If it's similar, it's probably driven by the norm, in which case, it is not *your* behaviour. You didn't choose it; you are simply acting out the collective pattern like a faithful worker bee.

What's wrong with the norm? There is nothing, in principle, wrong with going with the herd, if the herd is going in the right direction. In the case of busy, and responding to excess, the herd is definitely not going in the right direction. We need to find our own, unique responses to our challenges; we need to create a better way of doing and communicating and delivering. The answer does not lie with the herd.

Mindless 'choosing'

Have you ever noticed that if you are watching TV, or playing cards, and there is a bowl of crisps or nibbles in front of you, you keep eating until they're gone? You don't stop to think, have I had enough yet? You just mindlessly consume. Brian Wansink, Professor of Marketing and Applied Economics at Cornell University, wondered if this would still apply to food that wasn't so appealing[7]. He gave moviegoers buckets of five-day-old popcorn. One participant described the popcorn as 'like eating styrofoam'. He gave some participants a medium bucket and some a large bucket. Those with big buckets ate 53 per cent more popcorn than those with the smaller bucket, even though they didn't like it. Afterwards, when confronted with the evidence, most denied the size could have affected their choice. One person said, 'Things like that don't trick me.' He was wrong.

There is mindlessness in lots of our daily behaviour. System One thinking allows us to automate a lot of what we do, so that we have the energy to focus our conscious attention on other issues. This works fine most of the time, but in a world in which the default behaviour and social norm is frenetic busyness, we are mindlessly drifting to toxic levels of activity and consumption. The only choice any of us seems to be making is for 'More'; and so we reach out, mindlessly, for more dry popcorn; we grab, mindlessly, our smartphone, for more empty, unfulfilling activity.

Think about how you could impose limits on this excess. For example, you can limit time: how long each day will you spend answering emails? Or you could limit quantity: if you were only to attend three meetings a week, what would they be? Charles Handy, the business consultant, limits his income to ensure he doesn't take on too much work[8]. He agrees an upper and lower limit of income for any year with his wife and as soon as he has earned his limit for the year, he stops consulting until the following year. He has put an upper limit on his income to stop mindlessly reaching for 'More'.

How could you limit your mindless reach for 'More'?

How to make better choices

Once we accept we need to make more choices, we need to work out how to make the right ones. Making better choices, for most of my clients, isn't about what they need to do. Most of them are clear what they want to focus on 'if only they had the time'. They are clear that reactive busyness isn't effective and isn't fun. What they need help with is how to make the changes that will enable them to become more selective. How to stop entering the office, full of good intentions to work on an idea which could make a real difference, only to find themselves distracted, dissipated and disillusioned by the end of the day. This section is about learning to break that cycle and make the choices that will enable you to become more creative and effective.

Hot and cold decision-making

If I offered you two cheques, one for £100 which could be cashed in a month and one for £150 which could be cashed in two months, which would you choose? Most people would go for the £150. However, if the £100 could be cashed tomorrow, with the £150 not cashable for a month, would your choice remain the same? Most people in a real experiment would decide to take the £100, despite the fact that the second option is rationally the better choice.

This example demonstrates a form of hot and cold decision-making. In the 'cold' rational state, we would obviously choose the £150 cheque. However, once the reward is placed in a more immediate setting, temptation kicks in and we make a 'hot' and irrational decision. We can readily make good decisions when we are not facing temptation directly, but that ability disappears when staring it right in the face. As economist George Loewenstein explains, 'it's really easy to agree to diet when you're not hungry'.

I would struggle to find anyone who wouldn't immediately accept that they should be working on important things, rather than simply urgent matters. Most of those people will also be reasonably clear on what those important things are. Yet, day after day, on entering work, temptations loom. From the perspective of urgent versus important, most offices are very hot places: distraction, requests and pressures can be found around every corner. The immediate gratification of the urgent is just so much more tempting than the long-term benefits of the important. The attraction of small, simple tasks will always beat the bigger, harder, longer-term activities. The payoff of emptying your inbox and answering emails on your journey home will always feel more real than the benefits of taking that time to read or reflect. In our cold state we are clear what we should do and we can come up with good intentions; in our hot state, we are more inclined to think 'just one more'.

Stay cold, longer

I am always attracted to simple ideas. One of the simplest techniques for staying cold I've ever encountered is so obvious once you've adopted it. It is called 'Eat that frog'[9] in a book of that name by Brian Tracy. The concept is that if you eat a frog first thing in the morning, anything else you do that day won't be too bad! Essentially Tracy is suggesting that, before you open your inbox, listen to your voicemail or answer instant messages, you set aside a slice of time to work on the biggest, scariest, most important project you are facing at that time; by confronting the task head-on, everything else you need to do that day will seem easy.

One of the reasons this idea works so well is that, before starting work, we have a kind of emotional distance and therefore a better perspective on what matters. We are in a cold, rational state; and are more able to make good choices about the best use of our time and attention. When we arrive at the office and turn on our email etc., suddenly the temptations of the small, the urgent, send us spiralling into a hot state, and we get totally distracted from our main purpose. The habit of not turning on your email for a short time each morning, and using that time to focus unwaveringly on those areas you identified in your cold state really works.

Good choices take energy

Stanford Business School Professor Jonathan Levav and Shai Danziger, Psychology Professor in Tel Aviv University, reviewed more than a thousand parole decisions made by judges in the Israeli prison system. After hearing each case, judges decided whether to parole or not. In this situation, the higher-risk decision was to release, even if that option would please the prisoner and save tax-payers some money. On average, each judge approved parole in about one in three cases. However, a very strong pattern occurred: of those prisoners who appeared before a judge early in the morning, 65 per cent were paroled; of those who appeared late in the afternoon, only 10 per cent were paroled![10]

The explanation for this shocking, but very human, lack of consistency is something called ego depletion. We have only so much mental energy to go around, which means that when we've been making a lot of decisions, we get tired and begin to either avoid decisions altogether or take the less risky, easier option, like the judges later in the afternoon. It stands to reason that when we are incredibly stretched and busy, there will be choices we're not making, or situations where we're wrongly opting for the easy path. We might have to accept that at certain times of the day, we are going to be pretty poor at making clear, strategic choices about the best use of time.

Here are some strategies you can use to avoid this:

- Make your choices about how you'll spend your time first thing in the morning when your ego is not depleted.
- Take regular breaks, and have a small, healthy snack during each break to replace some of the glucose (the study above noted that there were spikes of better decision making during the day, and that these were always after meals or snacks!).
- Review your progress and focus immediately after each break.

Combat social norms

As we saw in the experiments with hotel towel recycling and the card comparisons, social norms are strong influences and it isn't easy to go against them – even when they're wrong.

We can use this insight to help combat the general social norm towards busyness. As well as making an effort to break away from colleagues and social peers who are taking the wrong approach to busyness, you should also surround yourself with people who respond more creatively to 'too much', so that you can be affected by their behaviour. Think about how you could spend more time and build deeper relationships with people who don't get sucked into mindless busyness, who make better choices. How could you spend less time with people who might influence you with unhelpful behaviours?

One specific strategy is to identify the behaviour we most want to change and find people in your organisation, in your personal life or in your family who model good alternative behaviours. Spend time with them, and build relationships with them. Ask them about what they do, observe closely how they do behave, how they think about busyness, do all you can to start making their approaches and behaviours the norm for you.

With any change, the starting point is to notice the issue and raise your awareness of the problem. Once you are clear about how the norm is shaping (unhelpfully) your behaviours, start experimenting with alternatives. The following conversation is an example of norms in action:

> You: 'Hi how are you doing?'
> Other: 'Oh, I'm very, very busy. How are you?'
> You: 'Oh, I'm very, very busy . . .'

Just for the fun of it, next time you're in that conversation, say you've decided not to be busy; say you've decided that you want to create time to think, instead of endless, mindless busyness. See what reaction you get: alarm, pity, envy . . . You'll get different reactions, but you'll get a reaction. Find your own behaviours, your own response to too much. Step out of the herd.

Un-choose greyness

Perhaps my biggest fear for myself, and the most common problem I see in others, isn't busyness; it's greyness. When there are so many options, so much opportunity, so many distractions and so much work, it is incredibly easy to overload your palette with too much colour. Given the finite size of your palette, the risk is that the colours will start merging together and, as we all know, if you mix too many colours together you don't get a rainbow, you get grey. To paint a vivid life, to have a vivid career, you need less colour rather than more; that means you have some tough choices to make.

There is a sense that busyness is not just a failure to make choices, but an avoidance of doing so to avoid losing out on something else. Think about how you behave at a buffet table: if you're anything like me you pile your plate high with all kinds of weird and wonderful flavours and colours and you end up with something you would immediately send back to the kitchen if a chef served it up. To avoid missing out on things, we pile our plate high with a bit of this and a bit of that. We would have a far better meal if we chose fewer items. If we choose chicken korma, we would be better off not choosing sweet-and-sour pork and the steak pie. Individually they are great; together they are a culinary disaster. Yet we choose all three to avoid missing out on anything and the price we pay is a rubbish meal.

Busyness is buffet table madness. This is true in our work, it is also true in our private lives. We choose everything and end up trying to do too much. Everything isn't really a choice. In fact, what we should be doing is un-choosing things: consciously and deliberately choosing not to do things, killing off options in our lives and work to allow a greater focus on fewer things. Instead of choosing more, we should choose less.

The truth is that no choice is neutral. Each time you choose something, you un-choose something else. So even our attempt to do everything (by not un-choosing anything) comes with a cost, a loss.

The loss we avoid by choosing everything is small but visible; the loss we experience through choosing everything is large and lasting but invisible. To compete against the visible and small loss, I work to make the invisible, visible. I become really clear on what I want to achieve in a week or month, and what I'll be losing if I don't create the time, or focus my attention. I make the big loss palpable. I develop a stronger aversion to the big loss than the small.

Choose one thing you'd love to accomplish or do this coming month in work, or outside. What would this mean to you? How would it make your feel? What difference would it make? What will you lose if you don't do this? What will you lose if you cast your attention away from *stuff* this month? What will you lose if you continue to be so cavalier, so wasteful with your attention?

To accomplish or do this thing; what do you need to un-choose?

Focus on the gain

Most executive teams really struggle with discussions over headcount allocation. In these teams there is always a tension between the loyalty they feel to the part of the business they lead and the collective goals of the leadership team. Leadership teams may seem to operate effectively for most of the time, making cohesive decisions on strategy or on areas of business management. Then, at certain points each year, decisions have to be made on the best allocation of resources across the wider business. At this point any veneer of a united team making decisions for the good of the wider organisation disappears. It's turf war! Individual leaders fight for their territory to protect their people and to preserve their ego.

I was introduced to a technique, which I believe was developed by General Electric, called the Pin Game. The essence of this activity is to start discussions by identifying what the team wants to gain (the business strategy) instead of what the leaders might lose (headcount).

Starting from the business strategy, you decide how many extra 'heads' (represented by pins) the business will need in order to deliver the agreed strategy in the form of new projects, expanded initiatives etc. Next you compare this with the overall headcount increase, freeze or decline that the business is aiming for that year. This now gives a number of heads to be found from existing teams and projects. Finally, making sure to never get into debate about individuals, the team looks at the allocation of pins and considers, based on the strategy, what the appropriate allocation of resources across the organisation should be.

The genius of this approach is that it bases staff allocation on strategy, not on how hard people are working. When people try to allocate staff based on spare capacity, they get stuck: nobody has any. They are deciding based on what their people have time for (according to how they currently work), rather than basing it on what they want to achieve.

The same tactic can be applied to deciding which areas you will choose to focus on, and which to un-choose. Do the following:

1 Over the next year, to make a real difference in your career, role or personal life, what do you most want to achieve?
2 How much extra time, as a percentage of your overall time, do you need to allocate to reach this goal?
3 Now, on the basis of what you want to achieve, where will you find this percentage of time? You can't simply say, 'I'll work harder'. Your time has to come from somewhere. What will you un-choose in order to step away from greyness, and choose a life of more depth and colour?

The tyranny of 'have to'

What's in a word? Quite a lot, actually. Language has long been considered a critical vehicle through which we understand and respond to our environment. For example, behavioural economist Keith Chen found a link between the language people speak (as their primary language) and their tendency to save money[11]. In English, if you are speaking about time, you need to adjust your grammar to reflect whether you are speaking about the past, the present or the future. In Chinese, you speak about the present and the future using the same words (this is not simply about distant languages: English is the only Germanic language that separates time in this way). He found that, when you controlled all other variables, people that speak futureless languages, like Chinese, save more money (five per cent more) than those that separate the present from the future tense, because the future is not a separate, distinct thing.

Language matters. The language you use, or more specifically the words you use in your chosen language, can influence your actions and your feelings. It can affect the level of control you feel and the way you prioritise your tasks. The way you choose to talk about your work and plans makes a difference. I want to use the words 'have to' to illustrate this.

When you say 'I have to', what kinds of activities get the 'have to' tag? In contrast, think about those activities that we 'should' do;

what's different about them? If you're anything like me, you disproportionately use 'have to' to describe activities of short-term benefit and little lasting significance – in Dr Stephen Covey's language, 'urgent but not important'. 'I have to get that report done tonight'; 'I have to respond to that email'.

'Should' is used for important but not urgent activities: 'I should design a better way to . . .'; 'I should reorganise . . .'. 'Should' gets used for life-related activity. We tend not to say I 'have to' spend quality time with my children or partner tonight; we say I 'should'. 'Have to' is more associated with work-related activity.

Why does this matter? It matters because in a world of too much you can never do everything. 'Have to' activities are in direct competition against 'shoulds'; and 'have to' wins every time. When we allow 'have to' a free rein, it drives out 'should'. When we don't take care of the 'shoulds', when we don't give attention to what really matters in our life, we give up a sense of choice and control in our lives; we allow the grey to spread across our palette.

Let's be clear, I'm not proposing that we deny any sense of personal accountability and stop following through on commitments. I am simply saying that 'have to' is a weapon we use in the battle of priorities in our own head and with our families. It is powerful, but it removes a sense of choice and it drives activity that tends to be more task- than values-based; in so doing it reduces our sense of mastery of our life. Observe how you (and others) use it. Catch yourself in the act of saying (or thinking) 'I have to. . .'; and pause for a moment. Ask yourself why you are labelling this activity 'have to': what is your choice in the matter? The consequences of not doing the 'have to' are probably very salient to you; but what about the consequences of doing it? What 'should' will be lost? Then make an informed choice on what you will do, not because you 'have to' but because you choose to.

Words matter. Notice the words you use; spot those that limit your options, and use words instead that recognise your power to choose. There can be little joy in a life dominated by 'have to'.

Trial and error: every decision is an experiment

I worked for a short time in the financial markets at an exchange called LIFFE (the London International Financial Futures and

Options Exchange). At the time I worked there, the trading process was 'open outcry': traders wore brightly coloured jackets (to show which bank they were working for) and stood around in 'pits', shouting and waving their hands. Each pit traded on one of the financial instruments, such as Italian Government Bonds. Each pit also contained 'locals' in red jackets. The locals traded their own money. Most were marginally successful; some were spectacularly successful. I thought long and hard about what made some people so successful. In the end I decided it definitely wasn't a deeper insight into the markets. I think a big factor in their success was that they made decisions. They seemed to make more decisions than others. Those decisions that turned out to be correct, they rode. When a decision turned out to be wrong, they made a further decision, cut their losses and got out.

It is tempting to think you can rationally plan your way out of busyness. You can't. Nor can you rely on all this psychological research to give you a foolproof solution. Your life, your work, your environment and the people around you are just too complex to fully predict what will work and what won't. Use the ideas in this book to experiment, to try things. Many ideas and strategies won't work for you. Discard what doesn't, and build on what does. Keep making choices, of one thing over another; keep learning; and find your own, unique path out of greyness, out of busyness.

The big messages in 'it's your choice'

You didn't decide to be endlessly, frenetically busy, it just happened, one email at a time and, like the Siamese fighting fish, we're in danger of a terminal case of consumption.

HOW WE MAKE DECISIONS

- Most of the 'choices' we make are made on autopilot. This is very biased and some of those biases have helped us to **sleep-walk our way into endless busyness**.

- **Busy is the default condition of modern life; it is also the social norm**; so without perceiving our choice in the matter, we drift into busy.
- In the absence of proper choices, **the only choice we make is to mindlessly reach for 'More'**; without considering the consequences.

HOW TO MAKE BETTER CHOICES

- **We make great choices when we're 'cold'**, but in the grip of temptation (when we're 'hot') all our best intentions disappear. So, **stay 'cold' for longer**, and make better decisions about your priorities.
- When our brain is tired, we're more likely to do the thing that requires less choice, less risk. That means **the busy, depleted brain is less able to make the choices to step beyond busyness**. Make your choices when your brain is fresh.
- **Use social norms to help you**; hang out with great (and un-busy) role models.

UN-CHOOSE GREYNESS

- **By choosing to do everything, we are un-choosing depth, immersion and impact.** To move beyond busy, we have to become better at un-choosing.
- In persistently choosing everything or 'more', we spread ourselves and our attention thin and **the colours blend into an unsatisfyingly grey life**.
- Our words can trap us and limit our choices. Beware the **tyranny of 'have to'**.
- Don't wait until you can make the right choices to find your way out of busyness; **try things**. Some will work; some won't. Those that work, continue.

Go-Do

EAT THE FROG, COLD

When you're fresh, on the way to work, decide what is the most important thing to work on that day (cold decision-making). When you arrive, don't turn on your email or listen to voicemails for the first hour and work on this task. If you can't cope with a whole hour, try at least 30 minutes!

UN-CHOOSE

Identify one thing you need to choose *not* to do in order to allow you to improve your performance over the coming weeks.

Experiments

SOCIAL NORMS

Identify people who seem to be better than you at managing busyness and spend more time with them.

OUTCASTING

Be the outcast: play with never saying 'I'm busy'. Find more interesting responses, and look at the shock and horror in other people's faces!

KILLING 'HAVE TO'

Try removing 'have to' from your language. You always have a choice about what you do, don't use language to justify your busy behaviour.

Chapter 3

Negotiate your life back

I t had been a long day at work. A middle-aged woman called Rosa made her way to an empty seat in the middle of the bus and sat down. The bus filled up. A few stops later, people were standing in the aisle. James F. Blake, the bus driver, decided to take action. He walked down the bus and asked Rosa, and three others sitting near her, to give their seats to the passengers who were standing. He asked firmly, but politely. The three sitting near Rosa got to their feet; Rosa remained seated saying, 'I don't think I should have to stand up'. Shortly afterwards, she was arrested.

This may seem an odd little story, but a little context will help explain it. The bus was in Montgomery, Alabama; the date was December 1, 1955; Rosa Parks was black and the standing passengers were white. In those days, white passengers sat in the front of buses; black passengers were only allowed to sit in the rear. Rosa had chosen to sit in the front row of the black section. As the bus had grown more crowded, Blake had risen to move the sign showing where the white section ended back a row; Rosa was now in a 'white' seat. Rosa's resolute, but courteous response to Blake had her arrested. Her response also led to the successful Montgomery Bus Boycott, which ran for a little more than a year until a US Supreme Court ruled that the Alabama laws requiring racial segregation were unconstitutional. The US Congress later described Rosa Parks as the 'mother of the freedom movement'.

As an interesting postscript to this story, after the first day of the bus boycott, scheduled to coincide with Rosa Parks' trial, it was decided that there should be a formal leader for the boycott effort. A relatively young and unknown man was chosen. His name was Martin Luther King. King later said of Rosa Parks' actions: 'Actually, no one can understand the action of Mrs Parks unless he realises that eventually the cup of endurance runs over, and the human personality cries out, "I can take it no longer"'.

In this iconic story, it is social injustice that Rosa Parks could no longer endure. Though an ordinary woman, she took a stand because the alternative seemed even more unendurable. In the same way, although instinct compels us to carry on at our frenetic pace, and busyness seems easier than trying to react differently, we may well reach a breaking point where refusing to go along with the norm seems the only reasonable response.

This chapter looks at how to stop the momentum of busyness by drawing a line under too much; how we must set boundaries; how we can say 'no'; and how we can negotiate our way out of busyness. In doing so we will build Mastery over our own lives.

When is enough, enough?

The information age hasn't just given us more information, communication, noise and busyness. It has also made it a lot harder to judge how much work people are doing – how much is enough. Firstly, work is never 'done': there is always more to do. Secondly, few things are standard: we don't spend our lives knocking out the same thing, over and over in the same way; things change week by week. This means that evaluating whether task A was more demanding than task B is often not a straightforward activity. If it's such a tough problem to assess whether people are working hard, how can companies and organisations tell whether their employees are working hard enough? How do we as individuals feel comfortable that we're doing enough? The solution managers have adopted is to push everyone to breaking point: set targets for individuals and keep raising them until you see people really struggle to meet them – then you can be confident that people are working hard. The solution we, as individuals, have adopted is to keep working harder and harder; filling every moment of attention with 'productivity'; and working and fretting until we collapse, empty, into a semi-vegetative state in front of reality TV.

What about at home? How do you agree with those you love on the best balance of your time and energies? Is it better to put a few extra hours of work in; do homework with your son; go to your daughter's soccer game; or go to the gym? Other members of your family can't fully understand your burdens, nor will you ever fully understand their perspectives. Many of the conversations resulting from a more imaginative response to a world of 'too much' will be difficult. The easiest approach is to try to do it all – at least at work – and at home to play the 'have to' card.

We've been stuck in this situation for the last 10 years. Over that time, the pressure cooker has been turned up: the demands have got greater, the emptiness deeper. The emergence of the ubiquitous smartphone has just cranked up the heat. We'll remain stuck here until the human personality cries out, 'I can take it no longer'. This moment, which I reckon to be about now, is the one this chapter aims to address. If you want something other than to be stretched to breaking point at work and only half present at home – read on.

Setting limits

On November 9, 1989, crowds of people from East and West Germany climbed onto the Berlin Wall and celebrated. This iconic moment was symbolic of the collapse of the boundaries which had separated country from country and divided the world. Walls separate, but they also protect, as Germany found in the early years of its reintegration: while the process was hugely positive, it didn't come without its challenges.

Since the fall of the Berlin Wall, boundaries have been collapsing all over the place. Email has destroyed boundaries of time, allowing asynchronous work: there is never a time that we cannot communicate with a person (even if they don't instantly respond). Smartphones and laptops have destroyed the boundaries of space that naturally segregated work and life for generations. The emergence of global superpowers such as the BRIC nations (Brazil, Russia, India and China) and electronic communications has meant that more people are doing more work, destroying limits around quantity. A lack of boundaries in time, space and quantity pose real challenges for us from a psychological and a negotiation point of view.

It is still possible to set boundaries; they just aren't automatic in the way they would have been in the past. It's now your job to draw the lines in the sand. Boundaries are critical in protecting ourselves from our mindless consumption, to help others understand us, and to free ourselves from our servitude to servers.

Are you reaching your limit?

To set boundaries we need to have an awareness of our limits. The problem is, we often don't spot when we're getting way too busy, unhealthily busy, until we're already there. In another Brian Wansink experiment on mindless eating, participants were invited to eat bowls of Campbell's soup[1]. What they didn't realise was that each bowl had been tampered with so that, as the person ate, the bowl secretly refilled. We might think we would continue slurping the soup only until we had eaten enough, and then stop. However, an awful lot of the participants just continued mindlessly eating. Ultimately, it was the experimenter who, out of concern for his subjects, put an end to the experiment. We can be a bit like the frog in the pot of water that is being slowly heated, not noticing until it boils. It's far better to notice early.

Nassim Nicholas Taleb, economist, wise man and author of *The Black Swan*, thinks a lot about nonlinearity. He comments that, as certain variables increase, their effect is not linear[2]. Take traffic, for example. When the roads are very quiet, a small increase in traffic makes little difference. Increases in the number of cars and trucks continue to have minimal impact on the flow of traffic, until the roads start to get more congested. After this, any small increase in traffic leads to much worse jams and gridlock. Taleb describes this relationship as a concave relationship. Small increases at the start make little difference, but as you go further up the scale, additional small increments have an increasingly large effect.

I think the relationship between the quantity of stuff we do and our experience of busyness is also a concave relationship. When we have little going on, a bit more demand makes scant difference to our busyness. However, there comes a point when any small additions to your demands can send shock waves of panic through every fibre of your being. You may feel you're already there! If you are, all I'd say is, don't go any further: it'll get worse. And if you're not panicking yet, but are still high on the curve, the benefits you'll feel from small changes will also feel significant. If you get too far up the curve, your ability to absorb new demands and to adapt will be decimated.

So here's a practical tool, which I developed a number of years ago, called the Busy Footprint. As we move up the demand curve, and things start to get too much, our behaviour begins to change. These changes often happen without conscious thought. These behavioural changes are idiosyncratic, but consistent in individuals over time. They can be thought of as a behavioural footprint of extreme busyness. The simple idea is that, if you can recognise your Busy Footprint, you can use it like an early warning system and take timely steps to readjust your limits, preventing yourself from tipping into the deepest depths of demand doom (and any other D words you can think of).

For example, when I start to come close to turning the corner into crazy busyness, I start drinking more tea, and adding sugar to it; I stop reading; I want baths rather than showers; I lose things; I stop listening. Your signs will be different. Over the years, I've found it really helpful to notice these behaviours for what they are: warning bells that adjustments need to be made. Bear in mind, I'm not talking here of changing from busy to calm, quiet and relaxed; I'm talking about moving from unhealthily busy to sustainably (if unproductively) busy.

What is your Busy Footprint?

Managing boundaries

At one of my events, I had a Corporate Vice President at Microsoft come to speak to us about leadership. I had expected a useful talk about the usual leadership challenges he had faced and the lessons he had learned. He surprised us. His opening few lines gripped the room: 'I have never missed my wife's birthday or the birthdays of any of my three children. I have never missed the first day or the last day of any school term. I have never missed my wedding anniversary. I have never missed the opening night of a school play'. This was just a small part of the list he reeled off. The room was full of senior leaders, all of whom had missed many of the type of special events listed by the CVP. They all wondered how it was possible for this man, running a billion-dollar business, in a global role, to be present for all those moments.

So we asked him. His response was simple: 'Because I'm good'. We laughed. He explained that he had earned the right to make choices like this because he performed to a high level. He then went on to explain the understanding that he and his family had come to – that while they accepted that demands on him would rise with his increasing seniority, certain moments were acknowledged as sacred and irreplaceable. He accepted he would travel a lot; he accepted he would work hard; he would not accept missing these moments. They were one of his ways of harmonising his work and his family life. In always being present for those moments, he demonstrated to his children and his wife (and himself) where his priorities lay. Finally, he explained that this value of his was part of his 'Rules of Engagement' with any manager. Before he agreed to take on any role he would negotiate certain agreements, certain ways of working with that manager. He would not take a job if a prospective new manager was unwilling to agree to his Rules of Engagement.

This story illustrates three core aspects of boundary-setting which I call respectively quid pro quo, make choices, and the pre-emptive strike.

Quid pro quo

What deal do you have with your employer? What do you offer and, in return, what do you receive? There is a concept called the psychological contract[3]. The psychological contract describes the (primarily) unwritten deal between any individual and their employer. It goes way beyond the basic transaction of a certain wage for a certain number of hours, to encompass all the elements of the implicit trade we make with our organisations.

The psychological contract has four elements arranged on two axes. One axis includes what your organisation wants (certain skills, knowledge, attitudes, activity, time, results etc.) as well as the things you offer (a certain skill set, expertise etc.). The other axis relates to your wants – money and perks, the way you are treated, enjoyment in your role, variety, relationships, pride etc. On the opposite side of the same axis are the things the employer will offer. Alignment across both of the contract's axes is a sign of successful employee relations and career management, both of which result from an ongoing series of negotiations between organisation and individual.

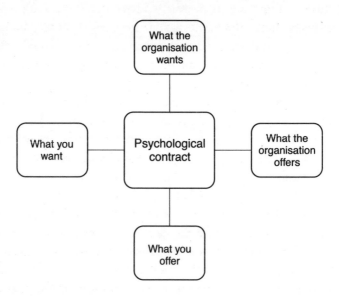

When there is a change in one of the contract's elements, the corresponding element on that axis will tend to adjust accordingly. For example, I was working with one company that asked me to look at two, seemingly disconnected, things: a real lack of proactivity in their staff, and a big surge in desire for career development coming through in their annual staff survey. When I started analysing what was going on, though, I realised that the offer from the employer had decreased over the last few years. A few years previously, this company had been the undisputed leader in its field; it had been *the* place to work. Over subsequent years, however, market share had dropped, sales had dropped and bonuses had dropped. At the same time, the amount of change and turbulence in that business had increased.

From an employee perspective, the company was offering less, so they were also now offering less. This didn't happen at a rational level; the employees recognised the challenges the business was facing and understood why lower bonuses and change were necessary, but psychologically a rebalance had to be made. The result was a reduction of discretionary effort, such as proactivity. As for career development, this was an attempt by employees to ask for an improvement of the employment offer – one which they felt could be met. As one person said, 'When bonuses were good, no one cared about careers'.

Coming back to our CVP, the psychological contract is a very simple quid pro quo: give more, get more. In his case, he performed well, and so the business was more than happy to be really flexible. Bear in mind, when I say 'give more' I don't mean do more email, do more hours and lose more weekends. I mean *achieve* more, deliver more results and innovate more. Success will never come through consistent withdrawals from the psychological contract; improve your offer, and your control and choices will also improve.

Make choices

I make no apologies for coming back to the word 'choices' again. Negotiating your response to demands requires you to make choices, and negotiating what you want in return also requires choice. In Chapter 2, I talked about 'How to make better choices' at work and 'Un-choose greyness'. From a psychological contract perspective, these sections could equally have been called 'Choose what I offer' and 'Choose what I want'.

What really hit me as I listened to the CVP was how wonderfully specific he had become over what he wanted. His role required him to make tough decisions each day, not only about his business, but also about the way he worked. He had been able to identify very specific moments that allowed him to feel connected to those he cared most about; they could accept his absences, confident in the knowledge that he would be there when it mattered most.

It really brought home to me that, in the same way that we can't do everything, we can't have everything either. Contentment stems just as much from the boundaries we set around what we want, and what we accept we are willing to let go, as it does from the boundaries we set on what we are prepared to offer.

Use your answers to the following questions as the basis for negotiating your boundaries:

- What do you (really) want when it comes to your deal with your employer?
- What's not important to you?
- What would you like, but are willing to let go of in favour of those things that are truly important to you?

The pre-emptive strike

The third aspect of boundary-setting is what I call 'the pre-emptive strike'. Let's imagine our CVP is out shopping for a present for his daughter's birthday the next day. He gets a call from his manager telling him that a real issue has arisen and he needs to attend a meeting with the CEO of Microsoft on his daughter's big day. Most of us might grumble during this call, but it would be followed shortly after by an apologetic conversation with our daughter, explaining why Daddy can't be there tomorrow. Some brave souls might explain about the birthday and ask permission, or even demand that they be excused from this meeting. From a manager's perspective, this response could feel irritating and even inappropriate. The response could be seen as a lack of commitment, rather than an expression of their values: 'the employee is being problematic'.

Now consider the case of the CVP. When situations like this occur, all he needs to do is remind the manager of their prior agreement. Both people are clear about the values of the CVP; both people are clear of the Rules of Engagement. The discussion rapidly shifts to a workaround solution to this issue; the refusal to attend this critical meeting poses a challenge, but is not a problem.

Prior agreements demonstrate how important things are to you, where your values stand. We respect individuals and leaders who have clear and strong values – people who live true to their principles. The pre-emptive strike sets out your ground rules and allows you to manage your boundaries, but diffuses difficult conversations in advance.

What are your Rules of Engagement? How clear is your manager about your Rules of Engagement?

Negotiate for your life

In 1962 the world stood perilously close to Armageddon. The Soviets had dispatched a shipment of nuclear missiles to Cuba. These were approaching the island country where they would be pointed at the US. President Kennedy had three options: let the missiles arrive in Cuba and just accept the threat to the US mainland; retaliate by bombing Cuba and launching an invasion; or start seriously negotiating. Sensibly, he chose not to ignore the threat. Thankfully, he chose not to launch an invasion since, unbeknownst to him, the Soviets had 40,000 troops in Cuba, and the Cubans had 250,000 well-trained troops ready too. Instead, he chose to talk. Through skilful negotiations on both sides, a nuclear war was narrowly averted.

We all have a choice as we face shipload after shipload of missiles, all pointing at us. We can't just ignore missiles or they may blow up in our faces. We can, however, as most of us have been doing, ignore the busyness. Alternatively, we could retaliate: we could hand in our notice or say 'to hell with this'. Or we could start talking. People are often remarkably resistant to talking and negotiating. They worry that they might lose out in the process, or that somehow starting to talk about an alternative response to busyness is revealing their dark secret: that they care about life beyond work. They worry that talking might place them in opposition to the needs of the business. But they pay a high price to avoid talking: they put up with way too much.

However, at some point, if you want to find a way forward that doesn't involve the ineffectual drudgery of busyness, or doing something drastic, you're going to have to start talking. When you get to that point, the rest of this chapter will help.

Don't haggle

An immortal scene from *Monty Python's Life of Brian* involves a desperate Brian trying to escape from a group of Roman soldiers who are chasing him. He goes to a market stall where he selects, and tries to pay for, a false beard as a disguise. The market trader can't understand Brian's behaviour and says, 'Wait a minute, you're supposed to haggle'. A gourd gets thrown into the bargain and the market trader asks for another 10 shekels. When Brian agrees to the price, the trader says 'No, no, no, no. It's not worth 10. You're supposed to argue! Ten for that, you must be mad!'

The sketch, funny and weird as it is, does point to two standard beliefs about negotiation: you're supposed to haggle and you're supposed to argue. Roger Fisher and William Ury, founders of the Harvard Negotiation Project at Harvard Law School, would disagree (in a non-argumentative fashion, obviously!)[4].

Imagine a business executive returning from a business trip. She has attended a 'Life Balance' seminar and, inspired, has decided she wants to improve her health and fitness. She walks into the house and announces to her husband that she's off for a long run. Her nearest and dearest – who has been single-handedly managing the home and children in her absence – reacts to this, expressing (in no uncertain terms) his desire for a break, immediately; he is off to meet his friends. Since that would leave no one to mind the children, both of them can't get what they want. The most common thing to do here is to haggle (or argue like cats and dogs).

In their book *Getting to Yes*, Fisher and Ury suggest an approach that results in two winners from the negotiation process. This is called 'Principle-based negotiation' and is based on two foundations: a focus on underlying needs and seeking agreements.

Focus on underlying needs

In any negotiation we have certain needs or principles we want met, and, in approaching a negotiation, we will identify ways to fulfil these needs. These are called our 'positions'. The negotiation, then, becomes a debate and trade-off between our respective positions. In the case of the business executive coming home from the seminar, her position is to go for a long run, right away. Her husband's position is that he needs a break, immediately. Clearly both positions cannot be maintained. There will be a winner and a loser, or a compromise (two losers).

Principle-based negotiations are based on building agreements founded on underlying needs rather than on haggling over positions. For example, if the business executive, instead of focusing on wanting to run immediately, talked instead about her desire and need to improve her work–life balance, her husband would almost certainly agree with that desire, and be supportive. At the same time, if her husband talked about how he had been run ragged by the children and had felt caged in the house for the last few days, she would recognise those feelings, and understand his need to get out of the house for some adult company.

Once an agreement is reached around underlying needs, the magic can happen. The wife and husband are no longer competing, pushing for their positions to be met. They are working together to find solutions to needs they both agree with. In the end, the couple above might agree to go out to the park together, with the children; they take a football, and have a game (exercise need fulfilled). In the evening, they get a baby-sitter and go out for dinner together (break need fulfilled). The fact is that most needs can be satisfied in multiple ways (multiple positions). If we start our discussion from the need, we can get creative, together, to identify solutions that fully meet both needs (instead of only partially meeting both).

Seek agreements

There is another reason this style of negotiation works too. Have you ever played 'devil's advocate'? The origins of the term stem from the Roman Catholic Church. When deciding if someone should be named a saint (a process called canonisation), the Church appoints a devil's advocate. Their job is to act a little like an investigative reporter for a tabloid newspaper: they have to search for all the dirt on the nominee, trying to find reasons why that person shouldn't be made a saint. Irrespective of their own views on the candidate for sainthood, their job is to argue the case against their canonisation.

When we play devil's advocate in normal conversations it's to argue a case just for the sake of the debate. Let's say, for example, someone is arguing that Diego Maradona was the greatest ever football player. You may be relatively neutral on the subject but, for the sake of a conversation, you argue the case for Edson Arantes do Nascimento, popularly known as Pelé. What happens next is interesting: the longer, and the more strongly, you argue for Pelé, the more you begin to convince yourself that the famous Brazilian number 10 really was the greatest footballer ever to play the beautiful game. This isn't because of your brilliant arguments either; in fact your opponent is becoming more convinced than ever that Maradona was the best. This is because of cognitive dissonance again: when we argue forcefully, our beliefs start to come into line with our argument.

When you apply this to a negotiation, the risk is that the very act of arguing, disagreeing or 'negotiating' based on different opinions can actually drive both opponents further apart, thereby reducing the chances of reaching a workable agreement that will satisfy both parties. Instead you should seek to find *agreement* in your negotiations to give you a better chance of finding a solution that will work for both people involved.

Let's say that you are about to renegotiate your boundaries. You want to spend more quality time with your friends and family. It's not that you want to do less work, particularly, it's just that the hours you work, the journey you make and the constant emails through the evening and weekend mean you are barely present at home any more. You could storm in and ask for a finishing time of 4.30pm (a position), given you have a long journey. Your manager will then have two options: yes or no. If she says yes, then you're okay; you might not have found the most creative solution, but you're better off, on paper at least (providing your manager didn't feel backed into a corner and irritated by your request). If she said no, where can you go? How would you argue to try to convince her? 'I want to finish at 4.30 ... [no] ... but I have such a long journey ... [no] ... I'm hardly seeing my children ... [no] ... don't you care about children?' It's a road to nowhere. You start off disagreeing, and get further apart as the argument gets more and more heated.

On the other hand, if the conversation is framed in much broader terms, you can build on agreements. 'My work and my family are both important to me ... [agree] ... I want to find the right balance ... [agree] ... will you help me find a solution that works for you and me? ... [agree] ...

So, in order to negotiate your boundaries in a positive, productive manner, you need to do the following:

- Before you start the negotiations, make sure you are really clear in your mind about your underlying need and how it differs from the positions you currently have in mind. It might be that your positions are fully and immediately acceptable, but in many instances this will not be the case.

- Put yourself in the other person's shoes. What are likely to be their underlying needs?
- Start by describing your needs and seeking to understand their needs.
- Look for agreement before trying to find a solution.
- Once agreement is established, get creative. Together generate solutions to meet both of your needs.

When compromise can help

Williams-Sonoma is a cookware company that makes high-quality cooking utensils. After having the same bread machine on the market for a while, they decided it was time to make an improved version. They released the new and improved bread maker at a premium price to reflect its higher quality and additional features. What happened next was unexpected: almost immediately, sales of the original bread maker doubled.

Researcher Itamar Simonson explains that this happens because consumers tend to prefer 'compromise choices'[5]. The new bread maker attracts your attention; it would be wonderful but is too expensive. You then recognise that the original model still makes good bread, and appears cheap compared to the new one; it suddenly becomes an attractive option. It makes you feel that you are making a sensible choice.

So let's imagine you have a burdensome report to do each week, which you feel takes more time to do than it warrants. You might put a proposal to your manager offering three options: the first is to keep producing the same report, the second is to produce a substantial but significantly scaled-down version, and the third is to take a bare-bones approach. Positioned this way, your boss is more likely to choose the middle option, which will still meet their needs, but save you a huge amount of time.

A foot in the door

Would being asked if you are likely to vote actually make you more likely to vote? The answer, according to social scientist Anthony

Greenwald, is yes. He asked this very question on the eve of an election. Those asked to make a prediction of their behaviour were 25 per cent more likely to vote than those not asked (86.7 per cent versus 61.5 per cent)[6]. This effect occurs because we're motivated to behave consistently over time. So, if we act in a particular way, or agree to something small, we become much more likely to act consistently with that action later. So, just after placing a bet, people are much more confident about their horse's chances of winning. Similarly, people who have agreed to a small sign being put up in their front window are much more likely to agree to a huge sign being placed on their front lawn at a later date.

If you want to make a change in your behaviour at work, and you want your boss to agree to it, start by making really, really small requests that would be difficult to disagree with. If these are accepted, your boss will be much more likely to agree with your real, and bigger request. If you do want to work from home one day a week, you might simply start by asking to work from home on a single, one-off instance. That will pave the way for a larger request.

Time to say 'no'

Would you kill someone with a lethal electric shock if a man in a white lab coat asked you to? Or would you say 'no'? In one of the most chilling psychological experiments ever, social psychologist Stanley Milgram began studying the effect of authority on people's actions back in 1961 (soon after the beginning of Adolf Eichmann's war crimes trial began in Jerusalem)[7]. The subjects were told that they would be 'teachers', and they should administer small electric shocks to the 'learner' if they got answers wrong. Each time the learner gave the incorrect answer, the voltage was increased by 15 volts (so the subjects were told – though no actual shocks were administered). The subjects were told not to worry; they were not responsible for any consequences. Despite hearing increasing screams and requests for the experiment to stop, 65 per cent of all subjects continued to do as they were told, up to the maximum shock: a massive 450 volts! They never said 'no'.

Work provides us with authority figures in abundance, all of whom can dictate our actions. Authority can reduce our need to take responsibility for our actions: being told to do something removes our need to decide. Additionally, saying 'no' to anyone, let alone someone more senior, is really hard. At some point, though, you'll need to use that two-letter word if you want to set boundaries and avoid the drudgery of the perpetual 'yes'.

The truthful 'no'

In 1901 Harry Houdini was handcuffed and locked inside an oversized milk can filled with water. Trapped, he only had a limited time before he ran out of breath and drowned. After much wriggling, he emerged triumphant to cheers from the crowd. This became one of his most iconic escapes. There's something about saying 'no' that brings out the escapologist in all of us. Being requested to do something we don't want to do puts us on the spot. After much wriggling and squirming, hopefully, we find our escape.

Let's imagine you've just been asked to attend an important business conference over the following weekend. What do you do? Do you tell your boss 'no' because you want to spend time with your family, or do you get creative? Our desire to escape can be so strong that we entirely fabricate a convincing-sounding story to demonstrate that we certainly cannot say 'yes': 'It's my second cousin's wedding. We were very close as children' or 'My long-lost school friend, who was with me in 'Nam, is visiting with his three-legged Chihuahua, who has dog leukaemia, so it might be my last chance to see her'. We can feel an almost irresistible urge to create excuses to get out of things. Our primary goal is to escape. This can help us escape from an awkward situation, but leaves us open to similar future conversations: 'Will you stay late to help me with my report tonight?' 'Oh, I'd really love to [lie], but [excuse coming . . .] I'm taking my budgie to the vet'. 'Ahh, that's a shame; how about tomorrow?'

While I'm all for creativity, when it comes to saying 'no' the truth is best. Escaping can help us to get out of awkward situations and is often an attempt not to damage the relationship, but it can lead us down a dead end; you can't keep on making up excuses. The truth may feel more challenging to say, but it can help to set boundaries and clarify your priorities.

Oh, and by the way, don't say 'I'm busy' as your excuse. It may be true, but it's not sufficiently explicit; it just sounds like a rude brush-off.

The thoughtful 'no'

One of the things that can prompt us to either say 'yes' when we want to say 'no', or to make up excuses, is the feeling that the spotlight is on us. When we get an unwanted request, a request to which we might want to say 'no', we can often say 'yes' simply because we can't think it through quickly enough. When the pressure is on we default to the safest option and say 'yes'. It might be that we need time to think through our reponse based on all our other commitments. It might be that we already know we want to say 'no', but just want time to think through our delivery. Either way, get out of the spotlight. Say 'Let me think about it' or 'Give me five minutes'. Then go and reflect in a cool, rational manner on your response. Assertiveness is not the same thing as quick thinking. Take your time; make the right choice; then have the conversation.

The positive 'no'

The starting point for saying 'no' effectively is saying 'yes'. The 'yes' is the big reason behind your 'no'. The Microsoft CVP would say 'no' to his boss's request, because he was saying 'yes' to being at his child's birthday. Having an important 'yes' makes saying 'no' a whole lot easier because it provides you with your reason for saying 'no'; it's your explanation. It also provides you with the motivation to say 'no'. When you say 'no' to busyness it's not because you want to stop being busy; it's because you want to become more immersed, more effective, more energised and more connected. Find your big 'yes' and you'll find your 'no'.

In his book, *The Power of a Positive No*[8], William Ury suggests thinking of your 'no' as a tree. The origins and the strength of the 'no' come from the roots. This is where you start in preparation and in articulating your 'no'; the rest of your 'no' is your big yes. This is followed by the strong, direct trunk, where you actually say 'no' clearly, simply and unemotionally to the relevant person. Finally, the tree branches out. The final part of the positive 'no' is to reach out to see if there is a solution, to try to make a positive proposal. Saying 'no' isn't simply escapology; it's also an exercise in persuasion. You may have just told your boss that you won't be delivering the report to her tomorrow, but you might end by saying that you'll have it with her by the close of the week.

To be clear, this isn't a proposal to soften your 'no'. Your delivery should be consistent with your big 'yes' and your clear 'no'. It shouldn't offer false hope either. Your 'no' can often be presented in the form of a third option. I mentioned creativity wasn't helpful when it comes to generating excuses, but it is really helpful here. Let's say you're being asked to develop a staff survey to assess training needs. Your role has nothing to do with training, but you do have some expertise in surveys. The reason you want to say 'no' to the project is that you are working on a major project launch (your big 'yes') and don't want to be distracted by survey development. After explaining your big 'yes' and stating your 'no' clearly, you want to close with a 'yes', a third option. You could say, 'Look, I'd be happy to act as an informal advisor on this. If you put your objectives and ideas together, come and see me and I'll give you my perspective. Would that help?'

The project management 'no'

In project management, they have something called the Triple Constraint Triangle. There are three fundamental constraints on any project; change one of these and it will immediately affect the other two. The model is shown below.

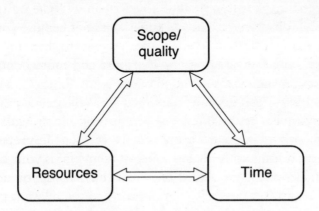

Imagine you're building a new sports stadium for the next Olympic Games. If the scope or quality is increased, i.e. someone decides 'Let's put a removable roof on it', it will have an impact on either the budget required or the time it will take to build the overall stadium – or both. Reducing the budget might be possible, but only if the scope is reduced and/or the deadline is lengthened. Given that there is a fixed delivery date for the Olympics, any changes to either scope or quality will have an instant impact on the resources needed (i.e. we'll need to get a lot more people on the job, quickly) or vice versa.

In the context of busyness, we might often be saying 'no' due to the overall press of work. You are saying 'no' to unrealistic expectations due to the other challenges you are facing. The project management 'no' involves explaining the implications of a 'yes'. It means saying 'no' to the demand as it was positioned, but leaving open a conditional 'yes' if the other person agrees to adjustments to the other constraints. For example, say you have been asked to prepare a presentation on your department's marketing spend in the last fiscal year by Friday. You may realise that this is not possible. However, you might say that you would be able to do the presentation if the scope was scaled down, the presentation was a week on Friday instead of this week, or if you get support to help you with this (or with your other work). This allows the 'no' to turn into a rational negotiation.

The big messages in 'Negotiate your life back'

We can't go on forever accepting more and more, doing more and more. At some point, for the good of our work, for the good of our families and for the good of ourselves, we will have to recognise when **enough is enough**.

The impact of more and more isn't linear, it's concave. At a certain point, a little more makes things a lot worse. Recognise the early behavioural signs of this; **spot your busy footprint.**

SETTING LIMITS

- Boundaries restrict us, but they also protect us. **In an unbounded world limits are not automatic**; we have to set them, and negotiate them ourselves.

- Manage your boundaries in three ways: **offer more to get more** in return; don't ask for everything – **be clear about which boundaries matter for you**; communicate your boundaries often, and before the time you need to enforce them – **the pre-emptive strike**.

NEGOTIATE FOR YOUR LIFE

- If you want to negotiate, **don't haggle!** Discuss your **underlying needs**, and the other party's. Build **agreement**, and from that agreement start to **identify creative solutions** that work for both of you.
- **Don't just offer one option**, but three; more often than not, people will choose the middle 'compromise' option. People like to act consistently. So, **ask for a little** and you make it much more likely, when you ask for something bigger, you will get a yes.

TIME TO SAY 'NO'

- A man in a lab coat persuaded normal people to give someone a lethal electric shock, just because they didn't want to say 'no' to an authority figure. **Learn to say 'no'** or suffer the consequences!
- The **truthful 'no'**: honesty is the best policy. If you make **creative excuses** you may hang yourself!
- The **thoughtful 'no'**: we often say 'yes' because we can't think of a good way to say 'no'. **Give yourself some time to think**. Figure out what you want to say; then go back and say it.
- The **positive 'no'**: behind every 'no' should be a big 'yes'. Focus on the **positive reason you are saying 'no'**.
- The **project management 'no'**: in every project there are three constraints – the **time** taken, the **resources** needed and the **quality or scope** delivered. The project management 'no' doesn't involve the 'N–word' at all. It simply involves a negotiation around constraints: if one changes, the others will need to change to compensate.

Go-Do

BOUNDARIES

Identify your boundaries: what are your limits? Once you've done this, identify three people to speak to in order set those boundaries (the pre-emptive strike).

RENEGOTIATE

Meet with one person in your life with whom you need to re-negotiate expectations. Focus on underlying needs and find a fresh, more healthy agreement.

Experiment

DOMINATE YOUR PHONE

Try switching off your phone as you leave work, and when you get home, leave it in your work bag. You're the master of your attention, not your phone.

BUSY FOOTPRINT

Observe your subtle behavioural changes when you start getting overloaded. Clarify your Busy Footprint and use it as an early warning signal. Tell those close to you about it, so they can spot it too.

Section Two

FOCUS

Success in the information age will be achieved by those who can differentiate themselves. This means focusing better on the big issues and setting your own agenda rather than allowing your email to do it for you. It means using a coherent strategy to set yourself apart from the crowd, thinking better by using your brain effectively, rather than fighting against it. It means making a real impact. This section explores how to achieve more by focusing on what you can do differently, what you can do better.

Racing in the wrong direction

In 1996, eight climbers died in a single day on Everest. It appears there was something of a traffic jam towards the summit and so progress was slower than expected. There is a rule on Everest that if you don't reach the summit by a certain time of the day, you have to abandon your attempt. On that day, these really experienced but frustrated climbers should have turned back, but instead they kept going. They reached the summit too late in the day, had to climb down in darkness and died.

Christopher Cave, a former stockbroker, heard about this and it bothered him[1]. It reminded him of what he'd seen happen in a lot of companies: a CEO would choose an ambitious goal and commit to it publically. Then evidence would start appearing that it was a bad idea. Instead of looking dispassionately at the new information and stopping to reflect on a better course of action, these businesses responded to their frustrated efforts with more activity. In effect, to avoid having to face the possibility that they were heading in the wrong direction, they just got busy and increased their efforts in the wrong direction. I see the same thing with individuals.

Most people today have a list of things they know they *should* do.

Yet they allow everyday flotsam and jetsam to fill up their lives, leaving no space for the things that will make a real difference to their performance, their career, their organisations. More specifically, they respond to the frustrations and pressures of life by redoubling their efforts in the wrong direction. They plough on, spending ever more time on email, doing more stuff – playing the wrong game instead of focusing on what is important.

An Industrial Age mentality

The essence of playing the wrong game goes back to an Industrial Age mentality. The primary goal in the Industrial Age was production: given a set level of quality, the more you could produce the better, and anything that could be done to increase efficiency was a good thing. Even though we've left the Industrial Age, most people around me still seem to be playing the 'More' game. The rules are simple: the people who produce the most (and are seen to be producing a lot) win. I've seen the 'More' game work, especially early on in people's careers. They work hard, they work long and their bosses notice they seem to be more 'motivated' than their colleagues. They start giving these people more to do: more work and more responsibility. This can become the template for career success.

However, at some point, these people hit the buffers. They get to a point where they are no longer competing against those who just want a job, not a career. Suddenly they find their competitors are also career-minded; are also hungry to progress; are also playing the 'More' game. It then becomes something of an arms race; with email response time, working hours and the sheer quantity of stuff produced being the criteria for success. When the 'More' game doesn't bring instant results, as their career progress slows, they do exactly what the climbers did: they redouble their efforts in the wrong direction, doing more and more until they either burn out or simply fade into the background. In a world of too much, 'More' is the wrong game: the right game is 'different'.

Chapter 4

Differentiate yourself

I n 1993, Continental Airlines launched its new, low-cost airline, Continental Lite. It opened to great fanfare as a specific move to compete against highly successful low-cost competitors, such as Southwest Airlines. Continental had many advantages: it had a large and wealthy parent company; it was offering some of the cheapest fares in the industry; it could meet the frequency of other low-cost airlines; it could allow passengers to transfer between flights without having to collect their bags; and seats were pre-allocated. It sounded perfect. Yet two years and $300 million later, Continental Lite flew its last flight. Partly as a result of this disaster, the mother company, Continental Airlines, came under hostile attack from Delta and Northwest Airlines. Ultimately, Northwest closed a deal that allowed Continental to maintain its brand, but all power transferred to the Northwest board.

Why didn't this promising new airline, with so many advantages on its side, become successful? Michael Porter, in perhaps one of the most famous *Harvard Business Review* articles ever, 'What is strategy?'[1] attributes the failure to a lack of strategic focus. Continental Airlines was a full-service airline, offering meals and the convenience of hassle-free transfers from one flight to another. It was catering for business passengers, and those who were less cost-sensitive than the target audience for Southwest. It had recognised, however, the strategic threat posed by low-cost carriers – and the opportunity. The airline attempted to be two things at once: a full-service airline *and* a low-cost provider.

However, in direct competition against Southwest, Continental struggled to do both full-service and low-cost. The company relied on travel agencies for its full-service business, but couldn't afford them for its low-cost option, so it cut agency commissions on all flights. In addition, the airline found it couldn't support the frequent flier benefits on its low-cost version, and so it reduced perks to members on all journeys. Flights were also frequently delayed at hub airports due to baggage transfers that other low-cost providers didn't have to worry about. The result: irritated agents, disappointed customers and late flights. Porter described Continental Lite's approach as 'straddling strategic positions'. It failed and the airline paid a high price for this failure.

Continental failed because it lost focus. Business strategy is all about how to succeed, in a competitive environment, when you have limited resources. It's all about doing things to differentiate yourself and making trade-offs in order to focus resources where they can make the greatest impact. To thrive in a world of too much means more than simply achieving a better work–life balance. It means to succeed in your career in competitive workplaces with a limited resource of time. To do this we can learn a lot from the behaviour of big businesses.

Differentiation

There are two big factors which affect your ability to succeed in your career in a world of too much. The first is that you have limited resources of time and energy. The second is that all of your customers (those people who will be making decisions about you which affect your career) are also over-stretched and distracted. The 'More' game fails on both counts because you are unlikely to be able to do sufficiently more than all your competition to deliver noticeably more or better results. You fail to stand out, and consequently you get forgotten.

To really succeed in a world of too much we have to differentiate ourselves. To do this we need to focus our limited resources on the areas where they will deliver the highest returns. To do this we can employ methods from the world of corporate strategy. We also differentiate ourselves by communicating our personal strategy and value clearly and memorably, so we influence decisions. Here we can use insights from marketing and the world of branding. This chapter will explain the alternative to the 'More' game; it will explain how to differentiate yourself by developing a strategy and communicating this simply as a personal brand.

Strategy means tough choices and focus

It may feel a bit odd to apply the language and frameworks of corporate strategy to you, your career and your life. Yet the world of corporate strategy is a great place to look for lessons on how to operate in a world of too much, as businesses have been grappling with this problem for a long time. Globalisation increased the scale of opportunity, but also the quantity and quality of the competition; product life-cycles decrease as innovation and market disruption accelerate; the consumer has become more informed and, with an ever-increasing number of product options, more fickle. Most companies face too much competition, change and choice.

Working with leadership teams, I have experienced, first hand, the challenges of making tough decisions in the face of seemingly endless options. The difficulty often isn't generating great ideas; it's saying 'no' to great ideas in order to focus on even better ones. This is essential because while great ideas and opportunities are seemingly endless, the resources of time, money or people needed to deliver them are limited. Companies can't do everything (as Continental tried to do); they need to focus in order to create and sustain a competitive advantage over their rivals. In hyper-competitive markets, companies that aren't focused lose. To help companies focus, to make the best use of their limited resources, they need a business strategy.

In the same way, on an individual level we can't do everything; so we have to make choices. In the section on Mastery we looked at having to choose because we *can't* do everything. Michael Porter would say we have to choose because we *shouldn't* do everything if we want to succeed. Using business strategy as a model for this will change your perspective on choice. These frameworks weren't designed to be used this way, but using the lens of business strategy can make it easier for you to ask questions about your priorities more objectively; it helps you take a broader, more 'strategic' perspective on your options and make better choices about how to use your time.

Making tough strategic choices allows us to bring the kind of focus and differentiation needed to flourish – to not just to cope or regain control, but to build a successful career. The choices discussed in this chapter are aimed at making a difference so we can stand out – choices that combine to form a personal strategy.

Operational effectiveness isn't enough

In an increasingly globalised world, it's harder to stand out amongst the competition. For Japanese companies in the 1980s, their secret weapon over Western corporations was an area in which they had developed fantastic improvements: 'operational effectiveness' – the practices that allow a company to create products better and faster, with fewer defects. Japanese companies seemed unstoppable as they churned out products more cheaply and to higher standards. Yet, after a decade of irresistible global domination, the tide started to turn for Japan. By the 1990s, Japan entered a decade-long recession, with zero growth, rising unemployment and deflation. Other countries around the world had copied the best practices of Japanese manufacturing and destroyed Japan's competitive advantage.

Operational effectiveness can provide important advantages over competitors, which can increase profitability, but it will rarely keep you ahead in the long term. Imagine a productivity frontier, which is the limit of productive capability, given the best practices and tools available at any one time. This productivity frontier will constantly shift as new technology is developed. These new technologies can be applied, at significant cost, but best practices spread quickly, and the immediate gains in productivity are also shared by competitors, so no competitive advantage is gained, meaning no increased profit.

In fact, what tends to happen is that, as all competitors get ever closer to the productivity frontier, the investment cost in making further incremental gains gets larger, and this eats into profits. It becomes an arms race in which everyone loses.

As an individual, the productivity frontier has shifted enormously with the arrival of each of the following: the computer, the laptop, the mobile phone, the internet, the smartphone and the Cloud. Each of these raised performance levels by allowing us to produce more. This has had three strategic impacts on the competitive advantage we have in our careers: firstly, because the productivity frontier has moved, we are all able to produce a lot more. So we do. This creates an ever-increasing amount of work for us all to do. Secondly, as we all get closer and closer to the frontier, our ability to differentiate ourselves on the basis of our productivity gets harder and harder. Finally, any further increments we want to make to our productivity in the hope of achieving ever-smaller advantages over our competition come at an increasingly large cost (especially if we remember Nassim Taleb's concavity).

The moral of the story is, there are only two ways of competing in a world of too much: productivity or differentiation. I suggest you do not compete on the basis of how much you can do; it's the fool's game of 'More' we've all been playing for the last 20 years. Operational effectiveness is necessary, but not sufficient; it's time for another game. It's time to achieve better by being different.

Being different: positioning and differentiation

It has never been more important than now to be different. In the agricultural era, competitive advantage came through ownership of land. In the industrial era, it came from productivity. In the information era it came through information, and the ability to capture and analyse it. Now, I believe, we're moving into a post-informational era, a period that the Nomura Institute calls the Creative Era[2]. Information is no longer valuable; in fact it's so ubiquitous it has become a commodity, or even free. The markets are so competitive and fast, products can be copied, services can be mimicked. People are so overloaded, and their information channels so bloated, that they struggle to focus on anything. Through all this, how do we choose what gets attention? What cuts through all the noise? In the near future, the only things that will be capable of providing you with a competitive advantage are difference, novelty and genuinely surprising or innovative things.

A strategic position describes the activities you choose to focus on, the problems you choose to solve for your customers. Differentiation refers to the degree to which what you do stands out from the crowd; the degree to which it is different. Developing a strategic position allows you to differentiate yourself in order to succeed; it helps you to bring real focus into the way you can uniquely add value.

Strategic positioning

Competitive strategy is about being deliberately different. Operational effectiveness means doing similar things to your competition, but trying to do them faster, or more efficiently. Intelligent strategic positioning, on the other hand, means doing *different* things to your rivals, or doing the same things in *different* ways.

Porter gives the example of Ikea. They serve young furniture buyers who want style at a low cost. This isn't unique in itself. What is unique is the way they choose to do it. You wander the showroom by yourself, with only a catalogue for reference, so there are no expensive showroom assistants to pay for; you collect your selections from the warehouse yourself, saving transport costs; and build your own furniture when you get home, saving in storage. These various savings allow Ikea to focus on delivering the maximum in style for the minimum in cost. In addition, since its target audience is young and in full-time work, the stores are open long hours and often contain free child-minding services. Ikea is different, not because its furniture is different, but because it has adopted a different strategic position in the market. Where rival firms are competing only on the quality or value of their furniture, Ikea has taken a different strategic position. It has gained a sustainable competitive advantage.

I talk to my clients about four sources of strategic positions from a career perspective: product-based positioning; audience-based positioning; niche positioning; and doing everything for everyone.

Only the first three of these are effective; only the last of these seems common in most organisations at present.

This wouldn't be a section on strategy unless I introduced something beloved by all business consultants everywhere: the 2x2 matrix! This shows the four positions you can take, based on product or audience, ranging from wide to narrow.

'Products' might be the range of products you offer; the variety of things you actually do; what you produce or the service you offer. Are you a specialist or a jack-of-all-trades? 'Audience' is the range of customers you support. These may be internal or external customers, but are you offering your service to a wide variety of audiences, or a highly targeted, specific audience? You can use this graph to identify which position you currently hold and then decide if it is the right one.

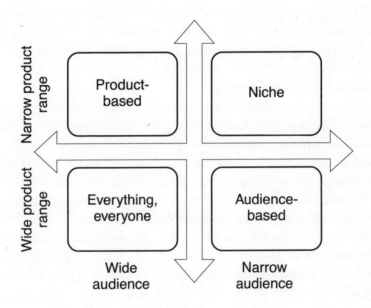

Everything, everyone

A restaurant I know had developed a good reputation for the quality and creativity of its food; however, it was struggling with its location. Finally it secured larger premises ideally situated to attract a lot more customers. In the first week it became clear that the demand in the new location was strong. But then it all started going wrong. To meet the demand, the restaurant decided to hire cooks from a well-known, low-quality, high-turnover restaurant. Rather than accepting that they needed to restrict their number of clients while they trained new staff, they filled the restaurant and the kitchen staff simply did their best. In addition, not all their new clientele were appreciative of the innovative haute cuisine, so the menu was 'dumbed down'. Rather than sticking to their formula of quality, interesting food, the restaurant tried to do everything for everyone. In a few short months, what had seemed like the glorious beginning of a very bright future was a distant memory. The restaurant lost its position in the market and failed to satisfy its customers; it closed shortly afterwards.

Trying to do everything for everyone is no strategic position at all. The business or person that adopts this approach spreads themself thinly and ends up delivering very little of real impact in the business. In trying to do everything and please everyone on limited time, they end up achieving little and disappointing all. This approach is often the most common position of those with serial busyness.

Audience-based positioning

This strategy was called a 'needs-based' position in Porter's *Harvard Business Review* article. It involves offering a wide range of products or services to a very specific group of clients. Take the example of a private bank which specifically targets a small selection of wealthy individuals. In targeting a small group of people, they can gain a deep understanding of their clients' needs and build a strong relationship. They offer the customer a one-stop shop of integrated products, all catering for people with very similar needs. They also offer this service in a way that is highly tailored to the needs and tastes of their target audience. A company basing its strategic position on audience-based positioning aims to beat its competition by using its deeper insight into the customer, tailoring its service to individual customer needs and building a trusting partnership.

Product-based positioning

This strategy is all about creating a very narrow range of products or services that will appeal to a wide population of people. Economists Kjell Nordström and Jonas Ridderstrale argue that there are only two effective strategies: to be 'fit' or to be 'sexy'[3]. 'Fit' means meeting a specific customer need better than anyone else. 'Sexy' means producing a product or service that has an emotional appeal – that stands out from the crowd because it is cooler, more desirable. Product-based positioning can come from either strategy. Henkel, the German company, invented the glue stick to allow people to easily and cleanly stick paper. They released Pritt Stick in 1969, which fitted a need (we didn't know we had) in schools and offices; by 2001 they were being sold in 121 countries. Apple are the obvious example of sexy. At the time iPods were becoming dominant there were many other mp3 players, but none were so cool. Product differentiation isn't simply about fit or sexy, though; it's also about focus and innovation. It's about doing very few things really well, so that they stand out from the competition in a crowded market. Apple CEO Tim Cook said: 'We are the most focused company that I know of or have read of or have any knowledge of. We say no to good ideas every day. We say no to great ideas in order to keep the amount of things we focus on very small in number so that we can put enormous energy behind the ones we choose.'[4]

Niche positioning

This is the least common of the strategic positions: to offer a very narrow range of products or services to a very narrow range of customers. Koenigsegg, the Swedish Hypercar manufacturer, do just this. They don't make many cars, but the cars they do make are at the extreme end of the performance and price range. Their Agera R model broke the Guinness World Record for a production car in 2011 by accelerating from 0 to 300km in just 14.53 seconds. In March 2009, the Koenigsegg CCXR was rated by *Forbes* as one of the 10 most beautiful cars in history. The very price of their cars means their target audience is narrow. A Koenigsegg CCX, for example, will cost you around $600,000. Their service matches their price. For example, their factory is based at an old fighter plane airport, which not only allows test drives on the runways, but also lets potential clients land their private jets next to the factory.

What should your positioning be based on?

When it comes to you and your career, what should you build your strategy around? Should it be a specific audience, whose needs you learn to understand and anticipate, and with whom you build strong personal relationships and trusting partnerships; or a specific thing you want to offer in which you focus on building exceptional, surprising or indispensable capabilities or services? My strong recommendation is that you ditch the 'everything and everyone' strategy and get a clear idea of where your focus should be – audience or product – before moving to the next section.

Differentiation

In his Father Brown series of detective stories, G. K. Chesterton included a short story called 'The Invisible Man'. The essence of the story is that all those involved (apart from Father Brown) are flummoxed by a murder that has been seemingly committed by an invisible man: no one was seen entering or leaving the house where the murder took place. The case is solved when Fr Brown realises that *the expected* often becomes *invisible* – in this case, the postman. When observers insisted that they hadn't seen anybody, what they really meant was they hadn't *noticed* anyone. The postman, because he was so entirely expected, was tuned out and forgotten.

The essence of strategy is differentiation: identifying how you can stand out from the crowd. This isn't just a PR thing. When everyone in our organisations is running flat-out, the greatest shortage in organisations today isn't time, but attention – focused attention. Have you ever noticed how you tune things out? You walk into a smelly room, but after five minutes you've got used to the smell and cease to notice it; you buy a new car and are terribly excited about it for the first few weeks, but after that it becomes simply the way you get to work; your house has a nice view, which you fail to see after a while. This process is called accommodation, and it is critically important to allow us to process our over-complicated world efficiently. Yet when something surprising is seen, heard or experienced, a part of the brain called the anterior cingulate cortex lights up. This is the error detection section of the brain and was essential to protect us from being eaten back in the day, by bringing all our attention to bear rapidly on that unexpected rustling in the bushes. We are primed, through evolution, to notice and give real attention to the surprising and the different.

This does, of course, have implications on our careers. If we do

what everyone else does – the expected – even with the best intentions from the managers and leaders of our organisation, we are likely
to be tuned out and forgotten. Unless we differentiate ourselves in
meaningful and useful ways, we blend into the background. When
we differentiate ourselves, we are noticed, remembered and valued.

Your choice over your strategic positioning – audience-based
or product-based – is an essential first step to clarifying where you
can focus your efforts to differentiate yourself. It helps because it
informs you of the game you want to play, of how you should try
and compete.

Audience-based differentiation

Could you differentiate yourself by understanding your target audience better than others, having stronger relationships and offering
them unexpectedly bespoke, easy or integrated solutions for their
needs? For example, Frank is a sales manager in a large media organisation. He has clients spanning a wide range of spend with his
business, but the majority of his business (about 50 per cent) was
coming from five per cent of his clients. When he reflected on the
way he spent his time, he realised that his time allocation bore little
relation to client spend. Frank was ambitious and cared deeply about
customer service, yet he realised if he wanted to make a real jump
in his performance he would have to recognise that all clients are
not equal. He had been allowing the requests and queries of his various clients to determine how he spent his time; he needed a
strategy.

He made a deliberate choice to make a radical shift in how he
spent his time, changing his allocation so he could spend more than
half his time on the five per cent. He didn't do this because the five
per cent were asking for it or needed it, but because he saw the five
per cent as his biggest opportunity. He met with them more, not to
sell, but to really understand their businesses and to build personal
relationships. He started to understand how he could transform how
he supported them. They were very busy, so he spent a lot of time
thinking on their behalf, contacting them proactively with media
stories and opportunities that might be of interest to them. His partnerships with his clients helped him to recognise that their
advertising needs were being met by individual media owners offering relatively narrow, standard products. He started to work with

other people across his own business or in other media and non-media organisations in order to deliver unique and innovative solutions for his clients, based on deep insight into their needs. He developed an award-winning solution by pulling together an airline, a travel agency, a TV company and a newspaper. He started to help them get integrated solutions to meet their integrated needs. He became the first person the five per cent would ring, not just when they had advertising they wanted to buy, but because they had an idea or a problem. By adopting this strategy, Frank transformed his effectiveness: his sales increased dramatically, his clients loved him and he differentiated himself in the eyes of his employer.

If you think this is the game you should play, reflect on the following questions:

- How could you bring much more focus towards your target audience? How can you change your time allocation to being strategically driven rather than demand-driven?
- How well do you really understand your audience's needs? This means thinking more broadly than the kinds of discussions they usually have with you. What are the problems you could help them solve, which they are not even discussing with you at present?
- How could you strengthen the relationship with your target audience? How could you build a stronger partnership with them? How much do they trust you, and how could you increase this?
- How could you broaden how you support your audience, so you can help in more ways? How can you make their lives easier, by integrating products or services into coherent solutions?
- How could you make what you do for your audience more unique and tailored to their needs?

Product-based differentiation

How could you differentiate yourself through what you do? What capabilities or areas of expertise could you develop that would truly set you apart? What service could you develop or offer that uniquely fits a specific need in your organisation or market, or that's just downright 'sexy'?

Amy works for a multinational food company which has grown through a strong sales culture and a capability to acquire and integrate other businesses. Due to the turbulence of the food industry, and also the acquisitive nature of her organisation, Amy noticed that there were a lot of change initiatives. As someone who had a low boredom threshold and was attracted to challenge, she felt working in change would suit her. Amy decided to get involved, but . . . she worked in finance.

Amy started to volunteer for any change initiative, which started to get her noticed. She demonstrated real commitment and not a little talent on these initiatives. She also proved to herself that this is where she wanted to go. With her manager's blessing, she completed a Master's degree in change management. She wrote a couple of articles for the internal newspaper and then in the trade press. She was proving herself to be increasingly useful and became recognised in the business for her ability to offer insights into organisational change backed up by sound financial understanding. Her breakthrough came when she was given a business (rather than financial) leadership position at a factory that was expected to be closed. She turned the factory around through a change programme which involved all the staff, alongside a series of tough decisions to stop the production of a number of long-established products. Next she worked with the CEO on the biggest acquisition in the company's history. She is now an MD, not because she was a good accountant or because she worked hard, but because she differentiated herself through a persistent focus on delivering change. It was her expertise in change, alongside her financial skills that made her stand out.

If you think this is the game you should play, ask yourself the following questions:

- What makes you uniquely useful to your business? What capabilities, expertise or experiences do you have that are different and valuable compared to those of your colleagues? What combination of skills do you have that is unusual and compelling?
- Where do your passions lie? What capability or expertise would you be willing to persistently invest in developing over the longer term?
- Which of your capabilities are most in need in the business or

the market at present? What capabilities will be most in demand in the future?

- How do you create opportunities for you to demonstrate your unique capabilities?
- How do you build a track record of success which demonstrates your strength in this area? What particular products or services will you develop or deliver?
- How is your capability driving innovations and change in the business?

Trade-offs

I remember watching a documentary about Ryanair, a successful European low-cost airline based on the model of Southwest Airlines. The programme was made in the early days of Ryanair. It was designed as a shocking exposé of the terrible customer service provided by the airline. It revealed passengers receiving little or no support from Ryanair after being stranded in obscure airports when their flights were cancelled; unexpected charges and fines; and rude and militant staff. It was quite shocking. At the end of the show, the investigative reporter got a short interview with Ryanair CEO Michael O'Leary to see how he would respond to all the findings. His answer was brilliant. He said, more or less, we don't do customer service; we do cheap flights. For me it was one of the strongest examples of clear strategic thinking I'd ever heard: he understood that there is a cost involved in providing good customer service – a cost which might increase fares. His strategic trade-off was clear: fly with us and you might not get the best customer service, but you will certainly get a cheap flight.

Frank and Amy had to make trade-offs to allow them to focus on their strategies. Frank had to manage the other 95 per cent of his customers as he deliberately reduced the time he spent supporting them. Amy had to find time for her change work, even if that took time away from her pure accountancy. We don't have unlimited resources so, if we want to succeed in a competitive workplace, we have to make some tough decisions. Making choices is a strategic activity. In fact, in my experience, trade-offs are at the heart of any good strategy. All organisations and executive teams are good at coming up with great new business ideas; very few are good at deliberately choosing not to do some things in order to go really deep into others. Yet that is what we must do if we really want to differentiate ourselves.

What trade-offs do you need to make:

- ... in your business?
- ... in your career?
- ... in your life?

A clear brand

In the world of too much, having a strategy is essential to bringing focus to your activity and delivering results when faced with too many possible options and the finite resources of your time and energy. However, this is only part of the picture. The other side of the equation is the way your strategy is received by the people who make the decisions that affect your career – your customers. You might have a beautifully focused strategy, but if you cannot communicate it in a way that gets remembered and influences decision making it won't make its full impact on your customers. For this we need to turn to the world of marketing and branding for inspiration.

Strategies are often complex and aren't terribly useful for communication purposes. The beauty of brands is that they articulate complex ideas simply. Being able to communicate your personal strategy in this way is a huge advantage in a world of too much information and too much communication. The simplicity of a personal brand helps to cut through all the noise. It clarifies and amplifies your value; it differentiates you.

(This section on branding stems from an ongoing collaboration with the brilliant marketing strategist, Damian Horner. Most of the best ideas in the coming pages are his.)

How brands work

Imagine you're shopping in a large supermarket and you're choosing a soup. In front of you are 300 options. According to economic theory, lots of choice is a good thing: it allows you to use logic to identify the best one for you. Following this theory, you would carefully scrutinise the labels, the contents and the prices to make a rational decision about which is the best soup for you. Three hours later you move on to the breakfast cereal aisle and start again. In practice, of course you don't.

What happens instead? One of two things, either you walk away, deciding you don't want to buy soup after all, or you substitute the rational option for the easy option. Instead of answering the question 'Which soup would be the ideal choice for me (and my family) based on my taste, health and price preferences?' you ask yourself 'Where's the soup I bought last week?' or 'Which has the nicest label?' or simply 'Where's the Campbell's chicken soup?'

This is an example of a phenomenon called *cognitive fluency*. Cognitive fluency is the ease with which we can process something: the degree to which a mental or perceptual task is easy or hard work. When making judgements we don't always think 100 per cent rationally. The brain often substitutes an easy question for a hard question. One of the criteria the brain uses is the cognitive fluency. We prefer, and feel more confident in, more cognitively fluent information.

Brands work by helping us make these mental substitutions and therefore make decisions easier and simpler. Each and every day we have too many choices to make; too many options. A big supermarket contains 70,000 brands. How can we possibly expect to go shopping and make fully informed choices on every item we buy. Faced with 300 soups, it's just not possible to read all the labels and objectively evaluate the contents of each. We've seen lots of Campbell's soup adverts, we remember eating Campbell's soup as a child, we know we like Campbell's soup, so we go straight to the selection from Campbell's soups and choose one of them; job done. Even though any number of the soups might taste better, be healthier or be cheaper; the easiest choice to make is the familiar choice; the brand you know and trust. It is for this reason that brands matter.

It's not about performance

Brands don't just influence our choices, they also influence our view of performance. Take taste, for example. You might think something as visceral as taste would be immune from the impact of branding, yet blind taste tests prove otherwise. In the United States, Budweiser has almost 50 per cent of the beer market: an astonishing dominance with so much choice available to consumers. If you speak to many Budweiser drinkers, they will imply they'd rather cut off a limb than sully their taste buds with the likes of Miller or Coors. Yet, in blind taste tests the majority of Budweiser drinkers cannot tell these three beers apart and certainly cannot recognise which is Budweiser. Taste matters, of course, but it's hugely influenced by the brand. Brands determine our preferences and choices.

You have a brand whether you like it or not

Branding is as relevant to our careers as it is to our purchasing habits. One reason for this is that people don't have enough information about you. Very few people see you at work enough to have a real and accurate understanding of your day-to-day performance. A second reason why brands are important is that it's difficult for people to retain what information they do have about you as they are also trying to hold information about everything and everyone else. Robin Dunbar showed that it is physically impossible to manage more than 150 real social relationships at once because our brains aren't big enough to hold all the information necessary[5]. This has become known as Dunbar's number. With the best will in the world, and even if the people around you had nothing better to do, it is just not possible for people to make all their decisions based on full and objective criteria.

Yet, every day, these people are making decisions about you which shape your career. These may be big decisions, such as whether they should offer you a job or what performance rating to give you. They may be much smaller: whether to invite you to a meeting or onto a project, to turn to you for advice, or what to say about you when you're not around. Given that they haven't got the capacity to make full and objective decisions, they substitute a difficult question for an easy one. They make their decisions based not on your performance but on your brand. Whether or not you like this idea, it makes no difference: your brand is already influencing your career and will do so increasingly as people get even more busy. Your choice is not 'Do I want a brand or not?' but 'Do I want to intentionally build my brand or not?'

Busy as a brand

Next time you're on a flight, watch and listen to what happens when the plane lands. Within seconds you hear beeps up and down the aisles, you see the desperate race to turn on smartphones, you start to hear the rapid tap of emails and texting, or even (my favourite) the call to say nothing at all to a friend or partner before the plane comes to a stop. I accept we're all busy people, but there is something in the urgency of the reconnection that speaks of something more than just an addiction to busyness. The truth is, busy isn't just a fact of life, nor is it a problem we all suffer; busy is also aspirational. In hundreds of ways each day we strive to demonstrate how busy we are. Our busyness is a live demonstration that the world cannot function without our presence in the global conversation. This aspiration stems from our deepest fears: that we don't really matter, that we are inconsequential and meaningless. Activity acts as a salve, a light relief from our deeper existential angst.

I talked earlier about how often we respond to the question: 'How are you?' with the word 'Busy'. As a little experiment, next time someone asks you this question, say 'I've got hardly anything to do these days', or even simply 'I'm not very busy'. You will notice the person you are talking to will adopt a look somewhere between pity and disgust.

Busy is a rubbish brand

When anything becomes common, frequent or ever-present, we stop noticing it. It's like a football team, dressed in identical red team shirts. The only person who stands out is the one wearing the green goal-keeper's jersey. We are primed to notice difference and novelty; sameness gets camouflaged into invisibility.

The same is true of busyness. Ask yourself, who do you know in your working life who isn't busy? There is nothing that can possibly be noteworthy, memorable or differentiating about busyness. It is not cool, it is not interesting, and, as I hope I have shown, it is not effective. Yet a scary number of clients I work with, when I ask them about their brand, start by describing how diligent or hard-working they are. It's like a dolphin that describes itself as a good swimmer! I understand how busy can be a response to fear, how it might help us to feel a little more needed and important, but it seldom does us any favours from a career perspective. For most people, and especially for higher performers, judgements are based on what results they deliver, what impact they make on the business and their ability to innovate. They are definitely not made on the basis of how busy they are. The only time when busy might be useful as a brand is when your performance is poor. Decisions on the performance of the bottom 20 per cent of employees might be heavily influenced by who seems to be trying hard, versus those that don't seem to care. However, if you are in such a role, you might be advised think about finding a job that's better suited to your skills and passions, rather than staving off the inevitable with ineffective activity.

Your strategic brand

If busy is a rubbish brand, what kind of brand should you replace it with? I am not suggesting that the answer is to be 'not busy' – you shouldn't replace busy with a vacuum, with an absence. In fact, the busy brand is really the vacuum; it says nothing about you other than that you have a lot on your plate. Instead what I suggest is that you build a brand that is based on the strategic position you have chosen, which will differentiate you and focus your activity on the things that matter. For example, if you have chosen an audience based position and your core contribution to your audience is 'creativity' then that should be your brand. A strong personal brand will help you to become known for how you contribute best, rather than the hum-drum ability to work long hours, write lots of emails and maintain a constant state of flurry.

Creating a strategic brand can really help bring your strategy to life and also articulate your unique contribution in that area. If you are able to build a strong brand, a brand that resonates with people, you will free yourself of the burden of the busy brand. You can start to differentiate yourself on the basis of your strategy and your contribution, rather than simply your busyness.

Make your brand simple

I mentioned earlier that one of the ways brands work is that they make something very complex much simpler to understand. So, when we think about what Volvo stands for we don't try and remember all the different models and all the different features in all those models. We don't run a detailed comparison of all these models with their nearest competitor in all markets. Instead, we hear the word Volvo and think 'Safe'. In making the brand simple to understand, more cognitively fluent, the brain starts to like and trust the brand more and allows the brand to influence our decisions.

When I work with people to help them develop their brand, they frequently struggle to make it simple. They strongly resist describing themselves using a single word or phrase and instead opt for a complex summary of what they do. Their argument is that as they have many skills and experiences it's not appropriate to 'dumb that down' to a single brand statement. Consequently they fail to make the tough choice to describe themselves narrowly, in the same way that many businesses fail to make the tough choices that will focus their resources. When they try to communicate information about themselves that is too complex, they fail to communicate anything; nothing is remembered.

In managing our brand, we are attempting to make things easy for people around us, to make it easy for them to 'get us', and in so doing, to understand our contribution and how we are differentiated. A good personal brand becomes something of an intellectual clothes hanger: all further information is hung onto it, but the brand provides the shape. It makes it easy for people to make sense of you, to understand you, to trust you, to explain you and ultimately to position you correctly for the right opportunities. So get over it! You might be a rich and complex individual; but your brand needs to be simple.

To bring this alive, I was once leading a session in Singapore with a bunch of high-potential leaders. During the day two senior leaders came to speak to the group. The first leader spoke about his role, some of the leadership challenges he'd faced and the lessons he'd learned that might be useful to the group. At three different points during his presentation he said, 'I make the complex, simple'. Each time his comment was relevant to what he'd been saying, a kind of summary of the point he'd just made. He wasn't bragging, either, just stating a fact. The next leader spoke clearly and eloquently, but at no point did he include a personal summary.

I was intrigued by the difference between presenting styles. At the end of the day I asked the group what they remembered from the two presentations. I asked about the second speaker first. The group remembered a variety of things, but there was little consistency. I then asked about the first leader. Without pause, and almost simultaneously, the group called out 'He made the complex, simple'. That leader had just landed his brand with the group. The group also remembered other things he had said as well, perhaps more than the second speaker, but underlying everything they remembered was an understanding of his core value to the business; they 'got' him. I suspect even if they'd met him months later, they'd remember his brand.

Your strategy, but on a really good day

Berocca is a type of multi-vitamin produced by Bayer and marketed in a number of countries across the world. One of their advertising campaigns shows a man in a suit get on his bicycle (one of those folding, travel ones), don his helmet, and start riding to work. Instead of the normal, monotonous pedal to work, the cyclist starts doing tricks: he wheelies, jumps and spins his way to the office. The advert then says 'Berocca. You, but on a really good day'.

I have talked about your brand supporting your strategy. Think specifically about what you do that is focused around your strategy. Your brand shouldn't just summarise the strategy, it should capture your greatest contribution in that area. In doing this it should be totally true, but describe you when you are at your very best: those days, or periods of time, when you rock!

To help clients do this I ask them to think of three occasions when they were brilliant. These occasions can vary from something as brief as a specific moment of insight to a presentation you gave or a meeting you ran to a day when you were on fire or a project you delivered successfully. Whatever duration these times were, identify three that you are truly proud of where you made a great impact.

Reflect on these three occasions (possibly with a partner) and ask yourself what you were doing or focusing on that made you so great at those times. In doing this, look for the common themes which made those moments really stand out.

Keep these themes in mind as you go into the exercise below. They will help you clarify a brand that doesn't just summarise your strategy, but captures the essence of your core contribution to the organisation.

Identifying your brand

A brand doesn't have to be a single word. It may be a word, or a phrase. Start with the thinking about your strategic positioning and how you want to differentiate yourself. Circle the five words in the table below that best represent you and your career strategy.

analytical	entrepreneurial	perceptive
assertive	expert	positive
big picture thinker	flexible	practical
'I connect the dots'	far-sighted	a problem solver
conscientious	firm	productive
cooperative	focus	purposeful
courageous	frank	high-quality
clear	friendly	quick-witted
clever	helpful	realistic
client-focused	honest	reliable
commercial	humorous	results-driven
determined	imaginative	risk taker
direct	innovative	sincere
disciplined	insightful	straight-talking
dynamic	logical	self-reliant
easy-going	methodical	team player
efficient	motivated	tenacious
energetic	on time	thorough
enthusiastic	organised	thoughtful
effective	original	unconventional

Once you've circled five words, either find someone to talk to or grab a sheet of paper and a pen and describe why these five best represent you. Once you have done this, reflect on any common themes or any aspects that felt truly significant to you. Combining your strategy with what came out of the previous exercise around your core contribution and this five-word exercise, write a short sentence, or even a single word, which describes the essence of your brand. Don't worry about making it perfect, just have a go.

Companies hire very expensive experts who spend months developing brands. It's not an easy activity. As a result, what tends to happen when I do this with clients is that they come up with something that feels pretty good; but isn't 100 per cent right. I call this first attempt your 'brand hypothesis'. Once you have written it, leave it somewhere so you see it regularly, talk about it with friends and colleagues. See if it works for you and them. Sleep on it, mull it over regularly, play with alternatives. You will probably find, over the coming weeks, that you get much clearer about what is right and not right about it. Then adapt it, refine it and, when you've got it right, start using it.

If it helps, here are a few examples of brands my clients have come up with.

- 'I join the dots'. This person was great at connecting people and ideas.
- 'Clarity'. This person was brilliant at bringing clarity to discussions and projects, summarising and getting to the key priorities quickly.
- 'No problem!' This client simply used the nickname he was given in his business. He persistently said 'No problem!' no matter what the request or how big the issue was. His colleagues jumped on his turn of phrase, since it captured his can-do attitude to everything and everyone. At the beginning of the process he had come up with boring words like 'Can-do' and 'helpful' before finally realising his nickname was a great brand.

Steal a brand

I'm a big believer in stealing with pride, or as Sir Isaac Newton would say, 'standing on the shoulders of genius'. The fact is that we are surrounded by thousands of brands. These companies have already done the hard work: they have already clarified and communicated their brand message. So, what a lot of my clients do is simply borrow an existing brand to represent their chosen strategy. One of the most common brands my clients seem to be choosing at present is Ronseal. Ronseal is a fairly unglamorous range of DIY products such as varnishes and wood treatments. Ronseal have built a brand around no-nonsense reliability and trust. Their slogan simply says 'Ronseal. It does exactly what it says on the tin'. For those whose brand is based around consistent delivery of promises,

'I'm Ronseal' works pretty well. Another common and more global brand seems to be 'I'm like Nike: I just do it!'

What popular brand best represents you and your strategy?

Build your brand

I start this section aware that you don't have very much spare time to market yourself. You may have even less desire to start promoting yourself, and elevator-pitching any unsuspecting executive to the point of submission. No matter how valuable you believe branding to be, you haven't got loads of time to do it, nor the appetite for bragging. So I will share a few simple ways of building your brand without killing your diary and annoying those around you.

Market research

Imagine two colleagues came up to you. One told you he was brilliant at closing deals; the other asked you what you thought he was good at. In the second scenario, the person happily answers your questions such as 'Why do you ask?' and 'What do you yourself think you're good at?'. Which person do you prefer? Which brand (and conversation) are you more likely to remember? I'm guessing you said the latter in both cases. We prefer to be asked our opinion than told anything. The first person is irritating, vomiting their inflated self-view all over you; the second gets you into a discussion during which, you not only become engaged with the issue but also ask for the relevant brand information. The second person's brand is also better remembered for two reasons: we remember answers to questions we have asked better than information thrown at us; the very act of asking a question prepares the memory for storage of the answer. The second reason we remember is that in the second situation we are active, in the first we are simply passive receivers; and we always remember routes better when we were driving than when we are passengers.

No one will ever mind being asked for their opinion on your

brand; on how you contribute best to the organisation. Most people will mind being told, without request, what you think. So . . . get asking!

Living up to your brand

Was Einstein good at organising?

The simple answer is, I don't know and I don't care. I do have a hunch, though: how can anyone with hair like his be organised? His contribution to the world wasn't because he was good at lots of things, but because he was great at one thing. History will not record his punctuality, or his ability at darts or his panache at throwing a party (by the way, I just made all these up, I have no idea if he was any good at them), it will remember him for his physics.

One of the best and most authentic ways to build your brand is also one of the biggest benefits you will receive from having a clear brand. Build your brand by living up to your brand. If your brand is aspirational, and represents your strategy (but on a really good day), living up to your brand is pretty useful. By striving in all interactions to be true to your brand, you contribute in the way you have decided you can contribute best and, in so doing, reinforce the brand and use it to differentiate yourself. This probably all sounds a little circular as an argument but because it is, and that's the genius of it.

In 1905 a new organisation was set up in the UK called the Automobile Association to help motorists avoid a troubling new practice of the police: stopping people who were speeding. Over the following decades the AA re-focused its efforts on supporting motorists in more valuable ways, most particularly in breakdown assistance. Following a piece of research, the AA identified that one of its key strategic assets was that people generally trusted and liked the men they sent to people's breakdowns. This led to a funny and successful advert. It showed a long-suffering driver, in a broken-down car, with two women in the back. The last scene depicted the car being driven by the AA man. The key message of the advert, said repeatedly by the women in the back of the car, was 'He's a very nice man.' 'He's a very, very nice man.' Some people hated the advert. I rather liked it (you can make up your own mind if you type 'AA very nice man advert' into YouTube). However, the crucial point here is the effect the advert had on the AA men.

Across the country, AA breakdown assistance drivers felt compelled to live up to the 'very nice man' brand. The company knew its greatest strength was its nice men, but in clarifying this, the existing strength became stronger.

For example, imagine your brand is 'clarity'. Once you have decided to make this your brand, you can constantly challenge yourself to live up to it. All your presentations, meetings and emails can be designed in such a way that they provide very visible clarity. Your emails become short and to the point, starting with the main point at the top and in the subject line. Your presentations become really simple and uncluttered, with each slide focusing on a single key point. In meetings you become the person who summarises the chaos, saying, 'So, for clarity, the three key points so far are ... '.

Your brand describes your greatness; and in living up to your brand, you become greater.

Consistency

In 1990, New York subways were dangerous places. Crime, and especially violent crime, was at an all-time high. But this was set to change because of a new strategy employed by Mayor Rudi Giuliani and Police Commissioner Bill Bratton based on the 'broken window' principle which says we are more likely to break the windows of a house if the windows of other houses in that street are already broken[6]. Using the theory as inspiration, Giuliani and Bratton hatched a plan. Instead of going after the perpetrators of violent crime directly, they started a very visible, very public display of law enforcement in other areas. They cracked down on petty crime like fare dodging and they removed the graffiti on the trains. Although they were concentrating on relatively minor crimes, they succeeded in presenting a consistent, visible and pervasive message to the public: this is a more lawful environment. The results were astonishing. Over the following decade there was a 75 per cent drop in felonies on the subway. Violent crime stopped because people saw lines of people being fined for not paying fares!

The small things matter as well as the big things. In the above case, cracking down on small crimes also reduced big crimes. The same is true for reinforcing your brand. And you can use this knowledge to your advantage. If you do really small things that reinforce your brand, people will infer that the big things are true as well. These small things are called 'high leverage signals'. One client I worked with from Shell had a brand around reliable, on-time delivery. He wanted a very simple way to consistently reinforce this brand. What he did was, I think, genius. He changed his voicemail message to say 'Leave a message and I'll call you back in three working hours'. Most importantly, he always did. I remember when I called him I couldn't help glancing at my watch as I left my message. I was timing him. Every time he called before the deadline, he reinforced his brand. Every time he returned that call on time, he built confidence that if you gave him a multi-million dollar project to run, he would deliver it on time.

Be playful with this. For example, I had one person who wanted to show that despite being a serious corporate executive he was creative and a bit of a maverick. He started wearing bright red socks under his company-standard pin-striped grey suits. I saw the business card of a divorce lawyer who wanted to show he could manage these serious affairs with humanity and, at times, humour. His business card had perforations down the middle (so it was easy to tear in half!).

What could your high-leverage signals be?

The big messages in 'Differentiate yourself'

You *can't* do everything and **you shouldn't do everything** if you want to succeed in your career. You need to focus with a strategy. Business strategies are useful because they are based on how to **succeed in competitive situations with limited resources**.

BEING DIFFERENT: POSITIONING AND DIFFERENTIATION

- There are **two ways to succeed**: through **productivity** (the 'More' game) or through **differentiation**. The best way is to **differentiate** yourself; do things better.
- There are four strategic positions you can take: everything, everyone; **audience-based; product-based; niche**. Everything,

everyone is the most common, and it's rubbish. Audience-based differentiation means serving the **unique needs of your key stakeholders**; product-based differentiation means developing **unique capabilities or expertise**.

- **Trade-offs**: Choosing not to pursue great ideas in order to go deep on others is hard, but that is strategy.

A CLEAR BRAND

- Strategies can be complex or difficult to articulate. **Brands help companies and people to communicate their strategy simply**, in a way that people understand.
- Busy is a rubbish brand. It says nothing about us and does nothing to differentiate us.
- Keep your brand **simple** and **reflective of you at your best** – you can even borrow an existing brand if it works for you.
- Make sure you **live up to your brand in everything you do** – it will ensure you perform to the best of your ability and build others' confidence in you.

Go–Do

STRATEGIC POSITION

Take a view. What is your strategic positioning: audience, product or niche? Once you are clear, draft an annual strategic plan to bring greater focus io your core strategic areas.

CLARIFY YOUR BRAND

Develop your own brand statement based on your strategy and understanding of your core contribution to your organisation. Once you have your first hypothesis, speak to five people who know you well at work and get their feedback on your brand. Reflect and adapt it.

Experiment

TRADE-OFFS

Try to stop doing things that are not core to your strategy. Some of these will cause problems; many of them will go unnoticed. By doing this you'll build up a clear idea of the real essentials.

BRAND REINFORCEMENT

Play with different ways to reinforce your brand. Use things like your email signature, voicemail messages or LinkedIn profile to subtly land your message.

Chapter 5

Think better

Your brain consists of just two to three pounds of a blobby tissue. It doesn't look much, but it is considered by scientists to be the most complex object in the universe. It contains about 100 billion neurons and a trillion support cells. To put that in context, you have as many neurons as the total number of people born in the entire history of the world! Now, to understand how much messaging is happening inside this blobby tissue, imagine that every person that ever lived is also fanatical about social media and has 7,000 friends on Facebook (each neuron is connected to an average of 7,000 other neurons) and sends between five and 50 status updates every second! (that's how active neurons are). Or to put that another way, in the time it has taken you to read this paragraph, your brain has sent about as many internal 'emails' as the entire world will send over the next year.

The brain is amazing. However, it wasn't designed for the modern working environment and all the challenges, distractions and stimulations of life today. The brain evolved for a different world: a world of simple choices; of limited information and distraction; a technology-free world. For example, our ancestors needed good memories to be able to recall if this or that animal would kill them, or how to find the way home after a hunting expedition. They didn't need to be clever and think about weighty problems of global economics, and they didn't have to multitask. Their brains developed to remember loads of stuff, but not to think about too much of it at the same time. In other words, we've got pretty good memories, but we're bad at thinking and juggling.

While biological evolution is very slow, cultural evolution can be astonishingly rapid. Our brains are little different to those of our ancestors thousands of years ago, yet our culture has evolved, bringing with it new tools and technologies that change everything as far as the brain is concerned. We no longer need a good memory (when was the last time you tried to commit a new telephone number to memory?): we have phones, tablets and computers to outsource our information to. On the other hand, we have never thrown as much information and complexity at our brains with as much speed. We have never pounded our poor overloaded neurons as hard and as relentlessly. We have never maintained a state of alertness as consistently as we do today, aided by our multiple pings and rings.

My concern is that these culturally and technologically driven changes have not taken into account what works for the human brain. We are seeing the incredible benefits in connectedness, entertainment and productivity, but are we also straining and misusing our grey matter? Since all these new capabilities were enabled through the wonder of technology, have we stepped back and asked, 'How can I use technology to support my thinking?' rather than, 'How can I squeeze a bit of thinking into the gaps when technology isn't battering my senses?'.

This chapter is an attempt to redress the balance. It will reflect on the cognitive challenges and pitfalls our brain faces on a daily basis. Based on solid psychological and neuropsychological research it will explain how to use your brain better. Being able to think better is not my recipe for getting more stuff done; thinking better will create the space for you to focus more time and energy on what matters to you and your organisation, to solve the big problems and to make a difference.

This chapter explains how thinking happens, and outlines practical strategies to help your brain work as effectively as it can – strategies which run counter to current practice in most offices today. First I'll explain how to concentrate and focus attention better once we're on task. Attention is under attack from every technological angle at present, but what should our response be? Given all the demands on the brain, it is incredibly easy for it to switch into neutral and procrastinate; especially over the big stuff. I shall explain the psychology of getting off the starting blocks faster on the things that matter. Finally, I'll explain the importance of *anti-focus*, as a way to massively improve your thinking power. Since the brain comes with no instruction manual, this chapter attempts to fill the gap.

A fussy brain

We all know the story of fussy Goldilocks who rejects the first two bowls of porridge, but settles on the third, which is 'just right'. It turns out our brains are also fussy. Amy Arnsten, a neurobiologist at Yale, has spent years studying the fussiest area of the brain: the prefrontal cortex. This is the front part of the brain, just behind the forehead, and it equates to about five per cent of the whole brain by size. The prefrontal cortex was one of the last areas to evolve, but it's critical for thinking. Without it you wouldn't be able to solve problems, prioritise, analyse, plan or be creative. As Arnsten explains, the prefrontal cortex 'holds the contents of your mind at any one point ... It's where we hold thoughts that are not being generated from external sources or from the senses. We ourselves are generating them'. The prefrontal cortex needs to have just the right conditions for it to function properly. Hence the reason Arnsten nicknamed it 'the Goldilocks of the brain'[1]. This chapter looks at how to create the right conditions for the prefrontal cortex. Thinking better can only happen when we are able to get our over-stimulated brains primed and ready to tackle the big stuff better, quicker and more imaginatively. Here are some strategies.

Efficient thinking

The central point I want to make in this section is that multitasking is bad. There are two ways in which we can multitask: one is to do two things at once; the other is to switch between tasks rapidly. You may think this is a timesaver, but you would be wrong. The brain is not built to do more than one thing at a time and neither is it designed to switch between tasks. It can do both, of course, but in doing so you think less well and less fast.

One thing at a time

Have you ever noticed that if you are walking while talking on your mobile phone and someone asks you a tough question, you stop moving while you think? You stop because you intuitively want to divert all your paltry mental resources to your prefrontal cortex. In fact, it was shown by the scientist J. C. Welch, in the late 1900s that thinking makes us physically weaker! Welch asked people to squeeze a lever as hard as they could, and measured the force they applied. Then the test was repeated, this time giving people a mental task to complete simultaneously. When people were thinking really hard, the physical force they could exert reduced by as much as 50 per cent![2]

The converse is also true. Harold Pashler, Distinguished Professor of Psychology at the University of California, had people perform simple physical and intellectual tasks in tandem. He found that the performance of a Harvard MBA student dropped to that of an eight-year-old child when the subject attempted to do more than one thing at a time[3]. Pashler would argue that part of the reason for this is something he calls dual-task interference: our brains are not designed to do two things at once, to multitask; we have a kind of cognitive bottleneck. The only way to work around this is to focus on one thing at a time.

Get it out of your head
Two Buddhist monks were walking together when they came to a river. Next to the river was a beautiful woman. She turned to the monks and asked them to carry her across the stream so she didn't spoil her dress. The first monk, knowing that touching women was not allowed, apologised but said no. The second monk, without pause, picked her up and carried her across the river. They walked on for many hours and miles. Then the first monk turned to the second and asked why he had carried the woman. To which, the second replied, 'I carried her a few steps across that stream; you have carried her many miles'.

At the start of the book I talked about the Zeigarnik effect and the drawbacks of mental churning when it comes to thinking. But churning can also have a more subtle effect. It can reduce our processing power. The second monk was only able to get into the Zen of his walk because he had closed the file relating to the woman. Open files clutter the brain and redirect energy. In his book *Getting Things Done*, David Allen describes the effect of carrying lots of open files as the 'monkey mind' – when our thoughts leap from task to task, from idea to idea[4]. Any time we are 'carrying' thoughts, worries, tasks in our heads, we are reducing our ability to think; we are becoming less effective.

In *Getting Things Done*, Allen suggests a simple tool for getting things off your mind that I love: 'buckets'. A bucket is something you throw stuff into. A bucket isn't a to-do list; it's just stuff. That's the beauty of it. There is no categorisation happening at all when you decide what goes in the bucket: big and small; urgent and important; shopping items, creative insights and actions. The important thing is that you always have your 'bucket' with you. You may be 'old skool' and like to capture things in a notebook, or you may prefer to use your smartphone, but whenever a task, important thought or action comes to mind, don't try to remember it – capture it in your bucket. You are not trying to do anything with it at this moment, just getting it out of your head to free up your prefrontal cortex to think better.

Buckets only work if we have confidence that we will respond to them, so clearing your brain takes trust. To make a bucket work, we need a habit of emptying it on a regular basis. If not, the brain will soon learn it can't relax. Most people I've worked with review their bucket daily, at specific chosen points. It's important to remember, when you review the bucket, that it isn't an action list. It is likely to represent the intellectual flotsam and jetsam of your mental meanderings. Seeing these items listed allows you to stand back and make rational choices. You will find that many items can simply be deleted; many you will put in what Allen calls a 'Someday/Maybe' file; others you will choose to do. Of the actions you decide are worth doing, some will either be individual tasks or larger 'projects' which might involve multiple actions. Individual tasks go in your to-do list, projects go into a projects file. The final step, for all projects, is to identify the next action. This action then goes into your to-do list.

This may sound complicated; it isn't. It is a simple discipline that helps you to get stuff out of your head, confident you will address what should be addressed. Doing this allows you to step back into the moment, focus, and think better about the things that really matter.

Externalise your thinking

Have you ever tried to play chess only in your mind? It's really hard, because not only do you have to decide the next best move, you also have to remember the positions of all the pieces. It's much easier to play when you can physically see the board. When you have a board, you free your brain from the task of remembering where all the pieces are; it can focus all its intellectual capability on developing strategies and making clever moves. The same applies to our thinking at work: anything we can do to externalise our thinking will free up more intellectual horsepower.

An example of externalising thinking is mind mapping. Often when we're trying to think through a complex problem we're trying to do more than one thing at a time. We're trying to hold all the different parts of the problem in our head, we're trying to manipulate the concepts and organise them in a sensible way and we're trying to solve the problem, all at the same time. Mind mapping and other, similar techniques encourage people to visually represent the various parts of a problem on a single sheet of paper or whiteboard which helps to delegate intellectual activity.

One of the most important intellectual tools I possess is my humble whiteboard. Time after time, when I'm getting a little stuck or entrenched in my thinking, I leap up and grab a pen. I write all the elements of the problem on the board, then I then start playing around with what I've written: drawing lines to show connections, wiping out and redrawing until it all makes sense. In doing this, I have freed my mind of the burden of holding all that information in my working memory. I have organised it externally, which allows all of my intellect to focus on solving the actual problem. My whiteboard makes me cleverer (or less stupid!).

Reduce your switching

Multitasking can mean performing two tasks simultaneously or switching rapidly from task to task. Each time we move between tasks, the brain takes a little time to re-orientate itself to the rules of the new task at hand. The time taken for this re-orientation creates what is called a 'switch cost'. David Meyer, Professor of Psychology at the University of Michigan, has found that, even if the cost of an individual switch of attention is small, the cumulative cost of regular switching is significant. He suggests that multitasking, in the form of switching backwards and forwards between tasks, increases the overall time needed to complete the tasks by 40 per cent[5].

The simple message of this is that we achieve more if we stay focused on tasks for longer. The more we switch backwards and forwards, the harder the brain has to work to re-orientate itself, and the slower we think. I call this strategy 'big chunking' to suggest that we chunk our time into big chunks of activity, not micro slices of tasks. This might sound obvious, but it doesn't feel it. In fact, quite the reverse: a small amount of dopamine (a feel-good neurotransmitter) is released when we switch, helping us feel potent, effective and efficient. The more we bounce between report-writing, phone-answering and email-reading, swatting tasks away, one by one, the more effective we *feel*. As the velocity of the demands increases, so does our dopamine. We have to learn not to mistake the buzz you get from multitasking for a rightly earned sense of effectiveness. This buzz perpetuates our illusion of efficiency; we delude ourselves into mistaking our ability to machine-gun disconnected tasks for working well. In fact, Jonathan B. Spira, an analyst at the business research firm Basex, highlighted the scale of the multitasking illusion. He estimated that extreme multitasking was costing the US economy $650 billion a year in lost productivity[6].

The impact that switching tasks has on productivity is seen most strongly for more intellectually demanding activities such as problem-solving, prioritising or planning. Your brain needs more time to get into gear, to grapple with the issues. Think of it like a new job. If you have been employed to perform a simple task, you will probably get up to speed pretty quickly. However, take on a big role and you simply won't be able to add value for months. I worked with a Brazilian VP in a major multinational who was taking on his first role in the Asia Pacific region. He spent his first three months doing nothing except chatting and learning. He recognised he needed time to understand before he could perform. Big, complex tasks are the same: you need time to kick the issues around before you can deliver value.

Break your day into big chunks of activity. The more complex the task, the bigger the chunk of uninterrupted time you should try and give to it. Of course life will intervene at times, the director will tap you on the shoulder and distract you, but your goal should be to maximise chunks of focused time.

... and it's not just a question of practice

If you're reading this and thinking quietly to yourself 'Okay, I get the general point, but I've multitasked for years ... I'm an expert', then I would ask you to think again. Multitasking is one of the few areas, intellectually, where practice does not make perfect. Researchers at Stanford University split people into those who were typically heavy media 'multitaskers', and those who multitasked less frequently. They expected to find that those with more practice multitasking, in switching back and forwards between tasks, developed a greater capability in this area. This is what normally happens in areas of human performance: with practice our performance improves. Surprisingly, they found the exact opposite[7]. Those people who multitasked a lot in their day-to-day lives underperformed on a test of multitasking ability; they were not as good at task switching. The reason for this is that serial 'multitaskers' were less able to separate the wheat from the chaff; they got more distracted by irrelevant and unimportant information. The more you multitask, the more distracted you'll be and therefore the worse you'll be at thinking. So go ahead if you want to continue, but don't say you weren't warned: multitasking is reducing your intellect.

How to avoid the switch

How often do you switch tasks at work? Whatever the frequency you just guessed, I would wager you are underestimating it. A Boston College study, published in the fantastically named journal *Cyberpsychology, Behavior, and Social Networking*, found that people underestimated their frequency of distraction by a factor of 10[8]. When working on a computer with a TV in the room, researchers monitored eye movements between the two screens. The participants estimated that they switched the focus of their attention every four minutes. In actual fact, their eye movements showed their attention switched every 14 seconds! One study of office workers showed that people tend to hopscotch between activities every three minutes[9]. This is worrying since researchers at the University of California found that workers took an average of 25 minutes to recover from interruptions like phone calls or answering email, and return to their original task[10].

Some distractions are unavoidable. A lot, however, are self-induced. If we're really honest with ourselves, a lot of the hopscotching isn't driven by necessity; it's because the novel is more exciting; and the simple is more attractive than a more intellectually demanding activity such as deep thinking. So we flip into our inbox, triggered by the ping of a new email; we flop into an IM chat instead of persisting in thinking through tough challenges.

It would be better to avoid the distraction in the first place. First on everyone's list here should be the email notifier in Outlook. Turn it off, or even better, turn off Outlook while you're working on a big chunk. You might turn your phone to silent or at least put the text notifier on silent. You could remove visual temptation. For example, my friend was regularly getting complaints from his wife about the degree to which he was 'present' when they were together: his smartphone was always there, luring him away from her. He agreed that when they ate out in restaurants he would no longer place the phone on the dinner table. It worked; he was less distracted. So don't place your phone on the desk and don't open your social media or IM on entering the office.

What distractions might you avoid and how will you go about avoiding them?

Machine-gun in bursts

To allow yourself to focus properly on chunks of activity, you also need to create the opportunity to address email and the simple tasks on your to-do list. I call this machine-gunning This may sound extreme, but I like to imagine blasting through email and messages, killing off these distractions, before returning to my key priority areas for chunks of time. I seldom find much that will change the world in my daily inbox; however, that doesn't mean I can afford to ignore it.

I have two rules for machine-gunning the inbox and other tasks:

- Choose a time. Machine-gun at certain, specific points of the day. For the rest of the day, the email is off and the task list goes unaddressed. You don't need a to-do list to tell you what's most important. You know that already (or, if you don't, it's not important).
- Time-limit the blasts. The nature of micro-tasks is that, if you are trying to get through them all, they can easily swamp your day. Give yourself a deadline. This not only protects your time for the important stuff; it also creates urgency to your blasting.

Stop procrastinating

Procrastination goes hand in hand with busyness. In fact, I would argue that an awful lot of busyness *is* procrastination. The thing about busyness is that it's a kind of displacement activity: it fills the gap that would have been filled by the thing we are procrastinating about. If, instead of working on big stuff, we sat staring out of the window for hours, we would feel guilty.

But if we dive into micro-tasks we feel productive. Micro-tasks such as email and texts are quick to do, and we get that sense of satisfaction (not to mention dopamine squirts) as we complete each one. The lazy brain prefers the easy over the hard, so we convince ourselves we're being productive. We tell ourselves, 'I'll just get on top of my inbox before starting project X.' But if we're honest with ourselves, we should be saying, 'I'll just mess around with some easy emails, because I can't be bothered to do project X.'

We need to shift the causal relationship. We tell ourselves that we don't get around to doing all the things that will make a real impact *because* we are so busy. In reality, we are busy because we are avoiding and *procrastinating*.

Everything that could make a big impact on your career or your organisation, such as your breakthrough opportunities or differentiating strategies, requires proper thinking, not just superficial processing. You're going to need to think deeply to fire up your lazy

System Two into effortful, sustained activity. Big problems need big thinking in order to wrestle them to the ground – and big thinking means a lot of effort. So here's the problem: big thinking is tiring; it's often the last thing we fancy, given how exhausting work and modern life are. So, when faced with a big thinking task, we procrastinate.

The Four Horsemen of the Procrastinator

In the final book of the New Testament, Revelation, Four Horsemen of the Apocalypse appear: Pestilence, Famine, War and Death. They prophesy a future of tribulation. I have developed my own Four Horsemen of the Procrastinator. Equally, these horsemen are harbingers of future troubles. Persistent procrastination is perilous, unproductive and profits few professional people! Avoid the significant stuff through inconsequential busyness (or looking out the window) and you are forgoing your opportunity and right to make your mark. The Four Horsemen of the Procrastinator are: Perfection, Mood, Fear and Dependence.

> **Perfection:** Setting unreasonably high expectations for yourself, wanting to get it right first time. The higher the bar people set for themselves, the greater the inertia.
> **Mood:** 'I'm not in the mood.' This horseman relates to those people who wait to be in the right mood before getting started at all.
> **Fear:** Concern about the consequence of not doing a good enough job, or indeed the increasing panic that the deadline is approaching and you still haven't started. Both types of fear can lead to procrastination.
> **Dependence:** This is dominated by the word *when*: 'I'll do it when I'm on top of my inbox'; 'I'll do it when I have heard back from Roberto'; 'I'll do it when I have all the information'.

Before we move any further, which of these horsemen has you in their grip most?

In the spirit of honesty, I'm a fabulous procrastinator! I often find myself being besieged by perfection, mood and dependence. Take this book, for example. I spent years on research, setting ridiculous levels of personal expectations as a form of procrastination over actually writing the thing. I regularly told myself 'I can't be creative now, I'm too tired'. Perhaps worst of all, I told myself I'd write the book when I was less busy (but more of that in Chapter 11). My point here is that we shouldn't be in thrall to the horsemen, but should recognise how and when we get 'hooked' and have strategies in place to deal with them.

Perfection

High expectations breed inertia. To overcome inertia we need to create momentum – one of the central principles of most approaches to procrastination. Get the ball rolling and procrastination evaporates. In their wonderful book, *Switch*, Chip and Dan Heath suggest that one way of getting into action is to 'shrink the change'[11] – to make it feel less daunting. The strategies to directly address Perfection are around shrinking the challenge at hand, and so getting started.

Create momentum
One way of creating momentum is to create the impression that you have already started. Alia Crum and Ellen Langer were interested in exercise at work. They looked at the working habits of hotel maids, and how many calories they burned. It turned out they were dramatically exceeding the recommended daily dose of exercise recommended by the Surgeon General. Crum and Langer then asked those maids if they thought they were exercising enough. Of these, 67 per cent felt they weren't, and more than a third thought they weren't exercising at all.

These maids were split into two groups. Both were told about the benefits of exercise. One group was also told how much actual exercise they were doing already in their daily work, including the fact that, for example, they burned 100 calories after half an hour of vacuuming. The other group wasn't told. Four weeks later, the first group had lost nearly two pounds in weight on average; the second group had lost no weight at all[12]. Knowing they were exercising already created momentum for the first group, it was easier to do a bit more because they were already in motion.

If you want to create momentum, spend a few minutes reviewing what you have already done in a relevant area. Start by remembering and recognising before you start to produce. For example, get any previous work out and start organising it. Pretty soon you'll be in the flow and off.

Alternatively, a tip for writers is to never finish your writing day at the end of a chapter. Always finish mid-chapter, mid-paragraph or even mid-sentence. That way you get momentum by continuing a previous train of thought.

Thin slicing

Marla Cilley, or, as she calls herself, 'FlyLady', is a self-help guru focused on housekeeping. She talks of the dread some of her clients experience when facing disastrously messy, dirty houses. It is overwhelming. Sure we want our homes to be immaculate and tidy, but we are stuck in neutral as we consider the scale of the challenge. She developed a policy of the 'Five-minute Room Rescue': you enter the dirtiest, messiest room in the house with a kitchen timer. You tidy and clean like fury, but only for five minutes; then you stop. What tends to happen is that people, since they're already in motion, keep going. Success in this task has shifted from overall task completion, to completion of an allocated time – a much more manageable goal.

I am a huge believer in regular, short bursts of activity to get momentum going. For me, five minutes is too short for intellectual tasks; I tend to go for 30 minutes to one hour. However, big projects can be a lot easier to start in 30-minute chunks every day – especially as the Zeigarnik Effect means you'll be thinking about the project all day!

Swiss cheese it

Dave Ramsey, a personal finance expert, would argue that procrastination gets in the way of debt repayment. People who have massive debts don't know where to start, unmotivated by the fact that they can only chip away at the money they owe. He has developed a unique approach. Most advisors would take the rational approach: identify where you are paying the most interest and focus on clearing those first. Ramsey recognises the need to create a sense of momentum. He asks clients to write out all their debts – on loans, overdrafts, credit cards etc. He then has them place the debts in order, not on the basis of interest payments, but on the basis of size. He gets people to focus on paying off the smallest debts first. The huge advantage of this is the feeling of momentum when the number of debts starts reducing. People can feel real progress.

Swiss cheesing is a variant on thin slicing, but instead of the small chunks of time, you target a small part of the overall task. You choose a small, specific piece of the overall activity and nail it – a bit like putting holes through cheese. Small chunks are easier to attack than big ones.

Mood

Our moods change regularly through the day, and many serial procrastinators allow mood to affect their judgement over whether they can or cannot start something important. Yet work comes at us independent of our mood. Our opportunity to impact our organisations will not wait until we're in the perfect mood. We have to deal with our mood so that it is no longer a cause of our procrastination. There are two approaches to this: either to make progress despite the mood, or to change the mood.

Making progress despite the mood

It is a psychological reality that as our mood changes we become ego depleted, or are just plain old 'brain dead' towards the end of a busy day. It is perfectly reasonable to accept, as we have all experienced, that at certain times we can really crack into a piece of complex thinking, analysis or writing. Other times, no matter how much we stare at the screen, we can't get off the starting blocks. The important thing here is to make progress despite your mood. In doing so, your mood might change, but even if it doesn't, you are further forward and gaining momentum.

Every big project has multiple elements of work associated with it. Some of those pieces will require intense concentration and activity from the prefrontal cortex; others are more practical, easier. Imagine you are facing an enormous data table resulting from a survey you commissioned. Your task is to put together a report on the outcomes of the survey. Whenever you look at the table, you get almost dizzy, trying to make sense of all those numbers.

Rather than getting tempted into procrastination by your inability to deal with the numbers, recognise that there are different types of task involved in the overall project, each requiring a different kind of mental activity. Decide what aspect you feel you *could* fruitfully make progress in, and make a start on that. For example, you could begin playing with the tables, hiding columns that don't seem essential, reorganising the columns etc.. Or you could start building the ultimate presentation, looking for images and visuals you think will be useful. Either way, you're moving forward.

My wonderful whiteboard

When talking about reversal theory in Chapter 1, I suggested some simple ways to change your motivation (flip between 'serious' and 'playful'). This applies to changing your mood too. Ask yourself, how do I change my mood? For me, movement, chocolate, music and play are the best ways. When I'm not in the mood, but know I should start work, I stick on upbeat tunes, get some chocolate (or the next best thing), grab my markers and I start playing on the whiteboard with ideas I want to work on. I change my goal from a serious, future-focused one, to one about enjoyment and playfulness. I ask myself, what would be really cool? (even though I know that is such an uncool thing to think!). Moods are transient; we don't need to be held captive by them.

Get the chemicals right

Neurons are not physically connected to other neurons. Electrical impulses pass down each neuron, but it is chemicals which do the leg work, passing messages from one neuron to another across a synapse. Synapses send signals which either tell the next neuron to do more of something, or less of something. Amy Arnsten discovered that the degree to which the prefrontal cortex is operating effectively depends upon the right balance of two chemicals: dopamine and norepinephrine. Without enough of these, you feel lethargic and bored. Too much and you feel anxious and stressed. Remember, the prefrontal cortex is Goldilocks, needing just the right conditions. These neurotransmitters have pretty complex effects, but in essence, dopamine is responsible for mood and pleasure; norepinephrine is responsible for 'fight-or-flight' – your sense of urgency or stress.

Once we understand that both of these neurotransmitters are important, we can take action to adjust them (without the intake of drugs!). If you feel 'not in the mood', it could be for a number of reasons. We may have the right levels of dopamine, but not enough norepinephrine, or vice versa.

Chemical levels	Symptom	What you can do
Not enough dopamine	Lethargy, boredom and a lack of interest and energy.	This is a classic scenario for reversal theory. Shift the goal to having fun, rather than task completion. Play a bit, and add some variety.
Too much dopamine	Scattered, restless and distracted, jumping from one thing to another.	Stay focused! Switch off all distraction. Remind yourself of the importance of the task, why it matters to you personally.
Not enough norepinephrine	A lack of urgency and impetus to get going.	Scare yourself (a little)! Visualise what could go wrong if you don't deliver on time. Set yourself goals to deliver certain things by a certain time. Get helpers to hold you accountable.
Too much norepinephrine	Stress, anxiety and fear.	Break the task into manageable chunks. Come up with a concrete plan of execution. Take a break and some deep breaths.

Fear

The fear we are talking about here is not life threatening and all consuming, it's nervousness about a big or visible piece of work; anxiety that you will fail. Fear is most definitely the province of norepinephrine, so see the table above for how to tackle it. However, in addition, we can use simple behaviourism to help us make progress in the face of emotion. We do this by creating a punishment that is more scary than the fear we feel through the task itself. At its core, behaviourism says punishments and rewards affect our choices by making a particular course of action more, or less appealing (or in this case scary). Ian Ayres, a Professor at Yale School of Management, makes use of this idea in his website StickK.com, which helps people to attain their goals by threatening to punish failure. People make commitment contracts on StickK.com. They identify a goal they really want to stick at, and then identify a penalty they will have to pay if they fail to comply. Apparently, the most common forfeit is a contribution to the George W. Bush Memorial Library Foundation! This means, when faced with the fear of the task, the worry that you might not do a good job; this is overcome by the greater fear of donating money to a charity you don't agree with. Your StickK.com punishment keeps you on the straight and narrow.

You can flip this and further fight your fear-induced procrastination with rewards for good behaviour. Ask yourself, how could you reward progress? What treat will you give yourself if you get X done despite your fear? Remember, immediate rewards work better, so don't choose a reward for the end of the project, but rather one for the end of this current working session. The same applies to punishments.

What will your forfeit be if you fail to deliver today? Who will collect that forfeit, and keep you honest?

Dependence

Dependence is all about waiting until some external conditions are satisfied: when something else is ready, or someone else has done something. It revolves around the word *when*. It feels like we are blocked, but really it's just an excuse. How do you get past *when*?

Making progress despite . . .

Earlier I mentioned how to progress despite your mood, by picking an aspect of the project for which your mood is best suited. In the same way, you can make progress despite whatever it is you are waiting for. Choose a component of your project that is *not* dependent upon this thing you are waiting for. Switch the focus from *when* to *can*: 'what *can* you do despite X?'.

Stop it! Now!

If the 'when' you are waiting for is more information, remind yourself that information can become an addiction. I'll say more about this in the next chunk, but just remember two things: the desire you feel right now to search a little bit more is probably based more upon the fact it feels good to do this, rather than because that extra information is necessary. Secondly, more information almost always makes the final piece of work more intellectually demanding to do: by searching more, not only are you using up time now, you're adding complexity and time later too!

Managing attention better

We've looked at how to think efficiently and avoid procrastinating. The other challenge is *staying* on task and stopping our attention from straying. In her insightful book, *Distracted*, Maggie Jackson[13] describes attention as the bedrock of society. Our willingness and ability to think deeply, to ponder the complex rather than the superficial, to be focused rather than diffuse, are critical not only to our thinking, but to our morality, our happiness and our culture. She worries that, culturally, we are losing our powers of attention: that our lives of distraction are reducing our capacity to create and preserve wisdom, that we're slipping towards a more ignorant period, even though this is being driven paradoxically by an abundance of information and technology. She believes this could have dire consequences. 'We are on the verge of losing our capacity for deep, sustained focus. In short, we are slipping towards a new Dark Age.'

Whether or not you believe we are moving to some kind of intellectually dumbed-down, cultural Dark Age, I think we'd all accept that the multiple sources of information, stimulation and demand hitting our brains today split our attention and disperse our focus. I would argue that attention management is far, far, far more important than time management. We can put in lots of hours at work, but our impact starts, our breakthroughs occur and our real relationships are built when we get the best from our attentional systems. In our distraction-rich workplaces, focused attention doesn't just happen; we need to make it happen. In fact, it would be hard to think of an environment better-designed to avoid deep thought and focus than most workplaces today.

This section begins from the assumption that we cannot hope to thrive and achieve all we dream of unless we manage our attention better. It suggests ways to help you improve your capacity for sustained, rich attention – the cornerstone to performance; if we cannot hold our attention in one place we will not be able to think with any depth or speed. Moving beyond that, this section explains the critical role of anti-focus, and how our ability to innovate and to differentiate ourselves emerges as much from anti-focus as focus, but never from distraction.

How attention works

Michael Posner is a professor, cognitive neuropsychologist, and one of the leading experts on attention. He describes attention as being much like an organ, with different parts that lead the orchestration of the mind. He identifies the three networks of attention as the orienting, the alerting and the executive.

The *orienting* network is designed to notice things in the environment and swivel our attention towards it. It spots the novel, the dangerous and the interesting, and directs the mind's eye towards it. It has been described by neuroscientist Amishi Jha as the 'flashlight of the mind'.

The *alerting* network deals with wakefulness. The alerting network establishes and maintains alertness, the levels of which relate to how much attention we have available. Our alertness determines our sensitivity to our environment: whether we tromp mindlessly through a field or drink in the scents of flowers and the colours of the grasses.

Finally, and perhaps most importantly, comes the *executive*. The executive is the decider, the director, the boss. Without the executive, our thoughts and mental experience would be chaotic, overwhelming and transient. The executive network allows us to have self-control, to make choices and to focus.

As you have probably experienced, our attention results from a constant push and pull between the 'top down' purpose-driven executive direction and the 'bottom up', stimulation-driven orientation and alertness networks. We are evolutionarily designed to be interruptible, to notice novelty and threat. In a world of too much, as the number, urgency and fascination of distractions increase, our attention cannot be taken for granted. We need to work at it.

Distractions and resisting them

As I sit here at my desk I have the world at my feet. In a way that wasn't available to even the richest rulers in recent history, I have instant access to a world of information, a world of television shows, a world of communication, a world of music and a world of weird videos of tight-rope walking dogs. Our attention systems, and particularly our executive network, is all that stands between a healthy, productive psychological existence and a meaningless life dissipated on a wave of information consumption. It's our executive networks against the world of too much – and our attention is losing.

We are interrupted and distracted a lot. It is easy to blame our work environments or other people for interruptions, but Professor of Informatics (the study of computer science and computer-human interaction) Gloria Mark found that 44 per cent of all interruptions were self-initiated: we interrupt ourselves.

This reminds me of a client I worked with a few years ago, who was working with me on a senior leadership programme. He was determined to become 'more strategic'. He explained how, in a production-focused business like his, it was difficult to get the time, free from interruptions, to think properly. He agreed to lock himself in his office the following day, turn off his phone and his Outlook, and create the time and space to think big. The following day, according to plan, he warned his staff that he would be unavailable and turned off all his communication tools. He sat thinking. Then he started wondering what he should be doing or thinking about; was he doing it right? He was finding it hard to think. Then he started worrying that he hadn't written anything yet. He was struggling with his lack of 'productivity'. After about 20 painful minutes, he 'sneaked' a quick peek at his email; then he heard an interesting conversation about a production problem happening outside his office and he opened his door and joined in.

Trey Hedden and John Gabrieli, neuroscientists from the Massachusetts Institute of Technology, explain that when we are focusing on difficult tasks, our brain interrupts us[14]. A part of the brain called the medial prefrontal cortex gets activated when we are not focused on external stimulation or tasks. When we're thinking deeply about a topic, it generates ruminations, thoughts or daydreams: the harder the intellectual task, the greater the desire to wander. So we think hard, the mind wanders and, hey presto, we're distracted. David Rock, the neuroleadership expert, cites research that shows people only hold onto one stream of thought for 10 seconds, before flitting off onto something else[15].

Look inside your own stream of consciousness for a few minutes.

How do we refresh our attention?

This was a question asked by psychologist Marc Berman, Jon Jonides and Stephen Kaplan and which built on Kaplan's earlier work into Attention Restoration Theory (ART)[16]. This splits attention into two types: directed and involuntary. Directed attention is effortful and focused, in which the executive system deliberately brings all our attention to bear on the project at hand. Involuntary attention is when inherently interesting things, such as the beauty of a sunset, capture our attention and re-orient our attention in their direction. ART suggests that, as involuntary attention takes hold, it gives the parts of the brain associated with directed attention a chance to recover and replenish.

Given the importance of our ability to focus, understanding how to refresh our capability seems pretty important. So Berman and his colleagues decided to test what types of breaks would refresh the brain best. To do this, they had subjects take a walk. Some walked through a busy city; others walked through a wood. The pleasant sights and sounds of the woods were expected to modestly attract involuntary attention, gently calling for notice; the city, meanwhile, would still attract involuntary attention, but of a more dramatic and intense nature. Which would refresh people more? The results showed that the woodland walk significantly improved cognitive performance; the city walk didn't. The reason for this is that, even though the city walk triggered involuntary attention, it also called for focused, directed attention too, to avoid being hit by speeding taxis, for example. As it required focus, the brain's performance wasn't rejuvenated by the urban stroll.

The moral of this story is not that we need the woods and trees, but that to replenish our ability to focus we should unfocus. It does little to cognitively recharge us if we switch our attention onto WhatsApp, the TV or Angry Birds; they all require focus.

Turn off, tune out, drop in

When Timothy Leary, back in 1967, called, 'Turn on, tune in, drop out!' he created a slogan for a generation. He was encouraging people to connect more to their humanity at an event called *Human Be-In,* a gathering of 30,000 hippies in San Francisco. Four decades later, to reconnect with our humanity, we need to do exactly the opposite.

Perhaps the biggest challenge to our ability to think well in today's world is what Linda Stone would call *continuous partial attention.* We pay partial attention to everything, continuously, because we don't want to miss anything. We constantly scan the environment of information, messages, stimulation and threat. We are always alert, constantly connected, and continuously trying to optimise efficiency.

To maintain this state of high alertness, we have to operate in a constant crisis management mode. That sense of impending crisis encourages us to be always on, working and connecting everywhere. In the size of doses we serve ourselves, continuous partial attention is fragmenting, stressful and empty. We feel overwhelmed and unfulfilled and it compromises our ability to think and focus. Continuous partial attention guarantees we never fully recharge our ability to focus, so we lose our ability to focus deeply. It's a bit like if you've been working all day, and at 4.00pm your boss brings you a big thinking task that has some urgency to it. You know that feeling of trying to force your tired brain into gear. That's the effect, albeit at a smaller scale, that being continuously alert is having on our ability to focus: it's making it shallower. Or, to paraphrase Leary, we never turn off, and we never tune out – and so we are unable to really drop into the moment, drop into meaningful relationships or drop into ourselves.

Time to not think

So far the arguments I have made have positioned the fragmented, distracted and shallow attention of busy at one end of the spectrum, and placed deep engagement and focused attention at the other. I have explained how the world of too much is eroding our attention and damaging our ability to focus and engage. However, this is not a full picture. In actual fact, there is another mental state that is under threat every bit as much in today's world as deep attention. A state that is also critical to our ability to thrive. That state is 'not thinking' or anti-focus.

One of the most significant findings from neuroscience in recent years is the discovery of the default network. This is the network of neural activity that fires up when we are not stimulating ourselves or doing anything. We expected a lot to be going on in the brain when we are busy, or when we are focused. We hadn't expected a lot to be happening when we were neither of these; we were wrong. In fact, quite the reverse is true: when we are not on task the brain becomes extremely active. The question we have to ask is, 'why?'.

When we are in the doctor's waiting room and there are no magazines we want to read, the default network fires up. When those subjects were walking through the woods, their default network was active. Or at times, even when we're trying to focus, it fires up (remember the Hedden and Gabrieli reference to internal distractions). In fact, the default network is responsible for all daydreaming, intellectual ambling and introspective thought. It might seem that this activity is a little light entertainment which the brain is kindly offering us in the absence of anything better. However, the default network is far more than a YouTube alternative. The default network is doing important work.

The brain needs time free from external stimulation to assimilate, integrate and regroup. The default network is doing a kind of mental housekeeping: filing and organising recent experiences for easy access later. However, this process is far more interesting than the simple filing of data. What the default network is doing is making associations between new information and existing thoughts, ideas and experiences. It seems to play with different connections, in order to integrate the new data meaningfully. This is where magic can happen.

A creative process

Have you noticed how often you have your best ideas in the shower, or when you're in bed? The reason for this is that, at those times, our default network is in full swing (possibly one of the few times these days). It is making fresh connections, and playing with alternative meanings in order to store the information. This process is, by its nature, a fairly creative process: creativity happens when new associations are made – new connections that take two or more pieces of information and combine them to make something totally fresh. Since the default network is playing with new connections, it's not surprising that, from time to time, it will happen upon some surprising ones – some big insights or 'eureka' moments. This fiddling with new associations by the default network is central to all creative thought.

I'll explore creativity in the next chapter in more detail, but for now I want to move to another function of the default network, because I think there is something more profound and fundamental at play here than the production of creative ideas. What is happening here is that the default network is *creating you*! If you look inside yourself and ask, 'Who am I?' your sense of 'I' comes from a collection of experiences, roles, beliefs, ideas, cultural associations and feelings. Somehow, from that tapestry of disconnected thoughts and memories comes a sense of identity. When we are on task, we generate input and stimulation for the brain. This information is raw and external. It is only when we give the default network time to play with it, associating it with our own experiences and beliefs, integrating it into our understanding of the world, that it begins to have meaning. Without this process you can't turn raw, external data into something more personal; into *your* opinion, *your* knowledge and *your* insight. This is the real work of the default network.

Busyness and the differentiation of you
This brings us right back to busyness: how much time do you have alone in your mind, to daydream or reflect, to amble and wander? We have talked about the impact of all the demands we experience in the world of too much: our racing, multitasking and cramming drives out focused attention and engagement. However, our world of too much stimulation may be having an equally big impact. We now have stimulation devices with us all the time, ready for any moment when we are not on task. On the road, this may be our phone, our iPod, Kindle or games console. At home, we have multiple additional devices to ensure our brains are never left on their own.

If I can use an analogy, focused attention and engagement are the food we need, to provide the energy and the nourishment to survive and thrive. Stimulation and consumption of media is like bubble gum, it keeps us occupied, but offers little. The default network is like the digestion system: absolutely essential to allow that food to be integrated and used to become part of you. I don't think we're doing enough digesting these days.

One of the big themes of this chunk is differentiation. To succeed in a world of too much information, too much communication and too much distraction, you have to be able to cut through the noise and be noticed. This may be because you are doing things differently, or doing different things. Either way, you need to have developed a strong point of view and deep insights. Powerful views and insights do not come from consumption of media and stimulation. And they don't come just from focused attention or engagement either. They come from the combination of deep attention and then reflection. When we focus or engage we gain rich information, thoughts and experiences; when we step back from the experience and mull it over we create our meaning, our point of view and our insights. The two processes should work hand in hand. The more deeply you're focusing and the more perspectives you are taking in, the more time your default network needs to integrate these.

What we need is time off from the screens in our lives. We need time for the brain to detach; time without input; time for daydreaming and musing. Author Evgeny Morozov has taken this to an extreme: when he wants to create space to think he locks his phone and internet cables in a safe with a timed lock; in this way he makes it impossible for himself to glance at his email or go online for the weekend or the week. Buying a safe might be a bit extreme, but, however we do it, when we turn off the TV and computer, and tune out the social media and phone, we can drop into ourselves. Then we have a chance to allow our brain to relax and wander; we have a chance to integrate, learn and excite ourselves again.

When we don't do this, no matter how much we try to focus and 'learn', we stay undifferentiated. I come across a lot of people who try to learn a lot; who watch talks on TED.com and read good books. However, when it comes to using this information it comes out as sound-bites and quotes. They haven't given themselves enough amble time to digest and integrate what they are trying to learn. As a result, they are simply remembering stuff, rather than being changed by it and growing. They remain the mouthpiece of somebody else, rather than developing their own voice: a voice that is informed and inspired by others; shaped by their own experience and passions; and integrated into their own, unique world-view.

Carving our own niche

The world of too much is a world of challenge, but it is also a world of opportunity and choice. The problem is, most of us are too battered by demands to think clearly. We fail to create the time and energy to focus meaningfully on opportunities, or make intelligent choices. When we are not on task, we plug our brains into stimulation devices to avoid thought. The result: we become busy, unimaginative drones. Careers and lives today are much more of a blank canvas than ever before; more of a creative process. We can make active choices over what we will pay attention to and what to ignore; what to do, and not do; what we will stand for; how we will make an impact; what level of risk we will take. We can intentionally carve out our own niche in the world, become the person we want to be and differentiate ourselves. Or we can relinquish this opportunity and drift.

It's a lot of work choosing our own path, making our own mark and becoming unique, but a lot of fun. We need to think better by bringing our focus out of the daily distractions; by not procrastinating over the big problems; and by giving ourselves the time to integrate it all and grow. If we can do that, we will be ready to start making a real impact.

The big messages in 'Think better'

Our working habits are driven by what is **technologically possible**, not what is **psychologically effective**. This is a manual for using the brain to think better.

The brain, and more specifically the prefrontal cortex, is fussy. It is where we do most of our thinking but it needs conditions to be just right for it to perform at its best.

EFFICIENT THINKING

- The big thing to remember if you want to think better is to **minimise your multitasking**. Switching regularly between tasks makes you slower and dumber, even if you feel productive.
- Do one thing at a time by getting things **out of your head** and **externalising** your thinking
- Cut down on the amount you switch your attention between tasks by **working in bigger chunks of time**, and **minimising distraction**.

STOP PROCRASTINATING

- **Busyness is a form of procrastination**: doing lots of simple, un-taxing activities rather than a few important ones.
- The four horsemen of procrastination are: **Perfection, Mood, Fear and Dependence**.
- **Deal with Perfection by creating momentum** through thin-slicing and swiss-cheesing.
- When you're '**not in the Mood**' make progress **despite** that by selecting useful, but easier tasks; **reverse your mood** with music or movement; and get your **dopamine and norepinephrine right**.
- You can **manage Fear** using rewards and punishments.
- **Overthrow Dependence by shifting from** *when* **to** *can*: recognise **information addiction**; and, for goodness' sake, kill your belief that you will do this when you are less busy. **Do it now.**

MANAGING ATTENTION BETTER

- Our **attention system** has three networks: **orienting** (noticing stuff); **alerting** (your reserves of attention based on wakefulness); and the **executive network** (choosing where to focus).
- The **executive network is essential to effectiveness**; to recharge our capacity to focus, we have to de-focus and gently stimulate our involuntary attention.
- When we maintain **continuous partial attention**, constantly scanning for threats, alert to information, we never give our focusing powers the chance to regroup and recharge.

- To form our own **point of view**, to differentiate ourselves, we need time to reflect, to integrate what we are learning. That means **time off-task**, un-stimulated, which allows the **default network** to become active.

Go-Do

BIG-CHUNK YOUR TIME

From today, create uninterrupted chunks of time so you can stay on task for longer. To help with this, cut off distractions by disabling the email notifier and your IM.

MACHINE-GUN EMAILS

Choose certain slots in the day to work through your emails and messages. This tends to be low demand work so choose times when you are not at your most alert and save your freshest moments for the important things.

Experiment

UNTHINK

Practise unplugging from all stimulation for periods of time. Give your brain a chance to integrate and recover by going for intellectual ambles.

ZEIGARNIK EFFECT

Use the Zeigarnik effect to your advantage. When you have a big task to do, don't start it cold. The day before, try working on it for a few 10-minute periods to 'open the file' and allow your subconscious to begin processing.

Chapter 6

Making an impact

Ever fancied a piano ... made of concrete? Or a concrete picture frame, bath or wardrobe? Making just about everything from concrete was the brainchild of perhaps the most brilliant inventor of all time, Thomas Edison. His concrete obsession developed when another project of his failed: extracting iron ore using magnets and massive crushing rollers. He was left with a village full of heavy machinery ideal for making concrete, he thought. So he started another project, the Edison Portland Cement Company, in 1899 (a company that went on to supply the cement for the Yankee Stadium). Despite lots of investment, in 1906 his cement production was losing money hand over fist. So he decided to create his own demand. In an after-dinner speech in New York City, he proclaimed to the world he was inventing concrete houses. These could be made from a single mould for just $1200 a time – cheap enough for everyone, even those in slums. They would come with bathtubs and picture frames, and yes, even pianos. They would never need repainting, and additional storeys could be added with a small adjustment of the moulds.

Does it sound too good to be true? It was. The early prototypes proved disastrous, and though moulds could be re-used, the initial investment for a builder would have been $175,000. In truth, why would anyone want to live in a house that had been nicknamed the 'salvation of the slum dweller'? Today, only 12 of Edison's world-changing concrete houses remain.

When we think of Thomas Edison we think of the light bulb, the phonograph and the motion picture. But for me, the most inspiring aspects of the Edison story are not the highlights, but the failures. Edison registered an incredible, 1,093 patents for items he'd invented, but of all these inventions, most were flops. Yet he made a huge impact on the world because he walked his own path. He didn't get caught in the treadmill of reactivity. He thought differently, questioned things and persistently experimented with new ideas.

There are three ways you can try to succeed in a competitive working environment: you can offer what you do at a cheaper rate, you can play the 'More' game or you can make an impact by doing things differently. Only the last of these will help you thrive.

This whole section is about focusing on the right game: doing things differently to differentiate ourselves. If we just want work, we can work cheaply, and retain employment through undercutting the price other people are willing to do the work for. However, when we compete in careers on price, the value people place on what we do soon starts spiralling downwards; the opportunities for career-enhancing development dry up; and we begin to be seen as a faceless, interchangeable resource. My guess is that most of us don't want to play that game, but what about the 'More' game? If we play the 'More' game, we can only succeed in the longer term through working longer hours, doing more stuff, and ruining our lives even further. I firmly believe that the 'More' game only works early in careers, when the competition is more ambiguous about their desire for a successful career. Once you are one or two steps up the ladder, everyone around you wants to succeed, and they're all playing the 'More' game too. This takes us right back to Michael Porter's findings (see p. 81): we will succeed through differentiating ourselves, not through operational effectiveness (the 'More' game). One of the fundamental shifts we need to make to differentiate ourselves is to move our focus from getting things done to making an impact.

In a marketplace that is so fast and disruptive, organisations will only survive if they can make an impact: by creating new ideas, new products and new services faster than their competition. Businesses are crying out for innovation. Yet inside those businesses, the inbox rules, meetings abound and people leap from task to task. Everything businesses do internally encourages drone-like behaviour rather than invention. Busy people, straining to get it all done, are unlikely to create the next light bulb (or concrete piano for that matter). They don't have time to think, let alone innovate. By focusing on impact we can demonstrate and deliver real value. We can prove our worth by making a difference, rather than by working longer and harder than others.

This chapter will explain the three principles of making an impact in a world of too much: focus; think differently; and experiment. They will not make you less busy; other strategies elsewhere in the book will do that. The ideas in this chapter are about how to succeed without the need to be busy.

Focus

Edward M. Hallowell, author of *Crazybusy* and expert in attention deficit disorder (ADD) likens the experience of busyness to that of people suffering from ADD. 'People with untreated ADD rush around a lot, feel impatient wherever they are, love speed, get frustrated easily, lose focus in the middle of a task or a conversation because some other thought catches their attention, bubble with energy but struggle to pay attention to one issue for more than a few seconds . . . feel they could do a lot more if they could just get it together . . . feel powerless over the piles of stuff that surround them, resolve each day to do better tomorrow, and in general feel busy beyond belief but not all that productive'[1].

Sound familiar? That description would apply to many of us in our daily lives. Being busy, rather than focused on the big stuff, is more akin to ADD than to the super-effective business executive we aspire to be. But focus is essential if you want to make an impact on your organisation or the world.

Do the big stuff first

There is a little experiment Stephen Covey used to do with rocks, gravel and sand. You take a big jug and fill it with big rocks. When you can't get any more in, you add the pebbles until you can add no more. Finally, add the sand. Empty the jug and do the same thing in reverse. Add the same amount of sand, then the gravel, then the rocks. You will notice, try as you might, that you will only be able to fit a small number of the rocks into the jug this time.

This is a well-known time-management demonstration that conveys a simple, profound and seldom-followed principle: focus on the big stuff first and fit the little stuff around it. When we think about managing our time, we often think about what we will do, or when we will do it by. We don't tend to think much about the order we will do it, but the sequence matters. It matters because we get tired, we get distracted and we often don't get through all the items on our list. The things we choose to do first, we are much, much more likely to get done.

It is too easy to adopt the 'if' or 'when' mentality: *if* I get on top of my emails I'll give some time to my strategic work; *when* I have more time I'll be more strategic. Actions of broader, deeper and longer-term significance are sequenced after the immediate and the small, and so they don't happen.

We only deliver real impact through persistent focus over time. Having good ideas means nothing; they have to be delivered, day after day, to deliver lasting value. If you want to differentiate yourself in this world of too much, if you want to succeed, put your strategy and your big ideas first.

What's your breakthrough opportunity?

A good place to start to focus is by identifying your 'breakthough opportunities', a concept developed by a colleague, client and friend of mine, Shannon Banks, a Director of Learning and Development at Microsoft. It started from a belief that as leaders progress up an organisation, hard work and good performance no longer matter, because everyone at those levels is performing well. At such levels it is difficult to break through; there is a lot of competition for very few positions. Those that do break through almost always do so because of something they did that caught lots of people's attention. This may have been a change they delivered; an unexpected piece of work they produced; a valuable innovation that they implemented. It was never because of their hard work to deliver what was expected of them.

You may or may not be in a senior leadership position, but in a world filled with distraction, we need to work harder to get people's attention; we need to make breakthroughs. In order to make a decision about where your strategic focus should be, start thinking in these terms. What could you do that would make a real impact on the business? What would raise eyebrows? What can you do which would have a dramatic effect on your career? Once you have your list, use some criteria for selecting the breakthrough opportunity to focus your attention on:

- **Impact on the business**: how much of a positive difference will this opportunity make on the business and your career?
- **Passion**: how excited or passionate do you feel about this opportunity?
- **Strengths**: which opportunity plays to your strengths best?

Copy the grid below and capture some ideas. Once you have identified all the possible ideas, rate each idea against the three criteria, given them a score from one to 10 (one being low and 10 being high) to help you decide where to place your focus.

Possible breakthrough opportunities	Impact on the business	Personal passion for this opportunity	Degree to which this would play to my core strengths	Overall score

What opportunity are you going to go after?

Focus on 'Horizon Two' – the middle term

Mehrdad Baghai and his colleagues from McKinsey and Co. introduced the concept of three time horizons in which to think about corporate strategy[2]. Horizon One is short term: managing the business over the next year. Horizon Two is middle-term: identifying and putting in place the next generation of high-growth opportunities. Horizon Three is long term: incubating the germs of new ideas that will sustain the business long into the future. You need to focus on all three horizons in order to succeed. For example, failed companies in the technology sector, giants like Kodak, Sun and Xerox, all invested heavily in Horizon Three; and they all continued to run their businesses effectively day to day using Horizon One strategies. The problem was, they failed to translate these long-term ideas into concrete realities. They failed to pay sufficient attention to Horizon Two.

Horizon Two, the middle term, is a dangerous middle ground. It's quite nice for executive teams to go for off-site meetings and dream up bold, wonderful-sounding visions and long-term strategies. Back at work, these same executives enjoy getting embroiled in the heart-pumping, adrenaline-fuelled thrill of the day to day. Somehow, what gets lost is the middle term. Part of the issue is that, when Horizon Two activities are assessed, they nearly always fall far short of the immediate payoffs Horizon One offer and are less fun than Horizon Three ideas. Geoffrey A. Moore, a Silicon Valley-based high-tech consultant recommends that any company wishing to survive into the long term needs to find a way of incubating and insulating Horizon Two ideas until they are ready to be applied[3].

How true is this for many of us busy folk? For most people, Horizon Two is a work that will start delivering benefit in three to six months. It's nice to think of big, vague aspirations and dreams (Horizon Three), yet it's hard to see how these translate to the throbbing tempo of daily life. With Horizon Two activities, the payoff is more obvious, more tangible, yet most of us still need to discipline ourselves to focus on these. When we hold up the immediate value we will get from replying to those 12 emails against what we will gain from putting half an hour into that long-term project that no one is chasing us for, the dozen emails will always win. Yet many of the things that are most important for us to work on, which we are confident will deliver the most value to us in the longer term, are Horizon Two projects. They may be projects, or intentions to improve your network, or self-development activities; they all matter; they all take time before they will deliver.

We need to find a way of protecting the Horizon Two projects which we know could be of major value soon, but just not yet. One way of doing this is by ensuring your prioritisation decisions are made 'cold' rather than 'hot' when faced with the temptation of the immediate reward (as mentioned in Chapter 2). For example, decide at the start of the week what Horizon Two tasks you want to focus on each day; then decide how you will avoid the temptation and distraction of the Horizon One (the everyday, the urgent, and the electronic chatter). Your best focus is not the immediate (Horizon One), but it's also not the really long term (Horizon Three); it's the middle-term activity that will deliver results in three to six months.

What Horizon Two activity could you bring more focus into to make a big impact? What can you do to stop getting sucked into endless Horizon One work?

Tracking important practices: a balanced scorecard

Robert S. Kaplan and David P. Norton introduced the concept of the balanced scorecard to the business world back in 1992[4]. At the time they were concerned that focusing solely on financial measures of performance was driving the wrong behaviour in organisations. There is a saying that 'what gets measured gets done'. While a total focus on the financials might have worked in the industrial era, they felt it was increasing myopia in the complex world of the early 1990s. In essence, the balanced scorecard helps organisations track what really matters. It accepts that people will seek to deliver the numbers, whatever the numbers are. So by starting to measure a more balanced set of things, you get a more balanced and sustainable set of business practices.

Things have moved on since the early 1990s, but the need for a broader view of performance has never been more important. Converting the corporate perspective to a more personal one, I would argue that the individual's equivalent of the financial measures used by companies to track their performance would be whether they had an empty inbox, were delivering everything on time etc. We track these (without having to write anything down) because they are so visible, so noticeable. These might be valuable things to track, but this does not provide a very balanced view.

Most balanced scorecards have four areas they track, one of which is financial performance. I keep a balanced scorecard on myself to keep reminding myself of where I want to focus. It has four elements. One is Delivery, my day-to-day business; one is Writing, which incorporates research and thinking; one is Relationships from a work perspective; and the final one is Energy, which focuses on two areas: emotional energy from quality time with family and friends, and physical energy. I am truly succeeding when I focus on, and make significant progress in, all four areas over a month.

What would your four be?

Keep perspective: zoom in, zoom out

On the April 20, 2010, Deepwater Horizon, a BP-operated floating oil rig in the Gulf of Mexico, exploded into the night sky, into the Gulf and into the media spotlight. The explosion killed 11 people. Five million barrels of oil gushed out into the surrounding waters over an 87-day period. The wildlife was decimated; the local population devastated. The public demanded answers.

Into this tragedy stepped the CEO of BP at the time, Tony Hayward. Despite the obvious horror and ongoing environmental degradation as oil continued to gush out of the deepwater pipe, day after day, Hayward failed to respond to the mood of the nation or to see the bigger picture. He seemed preoccupied with the impact on the management team and on himself, saying things like, 'I'd like my life back' and, 'What the hell did we do to deserve this?'. Rather than acknowledging BP's role in the disaster, he continued to focus on the small picture, such as trying to blame BP's rig operator, Transocean. In July he was sacked.

Rosabeth Moss Kanter, Professor at Harvard Business School, cites this as an example of a leader who failed to 'zoom out'[5]. She argues that a critical leadership capability is the ability to operate like a camera lens: to zoom in and zoom out. Leaders need to be able to see the world through different perspectives at different times. At times they need to see the detail, to make decisions or understand critical issues. However, they also need to be able to see the big picture. The challenge for a lot of leaders is to make sure they don't get stuck either in or out, but are able to move in and out appropriately.

When I talk about focus, I don't mean persistent focus on the details. Frenetic busyness is strongly associated with zooming in. When we're busy, we can get so caught up in the stuff hitting us, we're stuck zoomed in. Times of focused attention on the detail are critical, but without the practice of regularly zooming out to check perspective and priorities, we can end up doing 'stuff', rather than maintaining our strategic focus. People that are zoomed in too frequently tend to get overwhelmed by the detail; they can take things personally, seeing the 'me' angle first; they skitter between tasks, rather than remaining focused; they see every situation as unique rather than noticing common patterns.

When we feel busy and overwhelmed, zooming out can help us to see the map to stay focused on the bigger priorities. Here are some questions to help you to zoom out when you're stuck zoomed in:

- What matters most in the big picture?
- What can I do here that is most in line with my strategy?
- What is the impact on those around me?
- What do I need to do to retain my focus?
- When have I experienced similar situations? What can I learn from those about me?

Bigger picture beats detail

'If only I could get a little more efficient and a little more organised, my life and performance would be so much better.' This is what I call the efficiency myth. In actual fact, for many of my clients, I have seen the exact reverse. They have focused obsessively on getting more efficient and organised, developing tick lists, colour-coded emails, set up folders . . . I have a fundamental belief that, for most knowledge workers, it isn't about more or better tick lists, it's not about more detailed planning, or even doing more . . . it's about focusing on, and doing, the right things. The thing about being efficient and organised is that the stuff that naturally fits on a list, and is readily ticked as complete, is the little, inconsequential tasks. The very act of detailed organisation can drive you away from doing the things that matter.

We know that we can improve our performance by coming up with a plan, but what kind of plan is best? In a carefully controlled study, researchers were keen to understand how to help students improve their study skills through planning. Students were put into one of three groups. One group was instructed to make daily plans for what, where and when they would study. A second group were asked to do similar plans, only month by month. A third group made no plans. Monthly planners performed best in terms of improvement in study habits, grades and in retention of the good habits: a year later the monthly planners were still getting better grades than the daily planners (though both groups beat those who didn't plan at all).

It turns out that having a broader view of what you mean to accomplish is more effective and motivational. Zooming out does not mean having no focus. On the contrary, focus is often lost when we're too close to the detail. A psychologist asked a bunch of US army generals how they managed their affairs. A battle-hardened general, the only woman in the group, summarised her approach: 'First I make a list of priorities: one, two, three, and so on. Then I cross off everything from three down'[6]. Detailed to-do lists can be a useful dumping ground to get things out of your head, but they should not drive your focus. You need to zoom back out to your strategy, your priorities, to remind yourself of where your focus should be. It usually isn't hard, it's normally one or two things.

Think differently

My father-in-law ran a design course. When he gave students a project, they would typically produce their first attempt fairly quickly. On completion, he would approach them and ask if they were happy with their design. Irrespective of their answer he would reply, 'Good. Now put that to one side and create a Plan B'. . . and then he'd push for a Plan C. Inevitably the student would groan and moan. Also, almost as inevitably, Plan B would be better than Plan A, and Plan C better yet.

Making an impact requires persistent focus, as well as the ability to ask if there is an alternative approach. However, questioning the status quo isn't an instinctive reaction. The brain is a connection-making machine, creating thoughts and beliefs through neural connections, and then storing these thoughts by linking them with memories of past experiences and ideas. In the future, when we encounter related information, the brain makes an association with the stored memory, and fires up these existing connections in anticipation of applying an existing model to the new stimuli.

The process of retrieving existing models, to spot a pattern based on past experience, is pretty much effortless, and the brain does this readily. In fact, the brain is so good at associating previous ideas to new experiences, it can lead us to recognise patterns where none exists. Take abstract art. When you look at a canvas covered with random swishes and swirls, the brain can't help itself – it 'sees' meaning where there is none. We find ourselves asking 'What is it?' and simultaneously trying to answer that question. What was intended to be meaningless, we interpret. This is what the American science writer Michael Shermer calls 'patternicity'[7].

Our tendency towards patternicity also affects our ability to think differently and to create. When we encounter a situation or a problem, the brain's starting point is to reach for previously developed solutions. This is good and efficient, but the connections the brain makes aren't always a brilliant fit. This is another example of our tendency to rely on the automatic System One rather than effortful System Two thinking. Once we have found a pattern, more often than not we accept it; the brain puts a massive 'full stop' after it. It stops searching for alternatives and we move on.

In almost every situation we encounter, autopilot kicks in, spotting patterns and telling us what to do. In a business context, when we encounter problems, not only do we automatically apply previous solutions we've developed, we struggle to see that there might be another way, more than one idea.

As Emile August Chartier said, 'Nothing is more dangerous than an idea when it is the only one you have'. Having one idea is especially bad if that lone idea is the same as everyone else's in your business. We increase our chances of making an impact when we cease to accept the same full stop as everyone; and when we start looking for alternatives to solutions that everyone else is taking for granted. This section will help you to spot the 'full stop' in yourself and others ... and kill it. It will encourage you to cultivate discord, where there was unanimity; to challenge false simplicity; and to hold onto your doubt. It will help you to create the right psychological conditions to think differently and make an impact.

Beyond the full stop

The starting point to thinking differently is starting to notice the full stop in your thinking. How often do you accept a taken-for-granted assumption? How often do you re-imagine habits and processes you have been following for years in the light of business changes? How often do you park the obvious, tried and tested solutions for a little while as you try to identify very different alternatives? How often do you stop at Plan A? When you start looking, you will see full stops everywhere.

'I am not creative'

I hear this phrase all the time and it worries me. It's not so much the words that worry me, but the full stop. It's a big one. People label themselves uncreative, and that's that. They leave the job of being creative to those who were good at painting at school. In doing this, we have marginalised creativity to the agencies and marketing departments. Yet thinking differently and creating new ideas is a core business imperative for every department. I believe 'creative' is an activity, not a label. After reading this section I hope – if nothing else – you turn off your autopilot a little more often. This is at the very heart of the 'creative'/'not creative' divide: people who define themselves as creative are much more likely to consciously try to come up with creative solutions. It's not necessarily that they have any unique genetic endowments, but that they decide to look for other options more frequently, to move beyond the immediate and obvious solution. Creativity starts with the decision to try to create.

To question you need doubt

Read this statement: *Lizards love playing Sudoku.*

As you read the statement above an image of a lizard sitting in front of a Sudoku puzzle, probably holding a pen, popped into your head. In doing this, for a moment at least, you believed me. Daniel Gilbert explains that to understand anything we first have to believe[8]. Or, more accurately, to understand something we must first know what the idea would mean if it were true. So we picture it as if it's true. It is only then that we may begin to question whether we believe it *is* true.

Normally, however, we don't bother to try and disbelieve, because it's hard work. Believing is a System One process: fast, automatic and effortless. Doubting, on the other hand, is System Two: it involves engaging our prefrontal cortex, our conscious reasoning processes. So it takes an act of will, and considerable effort, to doubt. Information that is odd, or that we're alerted to, will prompt us to make a conscious effort of will to fire up our System Two in order to verify our belief. In the normal cut and thrust of daily life, however, the majority of data is received as unquestioned fact. In addition, because System One is unconscious, we're not even aware that we haven't properly analysed the information . . . it is just taken for granted.

System Two also has severe limitations as to how much it can handle at once. So, if the brain is busy consciously processing other things, there is less capability left for doubt – so even more information goes unquestioned.

Gilbert ran a nice experiment to show this. He gave people a series of nonsensical statements for them to remember, such as 'a dinca is a flame'. Some of the participants were also asked to hold numbers in their heads at the same time (thus using up some processing power). Later, those who had had to remember the numbers as well as the statements, believed more of the nonsense.

In a future facing unprecedented levels of competition, complexity and interconnectedness of global markets, companies will not succeed through increases in efficiency or by finding new solutions. They will get ahead by fundamentally changing the way they operate; they will make breakthroughs and disrupt the markets they are in. Such organisations will find a way to get staff to question the 'taken for granted'; they will question everything. And questions don't arise from certainty, they come from doubt.

Doubt is essential for creativity. John Keats, the romantic poet, recognised this and created a term to describe the ability to stay in doubt: 'negative capability'. 'At once it struck me, what quality went to form a Man of Achievement, especially in literature, and which Shakespeare possessed so enormously – I mean Negative Capability, that is when man is capable of being in uncertainties. Mysteries, doubts, without any irritable reaching after fact and reason.'

Thirty years ago German companies used to employ philosophers to create doubt in their businesses and identify fundamental questions. Who's doing that in your business today? In most of the organisations I work in, all I see is people too busy to question; too rushed to want anything more than a sound-bite; too distracted to doubt. We need to kill the management mantra 'Don't bring me problems; bring me solutions'. We have too many solutions. We should do all in our power to be catalysts of doubt, to expose the uncertainty beneath the surface of fake solutions. It is only through doubt that the next great breakthroughs will emerge.

How can you build your tolerance of doubt; your negative capability? How can you get better at seeking problems rather than solutions? How can you be a master of discord, and sow more doubt into your business?

Create the conditions

Okay, so you've spotted a full stop, and decided you want to reach beyond it, to be creative. How do you make creativity happen? In actual fact, you've already taken the first step towards producing more creative ideas: you intend to be creative. Neuroscientists have carried out brain scans of people as they approach a problem. They then compared the participant's mental activation prior to their tackling the problem with the quality of the solution they generated. Those who ultimately produced a sensible, somewhat obvious, answer to a problem had beforehand activated different parts of the brain to those who came up with more creative solutions. The key is in the switch. The anterior cingulate cortex helps people switch attention from one pattern of thinking to another, to experiment with one idea after the other. Those who ultimately came up with creative solutions entered the problem with their anterior cingulate cortex primed and ready. Without being open to playing with options and switching approaches, creativity doesn't happen. And without being open to switching, people reach the first full stop, and then move on to the next problem.

Listen for the quiet connections
Looking for a new, creative idea is a bit like feeding the ducks. When we hold a problem or question in our head, neurons start quacking to get our attention. Some are bigger and stronger and push right to the front; some loiter to the sides, making apologetic

little quacks. Mostly, the noisy, pushy ducks get the bread. However, the nature of creative insights is that they involve making fresh connections with unexpected neurons – the quiet little ducks at the side. To allow that to happen the brain has to listen for the quiet, distant connections.

The nature of a new insight means that you are making fresh connections between ideas or information. The obvious, tried-and-tested connections quack the loudest, driving us to an autopilot-like response. Creativity happens when you are able to go beyond the noisiest ducks to allow you to notice the other ducks. To help in this, the brain has an amazing technique. Neuroscientist Mark Beeman made the discovery that 1.5 seconds before a new insight the brain floods the visual cortex with alpha waves, effectively shutting off sight[9]. To hear weak signals from the distant, unexpected neurons, the brain goes blind. The brain is effectively saying: 'Shut up! I'm trying to hear something'.

We've all been in those situations when you're grappling with a problem and you have a sense that you're not far from a solution . . . you just have no idea what it is! At these points, your sight is really unhelpful. Vision is such a dominant sense; it swamps our limited processing power.

Amazingly, if you ask people who are straining for an insight how close they are to achieving it, their estimates are pretty accurate. So we do seem to recognise when an insight is close at hand; we just need to foster the environment to hear it. Creative insight is more likely to happen when you have silence, physically and intellectually. Too much neural noise will drown out the quiet signals you're trying to reach for. That is why the shower, the toilet, your bed, exercise or a drive can be so fruitful from a creative perspective. Each of these activities provides low level intellectual demand and little mental noise. They allow the mind to wander in search of distant echoes; they help novel and unusual connections to be made.

There are three things you can do to quieten the brain, so that you can hear and reach for the distant connections that give insights. The first is to de-focus, as discussed in the previous chapter, to allow the default network to fire up. When conscious thinking is turned down at times when we are off-task, the default network is well suited for hearing and jumping to the distant connections: it's why you have so many insights when you're out for a stroll. The second strategy involves getting the obvious out of your head. When certain ideas and obvious connections are shouting loud, it can help to write them down and go beyond them. As we discussed before, the brain can do one thing well at a time; if it's remembering or inhibiting obvious ideas, this stops it from listening. Getting them out of your head frees you up to listen.

Finally you can try what I call 'strategic snoozing'. Research shows that, if people are given a difficult insight problem to solve, and then given a pause of eight hours before being asked for an answer, those that slept during the eight-hour pause were much more likely to get the answer than those that didn't. I've taken this idea further, not only are periods of sleep necessary for generating new ideas, I also believe the morning snooze time is a highly creative period. When my alarm goes off, I often hit the snooze button and gently call to mind a big problem I'm thinking about. I don't so much think about it as allow it to gently enter my thoughts as I snooze. I frequently generate great insights in the process.

Slow down

In the opening section of the book, I suggested making time more visible so you could be more productive. Research consistently shows that when we are highly aware of time through having a big clock in front of us or through regular reminders of time, we produce more in less time. The reverse is true of creativity. Increase our time awareness and we'll decrease our creativity. So use time wisely. When you want to whip through tasks and emails, or hammer out that report, get the clock out. However, if you want to reflect and create something novel, you want to ponder on a problem and grapple for fresh insights, put the clock away.

... or speed up

W. H. Auden, the poet, was a drug addict. He relied on caffeine and nicotine, but these weren't enough. In order to get him into the right frame of mind for writing intricate lines of poetry, he needed something stronger. His drug of choice was an amphetamine, Benzedrine. He described the drug as a 'labour-saving device'; he became a prolific poetry-writing machine under the effects of speed. He isn't alone. Jack Kerouac, for example, wrote *On the Road* in a three-week writing session fuelled by Benzedrine.

Jonah Lehrer cites these examples and wonders why such a drug should be so valuable in creativity[10]. The answer, he suggests, is that only a part of creativity is the insight. A lot of the creative process is a slow, steady process of 'unconcealing' the idea; of grunt work. He explains that the amphetamine did nothing to increase the writers' insights, but it did help them to persevere. It helped them to write and write and write, to be edited at a later point.

Clearly I'm not suggesting the use of drugs, but I really like Lehrer's separation of creativity into insight and grunt work. Sometimes we just need to make a start on a task to reveal the solution. The process will either prove we're on the right track or that we need to try a different approach. Either way, we've made some progress. Think about how many times you have figured out what you really thought only once you were halfway through a report or project. It's the easiest thing in the world to pause our work until we get a killer idea, but sometime the ideas don't emerge until we're elbow deep in the work; and they don't appear like a lightning bolt, just a gradual realisation. Either way, insight or grunt, it's still creativity.

Get outside your head

You're stuck in a tower that's 30 metres high with a rope that's only 15 metres long. There is an open window, but no door. The drop is far too great for jumping. How could you escape?

This is a fairly simple insight problem (the answer, as I'm sure you figured out, is that you split the rope lengthways and tie it, so it is half as thick and twice as long). When the problem is worded in the third person, i.e. talking about a 'prisoner', 66 per cent of people get the answer right. When the wording is written in the first person (as it is above), only 48 per cent of people get the answer right![11]

When we think in the first person, we can be less creative. When we picture ourselves in a particular situation, a whole set of assumptions, norms and images tag along for the ride: we remember similar problems we've faced; we try to remember solutions; we look for familiar patterns, and when one seems to fit, we use it. When we think in the third person, on the other hand, we are more inclined to start from scratch. We think more abstractly. Our imagination flies faster and further, and so we are more likely to solve the problem.

When facing a full stop, pause for a moment and ask yourself: how would Bill Gates, or Ang Lee, or Gandhi approach this? You might be surprised at how fresh your perspective becomes.

Don't just look for answers in obvious places

Sometimes the solution to a problem can come from unexpected quarters. Devi Shetty is India's leading heart surgeon, but his skill couldn't help him achieve what he wanted to. He was overwhelmed by the sheer quantity of patients needing care; there was also the issue of cost: a typical heart operation costs $20,000–$100,000 in the US. He couldn't see a way of meeting the need while keeping it affordable. Many surgeons would have got 'realistic' here, recognising the fact that heart operations all over the world are expensive. Devi Shetty didn't accept the full stop. He looked outside of his industry and profession for ideas that might help him increase his hospital's productivity, while slashing the cost of each operation[12].

Shetty recognised that Henry Ford had faced a similar challenge in the early 1900s, and had solved the problem with the assembly line. Shetty pioneered a new medical approach by applying Henry Ford's principles of mass production to open heart surgery, creating economies of scale and specialisation. For example, training heart surgeons is normally a very lengthy and costly business; heart operations are complex procedures. However, in Shetty's model, each surgeon only performed a small piece of the overall operation, making it much quicker and cheaper to train them, and allowing them to rapidly gain very specific expertise. Using this approach, 40 cardiologists were able to perform 600 operations per week, for a tenth of the cost incurred by equivalent Western hospitals, but with the same success rate.

Another example is Cemex, a Mexican cement giant. Cemex noticed that it took three hours from receipt of an order to the delivery of the ready-mixed concrete – a delay that was costly to contractors. Cemex realised they could charge a premium if they could reduce this waiting time, and so they studied the way in which call centres dispatch paramedics. Based on this research,

Cemex fitted all their trucks with GPS and implemented practices that reduced waiting time from three hours to 20 minutes.

What these strategies have in common is that they both reached outside their company, industry, and even their country to find an approach that could be borrowed. Where might you look?

Ask more (weird) folk

In 1675, the Royal Observatory was founded in Britain with the aim of improving navigation at sea. The biggest challenge sailors faced was an inability to assess 'longitude' accurately: how far to the east or west a ship was. This was a critical problem for Britain, as the country's importance on the world stage largely rested upon its naval and trading strengths.

Naturally, the Royal Observatory brought in the experts. Who better to solve such a problem than physicist Sir Isaac Newton and comet expert Edmond Halley? Yet even those great brains failed to make much progress. The whole issue came to a head when, in 1707, Admiral Sir Clowdesley Shovell, wrecked four ships in fog on the Isles of Scilly, believing himself to be further west than he was. Tim Harford, the economist, noted that this incident killed more people than the sinking of the *Titanic*, and it forced the Royal Observatory to try a different approach[13].

Instead of relying on a few experts, the organisation looked for a way to get a wider variety of 'solutions'. They offered a prize of £20,000 for an answer to the problem (equivalent to £30 million today). The ultimate solution didn't come from astronomy, where the experts had expected it to come. Nor did it come from a noted expert. It came from an unknown carpenter called John Harrison. He developed a clock so accurate at sea that by measuring the sun, the longitude could be calculated.

The genius of the award was that it invited a huge amount of people, with vastly different backgrounds and expertise, for their ideas. In doing so, they ultimately came up with a great solution that the experts would never have reached.

A more recent legend has it that IBM, a business that has successfully reinvented itself a few times over, developed a strategy called 'skunking'. Executives recognised they needed to radically change, but they weren't sure how. They needed some different perspectives. The problem was, all those at senior levels, all the high flyers, were of like minds. So IBM looked for their organisational 'skunks'. They looked for the oddballs with V-neck sweaters, acne and beards. They looked for those who had never really fitted in, for the people who had always been different. They looked for a fresh perspective. It worked. Ideas and innovation don't come from sameness; they come from difference.

How diverse is your network? How many weirdos and oddballs do you have in your list of close business contacts? How well do you use this difference? I know, for example, if I really want help with a problem, the worst person to look to can be a fellow psychologist: they will see the world as I do. I'm better off speaking to friends in advertising, farming or the fire service for genuinely different views.

The killer question

Mihaly Csikszentmihalyi, then a Professor of Psychology at the University of Chicago, led a team to study Nobel Prize winners. In particular, he was interested in understanding how it was they achieved their great breakthroughs. What he found was counter-intuitive (at least to business today): finding the solution was easy; the hard part was finding the right question. Once the question had been discovered, ideas flowed freely[14].

Mike Marquardt is an inspirational colleague, professor and one of the leading lights in the world of Action Learning[15]. Action Learning was first developed by Professor Reginald Revans, a physicist by training, who recognised the challenges posed when bright people (many of his fellow physicians at Cambridge University were Nobel Prize Laureates) were discussing complex problems. It is a process where a group not only discusses the problem, but also actively reflects on its effectiveness as a group.

When working with Mike as he runs Action Learning groups, there is one question he asks repeatedly of his groups that always has a profound impact: 'What is the problem we are trying to solve?'. The question addresses the very heart of the issue with a lot of group discussions or problem solving: we spend loads of time and energy trying to find a solution and a plan; we spend almost no time trying to understand and align over the problem.

At certain points in the discussion, he stops the debate and has every person in the group, independently, write down the problem they think the group is trying to solve. It is astonishing how often, after many hours of discussion, people within the same debate are trying to solve different problems. By bringing this lack of alignment to the surface, groups have to decide what the problem is, or how they will progress towards alignment. Perhaps the most common piece of feedback I have heard from groups working with Mike is how amazed they are at the length of time they took to agree on the problem, and, once they had agreed, how easily the solutions flowed.

This question isn't just useful in action learning groups, or even on complex strategic topics. Time and again I find myself in meetings where we are debating energetically and I begin to realise we are probably not clear or aligned over the problem we are trying to solve. The question nearly always stops people in their tracks; it nearly always helps people to think differently; it nearly always leads to better, more creative solutions.

Experiment more

Tim Harford, the economist, illustrates the value of a deliberate trial-and-error process of experimenting, with a story from Unilever[16]. This story comes from the work of the geneticist, Professor Steve Jones, whose father was the scientist at Unilever who invented the ubiquitous household cleaning product Jif (now called Cif). It turns out, when you're manufacturing any detergent, the design of the nozzle is critical. Unilever were struggling to get this right. They called in the experts; but without success. In the end, they tried running a series of experiments. They built 10 different nozzles and tested them. They then took the best of these, and created 10 variations of that design, and tested again. After 45 further experiments, each time selecting the best nozzle and designing 10 further variations of that design, Unilever found a brilliant design: a design that no expert in the world could ever have designed.

Failure

Failure is an ever-present reality for most organisations; it is also becoming more common. For example, John Hagel, of Deloitte's

Centre for the Edge[17] (which advises companies on technology), calculates that the average time a company spends in the S&P 500 index has declined from 75 years in 1937 to about 15 years today. Our world is faster now, more complex with more competition; it is riskier.

One of the things that can get in the way of making an impact in your work is concern about getting things wrong – failing. Part of the reason we use familiar, tried-and-tested approaches is that they're safe. We can predict the results we'll get, or, even if we can't predict the results, we feel we won't get into trouble for applying a standard approach. However, I agree with Tim Harford: we won't really succeed, we won't make an impact, unless we accept that we will need to fail along the way; unless we are willing to intelligently experiment.

Can we try to prevent failure?

The best way to avoid failure is to predict the future. In a famous study over 20 years, psychologist Philip Tetlock analysed how effective experts were at predicting future events[18]. He gathered nearly 300 eminent experts, whose job it was to comment on economic and political trends. Collectively he asked them 27,450 very specific questions. He was interested to know how well experts predicted the future. His findings were startling. Their ability to predict future events was only slightly better than uninformed undergraduates. Also, deep expertise didn't help: for example, experts in Russia didn't predict future Russian events any better than those whose expertise was in Canada. More interestingly still, the most famous of the experts were the most incompetent.

If prediction doesn't work, does planning? Paul Ormerod, a British economist, analysed the pattern of mass extinction over the last 550 million years. He found a clear relationship between the scale of extinctions and their frequency: extinction events that were twice as severe were four times less common; events that were three times as severe were nine times less common[19]. Through mathematics, despite an ever-changing competition between species and changing climates, a distinctive signature appears. Ormerod then went on to apply this to the corporate world of business failures. He found a remarkable similarity between what he'd found through evolution and patterns in business. This raises the question, if companies fail in the same way that species become extinct, is the whole process random? What about good versus bad strategic planning? Through the power of mathematics, he built a model that allowed some companies to be successful planners, and he called this the 'planning is possible' model. He built another model called 'planning is impossible' which assumed no one could plan effectively. The results of the 'planning is possible' model looked nothing like the real-life data of business success and failure. However, the model that assumed 'planning is impossible' was remarkably close to reality! This doesn't necessarily mean that no companies can plan, but it does suggest that planning is unlikely to be a very effective tool to prevent failure.

The lessons from Tetlock's work with experts and Ormerod's study of company failures is that we shouldn't rely on our intellectual horsepower to avoid failure. Tim Harford, in his book *Adapt: Why success always starts with failure*, suggests that our world is just too complex to predict and to successfully plan. For example, a big city like New York or Rio de Janiero is likely to offer as many as 10 billion different types of products and it is said that even in a single Starbucks coffee shop, there are 87,000 product variations available. More products, in a more global market, with more interdependencies and more players in the game mean an ever-increasing level of complexity. We don't have the intellectual capacity, or the computing tools to analyse all the possibilities.

If we can't avoid failure, what can we do?

We have to choose our failures

There are only three ways to try to succeed in today's competitive workplaces. You can work harder than everyone else; you can charge less than everyone else; or you can differentiate yourself and do things differently. The best way to succeed is play another game – make an impact by doing things differently.

However, doing things differently necessarily involves taking risks. Is this risk worth taking? Are we better off doing everything in our power to avoid failure? I would argue that the best way to fail big in your career and life is to avoid failure. If you are doing the same thing as everyone else, you are less likely to fail in the short term, but you will go unnoticed. You will become a commodity trading on quantity or price, disposable and unsatisfied at work. The trade-offs you make in life to sustain your position in the face of similar competition (by working really, really hard or charging less) help to ensure you fail to achieve the kind of lifestyle you want to; fail to become the parent or spouse you aspire to be; fail to be the person you want to become.

Failure is unavoidable; but we can choose which type of failure we will accept. We can avoid failure in the short term, and in so doing, fail in the slow, steady, life-sapping manner many of us are, by allowing ourselves to be so busy. Or, by doing things differently, we can fail small and often, and through failing, succeed more in work and in life.

Doing things differently is not a recipe to avoid failure – it will result in more failure – but, if done right, it will also result in a lot more success.

Intentional experimentation

We are surrounded by living proof that failing small and often is a great way to succeed. In fact we ourselves are arguably the greatest examples of this fact. The most durable, time-honoured approach to succeeding in complex environments is also one of the simplest: evolution. More specifically, what works is variation and selection. Stuart Kauffman, a complexity theorist, has shown that evolution isn't just a sensible way to attempt to solve complex problems, it's the best possible approach[20]. Sexual reproduction and genetic mutation produce a lot of diversity or variation. Of these variations, some fail, some survive and some succeed spectacularly. Repeated over millions of years, great solutions emerge that would never happen through careful planning; but they work.

As Unilever did with the detergent nozzle, we can learn from the wisdom of evolution; we can try things, different things, and build upon those that work. The lesson from Edison is that the way to make an impact is not through genius and coming up with a single, world-changing idea. The lesson from Tetlock is that we won't make an impact through our deep expertise. The lesson from Ormerod is we won't make an impact through brilliant planning. If you want to make an impact, learn from evolution: experiment. Do different things. Some stuff will work; some stuff won't. Select the stuff that works and discard the stuff that doesn't; and then vary things again.

Try new things

The starting point of succeeding through doing things differently is to try a variety of things, rather than repeating or copying. Lu Hong and Scott Page developed a simulation with robot-like-creatures[21]. Some of these creatures were smart: they could do more and calculate more; others were incredibly simple and basic. They found in a computer model that a group of very similar but very smart creatures was much less successful in finding solutions than the simple creatures, providing the simple ones were much more diverse. The reason for this was that the dumb creatures, as a result of their diversity, did more different things; and in doing so, found more solutions. The founder of Amazon, Jeff Bezos, claimed a lot of his company's success was down to the willingness to 'go down blind alleys'. One such experiment, allowing small booksellers to sell through Amazon, now accounts for a third of the company's revenues. If you are trying to succeed, in your career or in solving a really complex problem, don't put all your eggs in one basket. The starting point is to build on your ability to ask different questions and think differently: try lots of different things and see what works.

What aspect of your work isn't working? What patterns of behaviour are you repeating? What are three alternative, untried approaches? Try them and keep the most effective.

Place small bets

A number of years ago, a large cosmetics firm in Japan called Kao was considering a fairly radical departure from their traditional products: producing floppy disks. They were worried about the consumer response to this, so before investing heavily in new production capability, they tried a little experiment: they bought a large supply of floppy disks of about the same price and quality they ultimately intended to produce. They then relabelled them as Kao-branded products. Only when they had received a good consumer response did they make the large investment in new machinery needed for production.

Chris Rock is one of the most successful comedians in the world today. He came to prominence performing in *Saturday Night Live* in the early 1990s, has appeared in a wide range of movies, and was voted the fifth greatest stand-up comic of all time by Comedy

Central. Chris sees failure as an integral part of the process of developing great comedy. He realises that a lot of his jokes will flop, and that he cannot accurately predict which ones will work and which ones won't. What he does to remain successful is that he constantly tries out new material at small venues. Most of his new material has to be dumped, but some of it really works. The stories and jokes that really work, that have been tried and tested, are the ones he successfully uses on the big stages.

If you're trying to make an impact by doing things differently, try your ideas out on a small scale first. A colleague of mine was thinking about significantly rebranding his company. He was nervous about how his major clients would respond to his new brand image. Instead of investing straight away in a new look website, letterheads etc., he had three very different business cards printed. Each one represented one of his new design options. He started giving these out randomly to new and established contacts socially, but not in important sales meetings. He carefully noted their response; he tried to explain each of the three brands. In the end, it became clear which 'look' was working best; he also found one of the brands was easier for him to explain (fortunately it was the same one). Finally, convinced he had found a strong new brand, he invested in making the full change.

If you want to try things differently, ask yourself how you can experiment on a small scale. How can you test your idea in a way that failure is not a major issue?

Know what's working

Making small bets is critical, but we have to remember that we all suffer from biases in decision-making. The most relevant one here is the confirmation bias. When we do something new we normally look hard for confirmation that we were right; we seldom dispassionately review its effectiveness. The next strategy involves putting in measures to objectively understand what works and what doesn't.

A Dutch charity, International Christelijk Steunfonds (ICS), wanted to fund a school assistance programme in Kenya[22]. Like any charity, they had limited resources and wanted to make the maximum impact. So they worked with three 'randomistas', Michael

Kremer of Harvard, Paul Glewwe of the University of Minnesota and Sylvie Moulin of the World Bank, to do some small trials. Randomistas are people devoted to using sound experimental conditions such as random trials, to make informed decisions. They selected 25 schools at random and supplied them with textbooks, and tested the impact. When compared with the non-selected schools, the textbooks made little difference. Rather than giving up, ICS ran a second experiment. Again they chose 25 further schools randomly and this time gave them illustrated flip charts. For a second time, the results were disappointing. Finally ICS gave the school children tablets to treat intestinal worms. Worm tablets turned out to be a great success, boosting height, reducing infection and cutting absenteeism. They were then ready to make a much larger investment, confident that it would make a real impact.

It's not always possible to run random trials and control groups for everything. However, it's remarkable how often a lot of what we do in work and in life is untested. We place huge efforts into developing a project, and as it starts to get delivered shy away from assessing its impact due to fear that it may not deliver the hoped-for results. More than that, we are much more likely to spot confirmation of our success. Our effort too often shifts to justifying and promoting rather than objectively assessing. Anything we can do to identify the criteria before we start and test earlier reduces the amount of wasted effort. Anything we can do to test things more objectively helps us to make more informed decisions on the best course of action.

Learn the lessons, objectively

Harford's final suggestion in *Adapt* is that we learn the lessons of our experiments, our experiences and our failures. When faced with clear evidence that something (like overwhelming busyness) isn't working for us, there are three psychological reasons that many of us don't learn from the evidence and try something different.

The first reason is cognitive dissonance. Let's say you have come up with a great breakthrough idea, which will automate a lot of the work the team does, that you are sure will transform your department. Despite having a lot of other demands on you, you have managed to prioritise your time on this. However, early feedback is far from positive. Your team are telling you the new process is more cumbersome; your boss is questioning the costs incurred. Could they be right? After all, you are bright, experienced and you gave the project a lot of thought. It is hard for us to simultaneously accept that we are capable and expert, and at the same time recognise that we've made a complete pig's ear of the project. So we tend to deny the feedback and press on.

Secondly, in the same example, the 'gambler's tilt' can kick in. The biggest risk for any gambler isn't getting over-confident when they're winning; it's taking too many risks when they've just made a bad loss. As Kahneman showed in his work on prospect theory[23], after a bad loss, people can take desperate risks in the hope of recovering from that loss; risks they would never take before that loss. Our very investment in a project can make us blind to the evidence; we become determined to keep on going, investing good money or time after bad. Like the gambler, our aversion to loss makes us lose more.

Finally, we have to avoid what the economist Professor Richard Thaler called 'hedonic editing'. This is the tendency to convince ourselves that the mistake or failure doesn't matter. You might tell yourself, 'What do they know?' you are the expert after all. This can take place on the small failures, but also on the very biggest: wasting our life by living a dismal, grey, stretched life, where we fail to make an impact in work, and fail to live the life we want outside. We mash up the good with the bad, like Mary Poppins' suggestion to take a 'spoonful of sugar' to help the medicine go down. 'I don't really mind working 13 hours each day and being constantly exhausted; it allows us to live here and have great holidays.'

Ernest Hemingway advised, 'Write drunk, edit sober.' When you are getting evidence that something isn't working, get sober! Success doesn't result from making the right guesses in the first place; it comes from trying things and then, in the cold light of day, identifying what works and what doesn't, and then responding accordingly. In a world of too much, you haven't got time for things that aren't working. Keep moving. Try stuff out. Keep discarding the things that aren't working, to allow you to try new things. Find the stuff that really has impact, then run with it. To mis-quote the great Muhammad Ali, *you have to float like a butterfly to be able to sting like a bee.*

The big messages in 'Making an impact'

Success comes from making an impact by doing things differently, not getting lots of things done.

FOCUS

- People don't notice the everyday; to differentiate yourself you need to make breakthroughs. Persistently focus on **breakthrough opportunities** that will have impact, that you're **passionate** about and that **play to your strengths**.
- The best timescale to focus on to differentiate yourself is **Horizon Two** – middle-term opportunities which will deliver results in **three to six months**.
- A **clear focus doesn't mean narrow**; get really clear on the three or four aspects of your work (and life) where you want to make the most impact; develop a **balanced scorecard** to track your progress.
- Great leaders can focus and refocus, **zooming into the details and zooming out to the big picture**.

THINK DIFFERENTLY

- The starting point of any impact comes from the willingness to ask if there is an alternative approach; the willingness to **go beyond the full stop**.
- Create the conditions for creative ideas by **slowing down**, giving your mind space to wander, to make **new patterns of connections**. Or by simply getting on with it; an awful lot of creativity **isn't about insight, it's grunt work**.
- Multiply your new ideas by **getting outside of your own head**, by borrowing ideas from other industries or by drawing on the perspectives of different, or even weird, folk.
- The hard thing in making a breakthrough might not be finding the solution, but **finding the right question**. Great questions lead to great solutions and greater impact.

EXPERIMENT MORE

- **Busyness can be a form of 'playing it safe'**: trying to keep everyone happy; doing what everyone else is doing.
- But failure is inevitable. We can either **open ourselves up to making small failures**, through trying to do things differently, and make an impact; **or we fail big** through failing to differentiate ourselves, failing to succeed and failing to lead the lives we want.
- A smarter way is to **intentionally experiment** or learn from evolution. Do things differently; select the stuff that works, discard the things that don't; but keep trying new things.

Go-Do

DO THE BIG STUFF FIRST

Start each day, week and month by working on the big, important things. Prioritise them by the amount of time you spend on them and also in the order you do them.

BALANCED SCORECARD

What would your balanced scorecard be? Choose three to five items to track that will help you deliver your strategy and differentiate yourself.

PLAN B

Stop that big piece of work you are doing right now for a moment and ask yourself, 'Is there an entirely different way of doing this?'. Continue to challenge yourself on every big piece of work: is what you're doing differentiating? Have you taken the time to identify Plan B?

Experiment

KILLER QUESTION

Try using this killer question in meetings and discussions: 'What problem are we trying to solve?'. It can have a profound effect.

FAIL

Practise failing constructively, to learn and remove your fear about failure. Deliberately choose an activity or project you think you are likely to fail at; enter it with an intention to learn.

Section Three

ENGAGEMENT

The first section of this book was designed to help you regain mastery over your life in the face of too much by building a sense of control and overcoming learned helplessness. It is difficult to respond proactively to the demands we face without first feeling masters of our own destiny: it is the foundation on which we can build a better approach to 'too much' and on which we can start to build effective strategies to help us thrive.

In my view, there are two core components involved in thriving. The first of these is achievement – the feeling that we are succeeding. In the second section we moved beyond *mastery* to achieving *success*; we went beyond simply *coping*, to *thriving*. We looked at how to succeed through focus and differentiation.

However, thriving is not just about achievement, it is also about our level of engagement in our lives. In this section I look at this second aspect of thriving. I want to outline how easily we can disconnect from all that really matters to us. This happens because of busyness, but disconnection is itself a driver for more busyness. More importantly, I want to suggest how we might thrive by building a life rich in engagement – both at work and outside of it.

Disconnection

How many meals have been ruined by one or other of you picking up emails or receiving calls? How many evenings have you wasted watching TV? How many important events for your children have you missed (that you probably could have been present for if you'd really tried)? How many days in the last month did you go to bed feeling you had really been the person you wanted to be that day?

I see a lot of disconnection around me: people switching off – a little or a lot – from their dreams, from their loved ones and from themselves. I see people start on career paths for all the right reasons, and day by day, email by email, drift away from what was important to them. It never happens suddenly, or even consciously. It's just that a lack of attention to these things, over time, takes its toll. As we disconnect we always have a very good story for why this is the case; most of the time, we may even believe this story, but there is a sadness that creeps into our quiet moments – a kind of existential angst whose one refuge is activity; busyness quietens (and dulls) the mind.

The problem isn't technology. We don't disconnect from our values because we can easily look at Facebook or email, or because we have so much great stimulation available to us via one of our many screens. The problem also isn't work. We don't disconnect because we have jobs that are simply too demanding. The problem is one of adjustment.

Gin and busyness

Clay Shirky describes how, in the early stages of the Industrial Revolution, society went through a shattering change[1]. Stable pastoral communities were ripped apart by a mass exodus of people to the factories. Cities exploded with rootless, rural immigrants who had lost their way of life, their communities and their constraints, and had no idea how to carve a worthwhile urban life. Caught up in this upheaval, people turned to drink. Specifically, they turned to gin. In what is often considered the first endemic explosion of alcohol abuse, gin consumption in the UK grew from half a million gallons to an estimated 50 million gallons. Gin was the people's escape from the emptiness of industrial life.

I think we're at a similar point in history. Clay suggests that TV has become our gin. I think it's broader than TV. I think we have lost a sense of purpose and depth; in its place we have gained stimulating, but unfulfilling, activity and entertainment. We've become disconnected from what is really important to us; detached from what matters, we are unable to muster the energy for sustained attention and growth. So we look for cheap fixes that ask little of us and give little in return – fixes which leave us feeling empty but craving for more.

'More' and disconnection

I talked a lot about the 'More' game in the last section: the endless (and futile) quest for success through productivity. 'More' also plays a big role in disconnection. The busyness provoked by our desire for 'More' causes us to neglect things that really matter, and an unhealthy triangle results. The three components of the triangle are busyness, 'More' (externals like money or status) and disconnection.

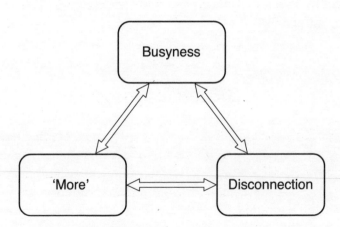

This is how it goes. We are driven to achieve success in the form of earnings, status and/or reputation. This leads to busyness as we strive for our external goals. By being busy we disconnect from our core values, and the people and activities that nourish us. This causes us to feel detached and hollow, so we fill the emptiness with more busyness, which gives us a buzz and more stimulation, but little real joy. And so we disconnect further, acquiring more connections on social media, but genuinely connecting with fewer people. We justify the busyness and disconnection because of our external 'More' goals; we salve our emptiness with materialism and consumption: 'I deserve this'. The external 'More' doesn't satisfy us, ever. We've replaced the protein of life with chocolate. It doesn't strengthen us or help us to grow; it doesn't satisfy; but it does whet our appetite for more.

In this section, I'm making a stand on behalf of depth over distraction, engagement over stimulation, genuine relationships over Facebook friends. It will help you to cut through the distractions of the world of too much by re-orientating yourself back to the fundamentals in your life: the sources of real happiness and wellbeing.

Chapter 7

The right success

ICI (Imperial Chemical Industries) had a glorious history. It was founded in 1926 through the merger of four companies, including that of Alfred Nobel's dynamite business, an organisation whose explosives allowed major engineering projects like the Suez Canal to become possible. For most of the 20th century, it rightfully earned a reputation as one of the most innovative companies on the planet, gaining 150,000 patents on many life-changing inventions and discoveries. Commercially, it was also one of the most successful companies emerging from the UK, dominating the manufacturing and chemical industries. At its zenith, it was the largest manufacturing company in the British Empire; it was commonly regarded as the 'bellwether of the British economy'. The ICI tradition was based on science and innovation. In 1990, its mission statement was to be the 'world's leading chemical company; serving customers internationally through the innovative and responsible application of chemistry'.

Through the 1990s, close to a century's worth of focus on science and innovation first, and profit and sales second, was overturned. Concerned about increasingly fierce global competition, and driven by ambitious CEOs keen to demonstrate their value to the market, the company became much more directly focused on maximising profitability and shareholder return. In 1997, ICI changed its strategy: the new strategy was summarised by the mission to 'be the industry leader in creating value for customers and shareholders through market leadership, technological edge and a world-competitive cost base'. No mention of chemistry was made. This new, profit-centred approach didn't work for ICI. After 80 years of scientific progress, innovative breakthroughs and sustainable commercial success, it experienced a rapid fall from grace. In 2008, ICI ceased to exist[1].

There was a reason ICI was so outstandingly successful for so long, and it wasn't its ability to manage the bottom line and the cost base. It was successful because of its deep expertise and passion for science. Chemistry was the heart and soul of the business, delivering innovation which, in turn, brought profits. In moving to a more directly profit-centric model, the business lost its vitality. The chemists weren't fired up by spreadsheets in the way they had been about test tubes. Saving money was less mobilising than saving lives. Inventory management just wasn't the same as invention. The last 10 years for ICI were spent scrambling for efficiencies and productivities as it increasingly relinquished its unique place in the market.

This story should stand as a salutary reminder of the perils of trading the heart and soul of a business for a balance sheet, productivity gains and cost efficiencies. It should also set off warning bells for you and me. In this chapter I'll clarify the corrosive effect of a perpetual focus on external, 'More' values. I'll then describe alternative, more engaging and rewarding definitions of success. Finally I'll help you to reflect on your own values – what are your core values, and to what extent are you living them? Overall, this chapter will challenge some common assumptions about goals and values. It will also help you to clarify where your focus should be in order to thrive.

Redefining success

I used the word 'thrive' in the book's subtitle because I wanted to emphasise a broader view of success. By 'success' I include financial rewards and positions of greater status. I also mean a lot more: an increased excitement in your work; deeper intimacy with your loved ones; and more joy in your life. It is the increased density of cherished moments, experiences that slice their way through the humdrum, searing an expression, a sunset conversation, a child's unintended joke into your longest of long-term memory. It is going to bed, calm in the knowledge that the world, your work and your family have seen the best of you that day, and feeling gently eager for the new possibilities of the morrow.

I told the story of ICI to go further than simply broadening the definition of success. I also want to crush an overly narrow, external definition of success. ICI shifted from 'better chemistry means success' to 'more profits mean success'. It killed them. I see a similar mentality in the people I work with today, and it's killing them too. Their actions shout a rapacious focus on the extrinsic 'More': more money, more status, more fame, more cool stuff or simply more than the neighbour! They push to improve their balance sheets and neglect their heart and soul, trading what could truly nourish them for 'More'. The problem is, when the goal is 'More', we can never be satisfied. 'More' is limitless and, as we get more, we have to make greater trade-offs to maintain what we have achieved. It's not working.

Instead we need a stronger engagement with what matters in life and a healthier relationship with achievement. We need this for two reasons. The first is that connecting to what matters is the essence of a happy, well-lived, meaningful life. The second is that when you are buffeted by too much, unless you hold tight to what's important, you'll be blown off course and be at the mercy of your environment. You'll be busy. In your hollow busyness, you'll become less vibrant and less impactful. You'll be a slightly rubbish version of you: without the sparkle, without the pride and without the joy. To hell with that! It's time to figure out a different way to thrive, a broader view of success. It's time to start smiling again.

'More' is not enough

Let me be clear: I'm no hippy – I'm a psychologist and a businessman. I just think you have to pay attention to the hard evidence that 'More' doesn't mean happier. For example, in a review of some of the evidence in the United States, David Meyers and Ed Diener comment that wealth has a remarkable lack of connection to wellbeing[2]. Even though Americans are twice as rich as they were in 1957, the amount of people telling researchers from the National

Opinion Research Centre that they are very happy has declined from 35 per cent to 29 per cent. Those in the *Forbes* list of the 100 wealthiest Americans were only slightly happier than average. When people were tracked for a decade, those whose income increased significantly over that time were no happier than those people whose income had remained stagnant. In fact, in cross-cultural studies, it is only in the very poorest countries like Bangladesh that wealth has a good correlation with happiness.

Not all values are equally valuable

Tim Kasser is possibly the world's leading researcher into the effects of materialism on wellbeing[3]. We often talk about people having different values, but many liberals assume that each person has a right to their own value system, and that each set of values is equally valid. Kasser would ask, from a psychological point of view, is this correct? More specifically, are some sets of values, some aspirations or goals, more beneficial than others? It's a pretty fluffy area, you might think. How do you create decent science from vague aspirations? To understand his research, I must first explain the three steps he took to clarify the question.

First, he analysed different people's values and found they tended to cluster into four groupings: *external or materialistic* (such as the aspiration for wealth, image and popularity), *personal growth* (learning, autonomy and self-esteem), *affiliation* (close relationships with family and friends) and *community feeling* (the desire to make the world a better place). Second, he developed questionnaires and other assessment tools to compare the relative importance of these values for people. If pushed to make a choice, as we are each and every day, what are our greatest priorities? Kasser was able to identify people for whom the external values were significantly more of a priority than the other values.

Finally, he had to identify what wellbeing means. He defined wellbeing in three ways: that people are more self-actualised (based on Abraham Maslow's model, this means someone who feels fulfilled and secure); they are more vital and energetic; and that they have less anxiety and depression.

His many studies with thousands of American adults and students showed a remarkably consistent pattern. Those who had stronger external than internal (growth, affiliation and community feeling) values – who aspired to be wealthy, have a great image and be popular – are less self-actualised, less vital, more depressed and more anxious. In addition, they complain of more headaches; rate the quality of their day-to-day experience more negatively; have less fun; are less satisfied in their life and with their families; are more narcissistic; and more likely to engage in substance abuse. Furthermore, these findings apply across the globe.

On one level, Kasser's findings are unremarkable. They simply confirm or amplify the old adage 'money can't buy you happiness'. Yet, on another level, they are shattering. Our whole society is driven by external values; our motivational systems at work are external; and our explanations to ourselves and our families for why we are so busy are external. What's also worth noting from Kasser's research is that it isn't how much money people have that matters, it's how much they *aspire* to be wealthy.

To answer the question posed at the start of this section, some values *are* more valuable than others. And of all the values, the worst of all, from a psychological point of view, are the external ones: wealth, image, status and popularity. So, if you want to ensure you lead a less happy and healthy life, strive for these!

Conspicuous consumption

Before he started Silicon Graphics, Jim Clark said a fortune of $10 million would satisfy him. Before founding Netscape, he thought $100 million would make him happy. Before initiating myCFO and Healtheon, he believed a billion would be needed. More recently he said, 'Once I have more money than Larry Ellison, I'll be satisfied'. Ellison, the founder of the software giant Oracle, is worth $13 billion[4]. How much is enough for you? Don't worry about answering that question, because as soon as you get close to reaching that amount, your definition of enough will have changed.

In 1899 the sociologist and economist Thorstein Veblen coined the term 'conspicuous consumption'[5]. He was using it in a narrow sense to describe a certain group of people who, in the Industrial Revolution, had become extremely rich. These people, the nouveau riche, were using money to visibly demonstrate their status and power.

More than 100 years later, we're all at it. Our desire for wealth isn't about a number on a bank statement; it's about how we appear to others. That's why other external values like status, image and popularity are all linked and each has the same effect on our well-being. That's why our desires for the externals are infinite – because we don't think of them in absolute terms, but in relation to others, and there are always wealthier people than us.

If you don't believe you're affected by this, think for a second: what would you prefer, a 30 per cent pay rise if you knew that everyone else in your team was getting a 50 per cent pay rise; or a 20 per cent pay rise if you knew no one else was getting any-thing? Now, swap 'pay rise' for holiday entitlement. Do you still answer the same way? If you're like most of us, you would have chosen the 20 per cent salary rise, and 30 per cent extra holiday. You'd happily forgo 10 per cent on your absolute salary to ensure you make progress in comparison to others. On the other hand, even though we might feel slightly disgruntled that others are get-ting more vacation, most people jump at the maximum holiday – the more rational choice. It appears that our leisure time isn't something we compete against others about. Externals are con-spicuous; they are relative and irrational; they are therefore infinite and insatiable.

'More' doesn't satisfy

Goal-setting has proved to be one of the most simple and robust motivational mechanisms we have. From that perspective, even if a drive to succeed in terms of external rewards, such as wealth or popularity, is associated with lower levels of wellbeing, there must be some satisfaction in working towards these goals, in making progress. In fact, surely one of the appeals of external goals is that progress is so noticeable. It's hard to track a change in your wisdom or your relationships, but you can easily notice a change in your bank balance. So does progress against external goals make us feel better, even if the end goal keeps moving further away?

In further research, Tim Kasser found that progress against exter-nal, materialistic goals made no difference to wellbeing – neither in the short term, nor the long term. On the other hand, making progress against more personal goals, such as relationships and growth, made significant differences to all measures of wellbeing, including drug use and self-esteem[6,7].

We all have a cocktail of values and goals which mobilise and drive us. In this first section I wanted to challenge what often feels a taken-for-granted belief that aspiring to 'More' is a natural and good thing. In today's world, it seems self-evident that we should sacrifice and make certain choices to get that promotion, or increase our earning power, but I want to place a question mark over these aspirations, and the sacrifices they ask us to make. The achievement of external goals such as wealth, status, power, popularity or fame is a hollow victory. It takes a lot from us to achieve them, we don't benefit from the progress we make and the finish line persistently recedes into the distance.

In fact, you could go a step further and state that success is theoretically impossible if judged from an entirely external perspective: it is relative and we will always be behind others. It is not something that can be achieved; it is only something that can be slavishly struggled towards – futile, punishing and empty. Which brings us right back to disconnection: the more we focus on external values and goals, the more we will be driven to sacrifice our time and attention for an empty goal, disconnecting from things that truly matter to us and which could nourish and complete us. In striving for more we become less happy and less healthy.

So what should we strive for instead?

A different success

If a thriving life is one built around deep engagement in what really matters – our core values and our closest relationships – then we need to define success differently. This next section will help you to reframe your definition of success away from a myopic focus on the external, and onto more engaging, sustaining areas.

Achieve indirectly

John Stuart Mill was a utilitarian, possibly the greatest of them all. Utilitarians believed the right course of action was the one that directly maximised happiness and minimised suffering. Having spent his life believing in a direct and simple approach to achieving good outcomes, Mill realised late in life that the best way to achieve something is often indirectly. In his book *Obliquity* (great title), John Kay argues that the same is true for successful companies and people. ICI were successful as long as they focused on chemistry and innovation rather than business success; Bill Gates and David Beckham succeeded, not by trying to make money, but by trying to be great at what they loved. When ICI switched their focus to business success and the bottom line, they shifted their orientation from a *learning* orientation to a *performance* orientation, lost their vitality and embarked on a rapid path to oblivion.

One of the most widely used distinctions in educational psychology is the difference between performance orientation and learning orientation[8]. Carol Dweck identified that some students were motivated towards task achievement and gaining approval from others; they tried to avoid failure and negative feedback. Other students were more focused on developing capability and improving; they didn't shy away from chances to learn through failure and actively sought feedback. Not surprisingly, over the medium to long term, learning orientation has been shown to lead to better academic success, as well as higher levels of enjoyment in studying.

Too much focus on success in external terms will make you unhappy and unhealthy. You will never feel you have 'achieved' success, and progress towards your goal will not improve your wellbeing. Focusing on success directly can drive us into a performance orientation. We seek to achieve by accomplishing what is asked of us, and keeping those around us happy. These very activities can drive us towards busyness. In any choice between actions, we take the more immediate, people-satisfying, problem-avoiding approach – behaviours which might actually undermine success. To me, that sounds like a pretty compelling set of reasons to *not* try to succeed.

On the other hand, a focus on personal growth and learning will bring with it specific capability, which can support our strategy in differentiating us and helping us to become more impactful in our organisations; and we also gain the satisfaction of developing true expertise. Learning, developing capability and failing can all take longer, but they are the true path to sustainable success.

The Nobel Prize-winning Indian economist Amartya Sen suggested that we should think of wealth not in terms of what you have, but in terms of what you can do. I would argue a similar shift is possible for success: that it could be thought of less as what you get, but what you can do.

How could you redefine your success in terms of what you can do?

It will make you less happy than you think

Imagine you were told that one of two things would happen tomorrow: either you would be hit by a bus and become permanently paralysed from the neck down, or you would win £27 million in the lottery. You were then asked to predict how happy you would be in a year's time as either a paraplegic, and as a multi-millionaire. How much of a difference between your levels of happiness do you think there would be? Dan Gilbert, Psychology Professor at Harvard, uses this example to demonstrate how bad we are at predicting happiness[9]. In fact, after a year, there would be hardly any difference in happiness levels! Hard to believe, but true. This is an example of what Gilbert calls the 'impact bias'. We massively overestimate the impact things will have on us, and the duration of that impact.

Gilbert, in a wonderful TED talk[10], cites Jim Wright, the disgraced congressman; Moreese Bickham, a man who was imprisoned for 37 years; and Harry S. Langerman, the man who didn't invest $3,000 in a small burger company run by a couple of brothers called McDonald. Each of these people believed they were happier as a result of their experience. Moreese Bickham even said of his time in prison, 'I don't have one minute's regret. It was a glorious experience'. Does that mean, as Gilbert jokes, that the secret to happiness is to become powerful then lose it all, spend a lot of time in prison and pass up the chance to make millions?

The real secret is that we don't just get happiness, we synthesise it. We have a psychological immune system that helps us to change our experiences so that we can feel better about the world. This process is largely unconscious. That's why, a year after the terrible accident, a paraplegic has regained their pre-accident levels of happiness.

How does this work? In a nice little experiment, people were asked to rank six prints of paintings by Claude Monet. Once they had done this, the experimenter announced that they happened to have a couple of spare prints; these just so happened to be the third and fourth choice. The person was invited to choose one of the two prints as a gift. They chose the third choice. At a later point, after 15 minutes, 15 days or 15 months, the preference test was repeated. Again, the person was asked to rank the six Monet prints. This time, their ranking was different. This time, the print they chose (previously ranked number three) had jumped up a place to second choice. The print they didn't choose (previously ranked number four) had dropped a place to number five. This is happiness synthesis in action.

What was fascinating was that Gilbert then reran this experiment with amnesiacs (people with no memory). Exactly the same effect was recorded. This shows the change in preferences wasn't because the subjects remembered what they chose. The amnesiacs couldn't even remember having done the test before. It means that the very act of choosing changed the structure of that person's preferences.

We come to prefer what we have and we can adapt and become happy with almost any situation (apart from persistent pain, it appears). It seems we are well suited to making do with stuff; that, no matter what the outcome, we'll work our way towards being happy about it. Those potential achievements, those balls you are terrified you might drop and that job you might gain or lose will have much, much less impact on your wellbeing than you think. Yet, we are completely blind to the impact bias and we sacrifice too much for successes that will provide too little in return. We all have great reasons to give up on the present in favour of a compelling-sounding future success (or to avoid a horrific failure), but success and happiness aren't found in the outcome; they're to be found in the journey.

So commit to what you value the most, focus on what you love and on where you are strong. If our justification to ourselves for crazy busyness is a future success, we are giving up our effectiveness, relationships and wellbeing on a flawed belief. Work hard, but don't sacrifice your present for the future; don't cut too deep into what really matters for you: it just isn't worth it. You'll find your way to happiness whatever you do.

Time affluence

There is a well-known management fable about two consultants who talk to a fisherman in a small Mexican village about succeeding in his business. They suggest borrowing money to buy more fishing boats. He asks, 'What for?', to which the reply is to make more profit to allow further expansion. This expansion, in their view, would continue until ultimately the business is floated (pun intended) on the NY Stock Exchange and the fisherman has the time to retire ... to a place just like the little fishing village he already lived in!

If financials and status aren't impactful on wellbeing, what does matter? What outcome would be worth aiming for? What would be truly valuable? In 2008, the Pew Research Center asked Americans to prioritise what was important to them. Sixty-eight per cent responded that having free time was very important, outpacing even the importance of having children (62 per cent) and a successful career (55 per cent). Time affluence, the sense that we have time to do the things we want, is the ultimate of luxuries in the 21st century[11].

If one definition of success is having the time to do the things that really matter to you, how might you achieve this? One way, of course, is to found, grow and float your company on the stock exchange and become so rich that you can afford to be idle. The cost in getting there may, however, be prohibitively high. An alternative is to be more careful about how you spend your time. Pause for a moment and consider how carefully you think about spending money. We deliberate long and hard before we hand over our cash. How careful are you when it comes to spending your time? Time is a much more scarce and valuable commodity, yet we cast it aside; we squander it shamefully.

If you want to feel more successful, if you want to increase your affluence, you might switch your attention from how you spend your money to how you spend your time.

What do you value?

So far in this chapter, we've talked about external, materialistic values being bad. We've suggested a few ways of thinking more broadly about success that don't include becoming wealthy, famous and cool, but what does this mean for you?

I have argued that a major driver of busyness is the aspiration for more: the materialistic, external desire for acquisition. It's easy to attribute the cause of this desire to global capitalism: in the modern world, the markets, the advertising and the norms suggest that we are better people if we have more stuff. However, I think there is another significant cause; it's just a little more subtle.

To explain what I mean, think about the setting of objectives at work. If you look at most people's objectives, these are a list of things that are easy to measure. Does this suggest that the only things that matter to job performance are things that are easy to measure? Not at all. It's just that things like improving communication are simply too hard to meaningfully measure, so we set nice, neat (relatively meaningless) SMART (specific, measurable, attainable, relevant, time-bound) objectives, such as to 'halve complaints by the end of the year'.

In the same way, materialism is easier to latch onto as a personal goal, partly because everyone else seems to be operating that way, but also because it's more readily measurable: $1000 is better than $500; an iPhone 5 is better than an iPhone 3; being a senior manager is better than manager. Material, external values are obvious, self-evident and easy to work towards – ready to use straight out of the box! As a result, materialism steps into the breach when we haven't worked out what our values are.

Personal values, on the other hand – clarity over what really matters to you – need more work. Many of us have vague notions of things that matter, nebulous clouds of concepts, ideas and goals. However, like light beams, unless they are really focused, they have no power to illuminate decisions and to cut through confusion. When our personal values and priorities are unsorted and unfocused, we default to the clarity of materialism.

This section will talk through a few simple activities to help power up your true values.

Do you *really* live by your values?

First, I'll start with being a little intrusive. You may have found yourself reading the sections about materialism and thinking,

'That's all very interesting, but I have my values in the right place'. I'm sure you're right, but I want to challenge you for a moment. In psychology we talk about *espoused* versus *enacted* values. Espoused priorities are what you *say*, when asked, about your values. Enacted values are what you actually *do*. In organisations, and in individuals, there is often little relation between the two. The evidence of your enacted values is how you spend your time.

Draw a pie chart reflecting all your waking hours in the last month. Use whatever headings you want, but to help, I have suggested a few categories you might use to split up your time.

Work – doing stuff, managing the daily grind	Work – working on things that really excite me	Work – learning, developing and experimenting
Family – 'processing' the kids (feeding, bathing etc.) and going through the daily routine	Family – quality, fun time	Family – important activity to invest in their growth or support them
Romance – special time with your loved one	Friends	Leisure – doing things that may be effortful but for their own sake, like a hobby
Household chores including things like shopping for groceries	Consumption – watching TV, surfing internet	Contribution – activity that makes a contribution to your community

Look at how your pie chart is divided. What does your actual allocation of your time say about your real (enacted) values?

What are your core values, and why?

Most of the lists of values people create, whether at a personal or a corporate level, are a waste of time. They are simply a list of nice adjectives that feel important to you. Here's my golden rule: when it comes to values, limit your list to two or three. Why? Values should direct attention, decisions and action. You can't possibly hold half a dozen or more values in your head at the same time. In corporate terms, values are one of the most central strategic decisions a business makes. They should be for you too. Take the time to identify your core values, those that energise you the most, and you will be able to draw on a lifetime of inspiration when you align your activity with them.

The Five Whys

Sakichi Toyoda is referred to as the 'King of Japanese inventors'. The son of a poor carpenter, he ultimately became one of the most famous industrialists in the country. Perhaps his most famous invention was the automatic power loom. This machine incorporated his principle of Jidoka, it stopped itself when a problem occurred. Later, he went on to found Toyota, where his focus on problem-solving continued. He recognised that getting to the root cause of problems was a powerful way to improve quality and fast track innovation. He developed a process which he called the 'Five Whys', which is now used in manufacturing processes all over the world.

The Five Whys is an incredibly simple process that gets under the surface of issues very quickly. You approach a topic and ask 'Why?' On receiving the answer, you again ask 'Why?' You do this five times. For example, let's say you were running a conference and halfway through the keynote presentation, the laptop delivering the presentation died.

The laptop died	Why?
It ran out of power because it wasn't plugged in	Why?
It must have become unplugged at some point and we didn't realise	Why?
Because we didn't check just before the keynote	Why?
Because we had a lot of things to think about, it's hard to remember everything	Why?
Because we didn't have a checklist	The root cause

I have often borrowed this approach to help people refine what's really important to them: the root cause of their passion, motivation and pride.

Identify three momentous times in your life. These should be three separate occasions. I suggest you do this both for out of work and within work experiences. Choose times that were memorable and significant. It might be because they were really important events in your life; or an achievement of which you are really proud; or a time you felt deeply and profoundly content.

Once you have your three moments, go through each one, asking the Five Whys. What you are trying to uncover is why these were so important to you. To make this easier, do it with a friend or family member. Have them ask you the 'Whys' to leave you free to reflect.

Understanding your whys can help you to tap into an incredible source of energy and motivation. Your whys point you to your core values – what truly matters to you will nourish and sustain you, and can direct and focus you.

Five and a half years ago I was approaching the big 4-0. Turning 30 hadn't been an issue for me at all, and I wasn't really expecting trouble over my 40th either. Then I started noticing a curious feeling. It wasn't anything strong like depression or frustration; but it was something. After a while I began to recognise this sensation as some kind of yearning, some kind of need that I was obviously failing to satisfy. On paper, everything was going well in my life; so what was this feeling? At around this time I sat down with a colleague and a coach. She started asking me about this feeling. Previous conversations I'd had on the topic with other people had focused on what I felt. Instead, she asked me 'why?' Why did I feel this way? I can't pretend that I came to a crashing revelation in that conversation, but it did start me thinking; it started me asking why. In time I came to realise the yearning was for something I'd never considered to be one of my values before: creativity. I might never have recognised it because I was always rubbish at painting in school; and it's also possible it wasn't important to me earlier in life. In truth I don't know. All I know is that around my 40th birthday I became aware that I wanted to create; in fact I needed to create. Over the years since that realisation, I have taken up photography and writing; I've even tried (joyfully but rather unsuccessfully) to paint. More significantly, the desire to create has fed into my work: informing my approach and inspiring my activity. I find it hard to imagine a life without seeing that creativity is at the core of what I do; and that clarity came from 'why'.

I'm about to turn 40. It's a natural reflection point and I don't feel unhappy, I just notice a quiet but persistent yearning.	Why has turning 40 made you yearn for something?
I guess it's because what I am doing is no longer enough for me, which is curious because I have succeeded beyond my expectations.	If you have succeeded, why is that not enough for you?
Because I am spending a lot of my time running big events, which are somewhat repetitive. Even though my clients are happy, my work isn't challenging me intellectually.	Why do you want to be challenged?
Because I'm happiest when I'm using my experience and learning to generate genuinely novel approaches or ideas. I don't get much of a buzz from producing good events any more. It feels like I am just reproducing experiences. I want to create.	Why is that?
Because creativity is really important to me.	The root cause

Hone your values

This activity will help you to hone your list of values, to move from a nebulous sense that stuff is important to you, to concrete, focused values that become your guide and compass in how you live your life. Here's how it works.

- From the list of 'values' below circle all those that really resonate for you.
- Add any values you feel are missing from the list in the blank boxes below.

Delivering results	Progression	Learning	Safety	Energy
Variety	Fun	Contributing to society	Peace	Change
Quality	Relationships	Integrity	Fulfilment	Recognition
Competition	Time	Belonging	Creativity	Pride
Interest	Status	Making a difference	Friendship	Wealth
Stretching myself	Wisdom	Reputation	Speed	Autonomy

- Now reduce that list to five (if it's not already that low) by prioritising the ones you feel are most important to you.
- Find someone to talk to. Explain your five values and why they matter to you. Have them ask you questions and probe and observe your energy as they do this. Through their feedback and through reflection get your list down to two or three.
- Now wear these for a while. If you've done the job right, they should feel vibrant, powerful. You might change the wording a bit, so it's in your language.

When you have established your values, use them. Remind yourself of them regularly. Reflect on the degree to which you live those values each day. One very compelling definition of success would be a life that was lived in line with your core values. If you reflect back to the espoused versus enacted activity earlier, how successful are you? How could you become more successful?

What's your purpose in life?

Sir Galahad was quite the man. Born as a result of sorcery, when Sir Lancelot was tricked into believing that Elaine of Corbenic was his beloved Queen Guinevere, he was raised by a great-aunt. On reaching adulthood he was reunited with his father, who brought him to King Arthur's court. On entering court, he was led to an infamous seat, the 'Siege Perilous', which had been bewitched by Merlin and instantly killed all who sat in it. Sir Galahad survived. Impressed, King Arthur took him out to a sword in a stone (a favoured pastime of his, it appears) inscribed with the words, 'Never shall man take me hence but only he by whose side I ought to hang, and he shall be the best knight of the world'. Galahad pulled the sword free with ease, to be proclaimed by Arthur to be the greatest knight ever.

What made the Sir Galahad legend so potent and popular through the Middle Ages wasn't his battles, conquests or sword-pulling; it was his quest. He, more than any other knight of the Round Table, is associated with the quest for the Holy Grail. Patiently Sir Galahad faces danger, he rescues maidens and saves Sir Percival, until, ultimately, he finds the Holy Grail. Sir Galahad had a quest that was important and worthwhile. It energised, sustained and directed him. Sir Galahad is a legend because he had a purpose and, no matter what tribulations he encountered, that gave him strength.

Joseph Campbell, the great mythologist, suggests that the Holy Grail represents our purpose in life – our own quest[12]. It is a mythical symbol representing the journey that each of us needs to go on to achieve what we are on this planet to achieve. Whatever you might feel about this, I think it's a great thing to ponder. Fundamentally it's a question that we all have to grapple with at some point. Once we are clear about our purpose, it helps steer our course towards greatness, towards achieving what we're are most uniquely able to achieve.

What's *your* purpose in life?

Imagine a different you

If you've ever suggested this to a child, you'll appreciate what an enlivening, engaging suggestion it can be. At some point we stop considering it ourselves. Why? We carry a (false) assumption that, once we become adults, and once we're in our careers, we already 'are' what we are. Rubbish. Our identities evolve and merge; they expand and diversify or they shrink and shrivel. This happens whether we shape it or not. Just think, for example, of all the roles you have in life. You may be an accountant; you may also be a father, a husband, a son, a dancer, a sailor and a charity fundraiser. We step in and out of roles every day. Our identity, the way we think of ourselves, is heavily determined by these roles. It is not just affected by the roles we play, but how engaged we are in these roles, and how aligned they are to our values. For example, you may be a father, but are you deeply engaged in that role? Do you dive deeply into your shared moments with your child, striving to improve as a dad? Or, do you process your children in a kind but expedient way between emails?

Here are three activities to help you re-imagine your life in a way that is more in line with your values, and as such, is more enriching and energising. Take the time to imagine yourself as a person living a different form of success, living an engaged and connected life, a life less enslaved to barren busyness.

1. What would a person like me do?

This is not a trivial question. James March, Professor of Political Science at Stamford, found that people make decisions based on one of two factors: the consequences (what will happen if . . .) or their identity (what does a person like me do?)[13]. In fact, the latter was used rather effectively to save the St Lucia Parrot. In 1977 there were only 100 of the parrots left in existence. Locals were relatively indifferent to their plight, destroying their habitat, hunting or trapping them. Then along came Paul Butler, a college student from London. He ran a campaign linking the bird to the St Lucian identity; he created the sense among St Lucians that 'we're the kind of people who protect our own'. Decades later, the St Lucian population embraced their parrot, poaching stopped completely and the species is now flourishing[14].

We are powerfully influenced by our sense of identity. What choices would you make differently in your life if you were the person you wanted to be?

2. Picture perfect

I mentioned that I have become interested in photography. One of the aspects of photography I've most enjoyed, and been most challenged by, is the process of selection. When submitting pictures for competitions, I would often have to select three images from hundreds. It's not easy. However, through the process, especially if you do this regularly, you really start to filter out what is important to you in an image – what you like about your photos. I think I have learned more about photography from the selection process than I ever did from taking the pictures in the first place.

The same process can be applied to understanding ourselves. I sometimes do an activity for leadership teams who want to build relationships. I ask people to identify five photos from their personal photograph files that collectively summarise who they are. The ensuing conversations can be rich, and people feel they 'get' team members much more deeply when there are images to look at. However, what strikes me is how often people come to me and explain how interesting and valuable a process the selection of the pictures was. It really forced them to make choices about what was important to them and their identity.

Now it's your turn. Identify five pictures which collectively summarise your identity at present. They may be actual pictures of you, images from the internet or from a magazine. Now repeat the activity, only this time identify images to represent what you would like your identity to be like. What does this tell you about your values?

3. A view from afar

In Chapter 6 I talked about the value of being able to zoom out. Research shows that people think more effectively when they view things from afar. For example, when people were given a problem and told to think of it as being a long way away (physically) they solved twice as many problems as when they imagined it was near at hand. The same effect is observed for chronological distance. Psychologist Jens Förster found that thinking about yourself in the future improves your ability to think abstractly and solve problems; you are able to gain some perspective[15].

Write a letter to yourself from a point 20 years into the future. Don't worry about what you have, or what job you're doing, in the future. Your task is to write a letter to your current self, advising on what you should do with your life, starting today. Where should you focus? What aspects of your identity should you build? Where should you engage most?

The big messages in 'The right success'

Our life has **meaning and a purpose** when it is built on our core values. These are the ultimate sources of our energy, creativity and resilience. A **life disconnected from core values soon loses its potency** and vitality. **We thrive when we are deeply engaged** in what is most important to us. **Success is a life of engagement** and meaningful connection, not wealth and fame.

'MORE' IS NOT ENOUGH

- **Not all values are equally valuable.** When people focus on external 'More' values, such as the desire for **wealth, status and popularity,** they are **less happy** and less healthy. Internally rewarding values, such as **growth, close relationships** and **community feeling,** are strongly linked to thriving.
- Switch your focus from **external** to **internal values** which make a big impact on your satisfaction and health.

A DIFFERENT SUCCESS

- Research shows that we might be better off trying to **achieve success (in worldly terms) indirectly.** So focus on the process of building your capability and expertise and success will follow.
- Whatever external gain or achievement you are striving for, it won't make you as happy as you think. So **commit to what you value most; don't sacrifice it** in the belief that the end goal will be worth it.

WHAT DO YOU VALUE?

- To lead a life in line with your core values, consider what these values are and whether they are **reflected in the way you spend your time.**
- Transform your values from an academic exercise to a **lifelong source of direction and energy** by identifying **two or three core values** to focus on, instead of a long list.
- **Identify your purpose in life.** Even though you're not Sir Galahad, you still need a quest to inspire you. **What's your Holy Grail?**

Go-Do

WHAT DOES THE EVIDENCE SAY?

Draw a pie chart which shows how you spend your time. To what extent is that in line with your core values? Make one change in the way you are spending time to bring it more in line with your values.

IDENTIFY YOUR VALUES

It's hard to motivate any kind of shift in lifestyle unless it's powered by strong personal values. Identify your core two or three values by doing either the 'Five Whys' (p. 188) or the 'Hone your values' (p. 190) exercise.

A DIFFERENT GOAL

If 'More' is not a great thing to work for; what should you strive for instead? Set yourself a clear goal to describe a different form of success. Tell someone you trust about this goal, and ask them to hold you accountable for delivering it.

Experiment

PICTURE PERFECT

Identify five pictures to describe the person you want to be and put them on your computer as your screen saver or desktop background to constantly remind yourself of a better identity to strive towards.

Chapter 8

From buzz to joy

W hat on earth can a colonoscopy – an unpleasant and painful experience – teach us about happiness? Quite a lot, as it turns out. Patients in the 1990s were asked to report their pain at 60-second intervals. This allowed doctors to draw graphs representing the overall pain experience of each patient. These graphs showed peaks of extreme pain, as well as indicating when sensation was merely unpleasant rather than painful. Now look at the graph below.

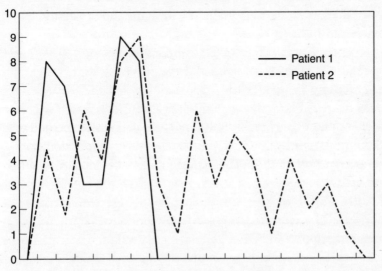

(This graph is illustrative, not the actual experimental output.)

It is easy to see that, as a whole, Patient 2 experienced more pain, and for longer. However, if you ask these two patients after the event to rate their overall experience, and their willingness to undergo the procedure again, Patient 1 would rate the experience as worse. The reason for this is that our memory of experiences is disproportionately affected by our last, most recent experience. Since Patient 1 had a very painful last experience of the procedure, they remember the event accordingly. Patient 2, on the other hand, had a much milder final experience, so they remember the overall procedure as not having been too bad. Daniel Kahneman explains this anomaly as being caused by two fundamentally different types of happiness[1]. We have an *experiencing self*, which feels our moment-to-moment joy, pleasure, discomfort and pain. We also have a *narrative self* which keeps the score and maintains the story of our life by capturing, interpreting and storing our experiences as memories. Put simply, it's the difference between direct and indirect happiness; between being happy *in* our life and being happy *with* our life. And there is very little correlation between the two. It is the narrative self that answers when we assess how satisfied we were with the overall colonoscopy. It is the experiencing self that feels the pain.

In the previous chapter I explained how to build a story of success that is more rewarding by replacing external, materialistic goals with values that are more personally meaningful and satisfying, and can enrich and nourish us. This was addressed to the narrative self. In this chapter I switch the focus to the experiencing self. While the expectations of the narrative self drive busyness, so the buzz of frenetic activity captivates the experiencing self. The narrative self needs deeper, better values, which we considered in the previous chapter. The experiencing self needs an alternative to the buzz; it needs more depth.

But why bother about the experiencing self? After all, the narrative self determines our broad direction, goals and overall assessment of satisfaction. However, it is the experiencing self that engages and connects. The experiencing self is all about the moment: what is happening right now. We might have great values, but unless we can be fully present and engage completely in what we are doing at the time, we will be unable to plunge deeply into moments.

Go deep

He loved the sea and so, in 1930, he joined the navy. But he wasn't satisfied with just skimming the surface: he wanted to understand the sea, to go deep. He started diving using a pair of underwater goggles, but, enthralled, he wanted more. Together with Emile Gagnan, an engineer, he built the aqualung, the first self-contained underwater breathing apparatus, and, in so doing, invented scuba diving. Leaving the navy, he set off on a lifetime's expedition into the sea, exploring and discovering. He was the first to recognise that porpoises could use echolocation, and he made films such as the Oscar-winning *The Silent World*, introducing millions to the realm beneath the sea's surface. He went deep, and in so doing, lived a life of adventure and joy; he inspired a generation, started the scuba industry, and pioneered marine conservation. His name was Jacques Cousteau.

If there's one word to remember from this chapter it has to be 'deep'. We live in a world that's scattered and diffuse. Messages, information and stimulation hit us from every angle, at every second. Our attention is pulled in every direction, never really sticking. We are constantly scanning for the next thing, skipping onwards, only half-present. We seek information in sound-bites, relationships in snatches and activity in bite sizes. We want life in thin slices; we want the buzz of busyness.

Ultimately, however, the buzz of busy is hollow. In fact, you could argue that buzz is the opposite of happiness. Pretty much everything good happens when we go deep: our experiences are richer, our relationships are better and our thinking is more insightful. We are more immersed, more connected and more satisfied. Happiness results from real engagement rather than distraction. It comes from depth rather than diffusion.

This chapter is an ode to depth. It will fire a shot over the bows of the superficial, the shallow and the fractured. We're racing across the surface of the sea, eager to get to our destination, mistaking the fizz of stimulation for the true joy of immersion in the moment. We're oblivious to what we're missing. We need to cut the engine and dive into the wonder and colour of the depths below, but before we can do that, we need to deal with our need for the buzz.

Beat your addiction to the buzz

Let's be honest; it can feel pretty good to be busy. At its best, the feeling as you leap from activity to activity, adrenaline flowing, can be similar to the feeling you get from competitive sports. And there is also a chemical reason for busyness: when we get an email notification, take a quick glance at our smartphone, or surf to another site the brain releases neurotransmitters. Edward Hallowell and John Ratey from Harvard have found that those quick fixes give us something like the 'dopamine squirt' provided by addictive drugs[2]. This means that, aside from all the compulsion to keep on top, email and social media have become an addiction! Busyness is not just a result of having too much to do; busyness is a buzz, and we're addicted to the buzz.

The root cause of addiction

Since the Second World War there has been an increasing, global epidemic of all kinds of addiction. Bruce Alexander, one of the world's leading researchers into the subject, claims that we are looking in the wrong places to address this crisis. Counsellors and social workers succeed in getting only a small percentage of people off their addictions. Police and armed forces gain minor, pyrrhic victories as they lose the 'war on drugs'. The underlying cause, he suggests, will not be found in medicine but in the social sciences[3]. The root of the problem is one of 'dislocation': a sense of a loss of identity, a lack of meaning and a weakening of culture. Building on the work of Hungarian economic anthropologist, Karl Polanyi, he suggests that dislocation has spread as the needs of communities and individuals are replaced by the needs of the market and the global economy. This has left people grasping for meaning wherever they can find it: in substances, in shopping, and in busyness.

Information addiction

For very good evolutionary reasons, the brain likes information and novelty. Information that helped an early hominid find food or understand its environment better could be valuable, as would the early detection of predators. So, over the millennia, the brain evolved to give little rewards whenever new information was found or something unexpected and novel was noticed. This reward is not just our good friend dopamine, but also our own internal opiate system which can induce a kind of blissful stupor (as the hours pass in Google searches). As we become addicted, the brain gets into a wanting cycle: it wants the reward, gets the reward, and as soon as it is rewarded, it starts wanting again. The dopamine system is never satisfied. We want information, so we do a Google search; as soon as we are rewarded we feel compelled, irrationally to seek that reward again, so one search follows the other. As neuroscience professor Kent C. Berridge says, 'As long as you sit there, the consumption renews the appetite'[4]. The same is true of the ping or vibration of a text or email. Since the brain rewards the detection of novelty, and since by definition most calls, emails and WhatsApp messages are unexpected, they elicit a reward.

Find a substitute drug

In the run-up to the Second World War, Germany developed the synthetic opiate methadone as a reliable local source of painkillers. These days, methadone is commonly used as a substitute for heroin. It can be medically administered and has longer-lasting effects than heroin, so it helps people gradually reduce their drug intake. At the end of the day, drug taking is pleasurable; it destroys lives, but the buzz is great. Methadone helps to gradually reduce dependence upon the high.

While busyness also destroys lives, the buzz, likewise, feels good. What's your methadone, then? If you like the buzz of information and the rush of frenetic activity, how could you replace that in your life with something less damaging? Berridge makes the distinction between 'seeking' and 'liking'[5]. It seems that dopamine is most strongly released through seeking rather than liking. Hence the compulsion to check Facebook every 15 minutes and persistently do one Google search too many.

If you want to scale back your buzz, or manage it in a more planned and recreational manner, you have two choices: you can find your dopamine elsewhere, or you can replace your dopamine with the methadone of liking (see the next section 'The joy of engagement').

Here are five ways to boost your dopamine levels without resorting to information-seeking and busyness:

- The first place to seek dopamine could be your diet. Foods rich in tyrosine, such as almonds, avocados, bananas, meat, poultry and sesame seeds can be turned into happy fuel.
- Exercise increases blood calcium, which stimulates dopamine production.
- Get plenty of sleep: dopamine production drops a lot when we're tired.
- Set micro-goals. Dopamine is part of the reward we feel when we achieve a goal. Set a goal to avoid email and social media for the next two hours!
- Failing all those, how about some great food, some laughter or some sex!

Substance abuse and addictions mess up lives. They suck the colour out of them, destroy careers and damage relationships, hurting those we love. While calling our habit of busyness an addiction may be stretching it, there are parallels. Information-seeking and responding to inputs feels good, and leaves us wanting more. The effect of persistent busyness is similar to that of persistent substance abuse on our lives and relationships. Most people who have too much of a habit fail to recognise they need to change.

When it comes to information-seeking, do you have an unhealthy habit? If so, what's your plan for kicking the habit?

The joy of engagement

Attention loves novelty; it's drawn to it like a moth to a flame. The brain, on the other hand, doesn't like disorder and chaos. The brain likes it best when everything lines up: our goals, our thoughts and our attention. When novel information arrives, by definition it's inconsistent with our current thinking, our present goals. When we face a lot of novelty, we get knocked off course, distracted from our goals and preferences; energy is diverted from our priorities and we are set on different, less satisfying tracks. Rather than enjoying smooth, focused, integrated thinking in which we feel in control of our consciousness, our thoughts become chaotic, hurried and splintered. This mental state is called psychic entropy; it is unpleasant and ineffective. This mental state is also called busyness.

So what's the alternative? Retire to a mountainous hermitage, away from the 21st century and its temptations? The answer started with a beeper in Chicago. Mihalyi Csikszentmihalyi, a Professor of Psychology in Chicago, wanted to understand happiness[6]. Like Cousteau, he wanted to go deeper; he wasn't satisfied that questionnaires asking about life satisfaction were really capturing the essence of happiness. So he got an awful lot of people to carry beepers which sounded at random times. Each time the beep sounded, subjects were tasked with capturing their actions, feelings and thoughts at that exact moment. Through capturing hundreds of thousands of these, his team built up a clear picture of the day-to-day experience of happiness; when it happens and why it happens.

One of the first things he found was a challenge to the stereotype: happiness is not lying on a beach sipping cocktails . . . We have this view that happiness is pleasure: it's about relaxing, luxuriating or feasting. He found that people's biggest highs, their peak moments or times of optimal experience weren't passive at all, but highly active. He described these times as *flow* experiences. When we're in flow, we are totally engrossed and immersed in our chosen activity. We lose all sense of time; we lose our sense of self (or the internal dialogue stops, anyway). Flow experiences are the very opposite of psychic entropy: our intentions, thoughts and actions are perfectly aligned; our consciousness is coherent and organised. This might be the semi-meditative state you get into on a long cycle ride, the quiet focus you find as you rebuild the car engine, or the laughter and giggles of a night out with your friends.

Busyness gets in the way of flow experiences in three ways: we jump from task to task, without giving ourselves enough time to become deeply engaged; our attention is scattered as we constantly scan the environment for new inputs, preventing full immersion; we tend towards the superficial and expedient approach, rather than a more engrossing, thoughtful and skilful one. Our opportunity to experience flow is reduced through frenetic, divergent activity.

Flow is the antidote to an addiction to buzz. It is also the antidote to psychic entropy, the disconnection of busyness. We achieve real happiness through deep engagement in what we are doing, whatever it is. We don't need to wait for life to get less frantic or more interesting; we can start by deciding to focus, 100 per cent, on the job at hand – to engross ourselves fully by stretching every fibre of our being to improve or excel in that task or activity. The children's bath time, the monthly sales report or the washing up all offer opportunities for great happiness, but only if we sink our attention into them with reckless abandon. An over-full workday and a long commute are transformed if they are structured into chunks of deep concentration to achieve a meaningful goal; if we resist the temptation to flip flop, distractedly onto the next thing; if we do only one thing, rather than dipping in and out of Facebook or our inbox.

Happiness doesn't just happen; we have to work at it. However, unless we do put in that work, we are unlikely to energise ourselves enough to face the world afresh, with vitality and creativity. When we put in the effort to engage, we are rewarded with flow.

How to achieve flow

If you stop and think about your own moments of flow, you will soon realise that peak moments are never guaranteed. You may passionately love cooking and frequently experience flow as you whip up a soufflé or a sweet and sour. There may also be times when you're just not feeling it, when, no matter how much garlic you crush or fruit you flambé, you are just going through the motions.

Flow is never guaranteed, but there are some conditions under which it is most likely to happen, which we'll look at now.

Challenge
The first component of flow experiences is that of challenge. When we stretch ourselves and our skills we are more likely to engage deeply. This might come from competitive sports, a fierce debate or artistic activity. Or it may come from something more mundane in which you have found a way to challenge yourself. I am reminded

of my Aunty Dymphna. As an early teen I was tasked with drying the dishes along with her after a big family meal (big family = lots of dishes!). I was horrified when I saw the sheer quantity of crockery and cutlery awaiting us while I knew my siblings and cousins were off playing but I hadn't realizsd that I would learn a valuable lesson. Dymphna attacked the drying up with an efficacy I had never experienced before. Her trick was, instead of drying a single plate at a time, she'd dry three simultaneously. She would do the same with knives and forks. I started aping her and soon found that by challenging myself to do three at once, not only did I get through the dishes a lot quicker, the time flew. I had discovered how to get into the zone while drying dishes!

Goals

Goal-setting is really just another way of increasing challenge. Instead of increasing the task's difficulty, we can set parameters around the task that make us stretch to achieve it. By doing so, we can even transform the process of answering emails from a cause of busyness to a flow-inducing activity. Here's how it works. Set aside a specific time in the day to deal with email. Then, once you have seen how many emails you have, set yourself a goal. For example, 'I'll respond to or delete all new emails within 32 minutes'. Then get a big clock to time yourself, cut off distractions and go crazy. What happens is that, as you are trying to achieve a tough goal, you also start thinking about new strategies for improving your efficiency, which engrosses you further and pulls you into flow.

Concentration

When an activity requires all your attention it brings organisation to your consciousness, triggering flow. Rock climbing, playing chess or writing poetry all involve focused attention and so make flow more likely. We can also help a less engrossing task to capture all our attention by focusing on the details or an aspiration.

I used to row for my university. Often we'd be rowing on cold, wet, windy mornings. You'd get into the boat, knowing you had a hard session ahead of you, wanting to be in bed, or back at home or pretty much anywhere other than where you were. As you started to row, you could feel the aches from the previous day's training, you felt exhausted before you even began. Then, at some point in the first five to 10 minutes, flow would kick in and you would forget all that. Consumed by the rhythm, focused on the micro movements of the rower in front, trying to get the timing of the catch (the point at which the blade enters the water) in perfect sync, driving the legs down, finishing the stroke with speed, exiting the water in sync and then gliding, with grace and finesse towards another synchronised, powerful catch. Rowing is an endless quest for the perfect stroke; an intense concentration on your actions, the movement of your crew members and the feel of the boat. Rowing is hard work; but it is also deep concentration. As one stroke merged into the next, so I would glide into a flow state. It was difficult to think of anything else when sunk so deeply into the moment as this; all my consciousness was wrapped in the activity, and the resulting psychic organisation, those flow moments, live with me to this day.

Feedback

Optimal experience happens when we're involved in a feedback-rich activity, and when we pay attention to that feedback. When you play tennis you get feedback from each shot, knowing instantly how well you swung your racket. If you are playing with the intention of improving, this feedback makes you strive to hit better, which absorbs your attention and elicits flow. As the musician plays her violin, she hears how well her fingers and bow combine to create the concerto. The gardener relishes the daily signs of growth – a tribute to their ministrations. When we observe progress, we are rewarded with joy.

Depth and engagement require commitment

The world of too much can lead us to keep our options open: to try a bit of this and a bit of that, to wait for something better. Overwhelmed by choice and opportunity, we can hedge our bets. We don't simply bounce from task to task at work; we bounce from hobby to hobby outside of work. We start sailing, and are feeling quite good about that until we hear about a friend who is kitesurfing, or water-skiing.

Dan Gilbert wondered if keeping our options open would increase or decrease happiness[7]. He had students on a photography course take pictures of things that were important to them using a film camera. At the end of the course they were asked to go into the dark room and print up their two favourite pictures. Gilbert would then ask, 'Which one would you like to give up?' One group of students were told that if they changed their minds, they could swap their choice with the other picture. The other group of students were told that they had to make a decision, and that there would be no option of changing their minds, since the photo would be sent away immediately for assessment, never to be seen again. Gilbert followed up with the students to determine how much they ended up liking the picture they chose. Those who were stuck with the picture, who had no option to change it, ended up liking it an awful lot. Those who had the option to change it didn't like the picture much at all.

We enjoy things more when we commit and stop keeping our options open. Yet we are entirely oblivious to this fact. When Gilbert asked these students which photography course they would prefer to enrol in – the course in which they could change their minds, or the one in which they had to commit – two thirds of all students chose the course that would make them less happy with their ultimate photograph.

In his wonderful book *Mastery*, George Leonard[8], an aikido expert, bemoans the fact that so many of us fail to commit to pursuits, activities or areas of expertise in the longer term. We get enticed by new sports and hobbies, thrilled with the initial steep learning curve. When our progress slows, as it always does, when we plateau, we lose interest and seek new activities. We miss the point. True joy, deep engagement and real mastery come from the journey, from the practice, from the persistent immersion in a pursuit; they come from commitment. This applies to hobbies and it also applies to careers and areas of expertise. My world changed when I decided to really commit to my subject; when I stopped trying to have a successful career and started trying to be a better psychologist. The change was subtle enough at first, but as I built my knowledge, so my interest grew; I started falling back in love with psychology. Then, projects started being transformed with the insights I was gaining, the conversations I was having changed and amazing opportunities started appearing. My career and life satisfaction were transformed. None of this came through working harder; it came through commitment. The deep engagement brought joy, but it also brought opportunity. Jacques Cousteau committed and through commitment he was rewarded with a life of engagement, a life of flow.

Inhabit your three seconds

When René Descartes provided the inspiration for the Keanu Reeves blockbuster, *The Matrix*, back in 1637, he was clear about one thing: the only thing we can be absolutely certain of is our mental experience ('*Cogito ergo sum*' – 'I think, therefore I am'). The world we experience could be real, a dream or the 'Matrix', but our thoughts regarding it – our attention – are certainly real. Whether or not you're a fan of René (or Keanu), Descartes captures something important: our experience, our attention is all we have.

If our moment-to-moment experience, our attention, is all we can be certain of, how long does it last? How long is the 'present' tense? From a psychological perspective, the present lasts about three seconds. Outside of those three seconds we think of experiences as the past or the future; we are not directly experiencing them as now. You could argue that the whole of your life is one long three-second bubble; it's all we really have. All of our attention is found in those three seconds, so it is important we maximise them. Flow isn't the only way of enhancing your present tense. This section will look at other ways to dive more deeply into the moment; to live and experience your three seconds more deeply.

Replace time with attention

In the last chapter I highlighted the value of time affluence. Time is precious, and time allows us to experience the basic goods more fully. However, I think we can focus on time too much, and in the wrong way. Firstly, time is never an end in itself; it's a means to an end. And, quite frankly, the end in question here is attention: if we can free up more time, we can devote more attention to important and enriching things. That is a truly worthy goal, but we don't necessarily need to create more time to gain richer attention. We can simply start focusing. Secondly, since time is precious and scarce, we have focused on maximising it, saving it, managing it. While all of these practices may be helpful (in moderation), the very act of managing time can lead us away from the path of engagement and rich attention, towards a multitasking, thin-sliced, fractured existence.

It makes it unnatural to stop and stare, to pause and enjoy. Our ubiquitous urgency drives us on to the next thing. Our concern that we might miss something makes us miss out on really appreciating anything. As a result, our moments when we're not caught up in frenetic activity lose their power and their joy; quiet time, simplicity and slowness lose their attraction. Real joy requires full, undiluted attention, and that's something we're not in the habit of doing: we don't practise being totally present. When we 'have a moment' we fill it with the help of our smartphone. We top up experiences with more stimulation: we multitask for pleasure as well as for productivity. We surf the internet or look at Facebook while speaking on the phone; we tweet while watching TV; we email while playing with the kids. In losing our ability to go deep into the moment, our moments are no longer enough for us in themselves without artificial additives. Unless we regain the ability to notice, to savour, we will be sucked ever more into unrewarding and unsustainable busyness.

Stop for a moment and recall your best moments over the last few weeks. Without exception these will be times when you shone the flashlight of your attention fully onto something; when you dived into the moment and were fully present. Improving your happiness and wellbeing doesn't have to be complicated, but it does require us to recognise that attention-splicing undermines our focus, weakens our ability to fully experience joy and squanders our three seconds.

Savour the moment

Being fully present in your three seconds is one thing, but how good are you at taking it further – at really savouring the moment? How good are you at lingering appreciatively in an experience; at bringing your full attention to bear on the moment, the sensation or the thought? A life of high-octane busyness can diminish our ability to stop and notice, to *feel* rather than *do*. When we're busy our attention stretches forward beyond the limits of the present into an uncertain, unfeeling future. Through busyness we vacate our three seconds, leaving behind only the husks of split, stretched and partial attention.

Fred B. Bryant and Joseph Veroff from Loyola University are the founders of the savouring movement[9]. Through their testing of thousands of undergraduates they have found techniques which promote savouring. Since our frantic lives diminish our ability to be present and savour, consider these three exercises in bringing you back into the present.

1. Happy attacks

Barry Horner, my father-in-law, is an artist and an inspirational figure. He has developed a fantastic little habit that, quite frankly, I, and many around him, have stolen. At seemingly random moments – during dinner, a conversation, or an activity – he will call out, 'I'm having a happy attack!' He does this when he notices he is really enjoying that moment. This works on three levels: it helps him to amplify and savour great moments as they happen (how often do we realise times were great only after the moment has passed?); it is generous, inviting others to relish the moment; it is sticky – such a simple behaviour easily becomes a habit. Speaking personally, my wife and I have taken this habit on board so fully that when we bought a little dinghy, we called her 'Happy Tac'! (Apologies for the bad pun, but the name still makes us smile.)

Inadvertently, Barry hit upon his own version of what Bryant and Veroff would call 'sharing with others' (I prefer 'happy attack'). The single biggest predictor of pleasure is the ability to tell others about your joy in the moment.

Start noticing and calling out your happy attacks!

2. Sharpening perceptions

This is the deliberate attempt to focus on certain elements of your present experience and the blocking out of others. This may involve paying particular attention to the drumming in a favourite rock track; noticing all the different colours and hues of green in a forestscape; or trying to discern the song of a specific bird. On a personal level, this happened for me by accident. My work involves a lot of travel around the world – often to amazing cities.

I was struck by how unmoved I was by some of the sights I saw in incredible cities like Istanbul, Hyderabad or Lima. I would often, out of boredom and tiredness, drift back to my hotel room and work. I realised why this was: without Dulcie, my wife and best friend, I wasn't able to savour the moment to the same degree: I had no one with whom to share the experience, no one to call out my happy attacks to. By chance, my father-in-law Barry had started a photography club at the same time. I had no history of artistic ability or even visual fluency; all my photos up to that point were the worst kind of holiday snaps. However, for the fun of it, Dulcie and I decided to join. What I hadn't expected was that this simple act transformed my travel. I now had a mission when I was out and about in strange and exotic cities. I wasn't simply seeing the sights; I was looking for great photographs. As my camera lens focused and zoomed, so did my attention. I drank in the sights, hungry for more. I initiated conversations with locals (whose photo I wanted to take) whom I would otherwise have passed by, oblivious. I learned to truly savour the travel and the cities; I was excited and energised by what I experienced. I stopped drifting back to the hotel room.

Consider a potentially pleasurable activity that you have lined up today. How could you direct your attention onto a specific aspect of that experience to help you savour it more deeply?

3. Absorption

'Shut up!' This technique for savouring is the deliberate quieting of the internal dialogue in your head. We now appreciate that not thinking is a deliberate act: the natural state of the brain is to bounce and jump between thoughts, images and memories. Collectively, these inner distractions take you elsewhere intellectually. Absorption is the attempt to stop thinking and immerse ourselves totally in the senses. An example might be the experience of sinking into a deep bath, taking the time to notice the touch of the hot water on your skin, feeling the bubbles and the ripples and sinking into the gentle embrace as the warmth seeps through to your core. Or it might be intensely focusing on the taste of a fine meal, straining every aspect of your attention to wallow in the unfolding flavours. Both these experiences stand in stark contrast to jumping into a bath and reaching reflexively for a celebrity magazine, or simply chewing and swallowing your meal, barely noticing the flavour and the texture.

What sensory experience could you wallow in and, by sinking all your attention into your feelings, use to quieten your overactive brain (at least for a few minutes)?

Less is more

I went on a couple of stag weekends a few years ago. On one of them we flew to a foreign city for a fun-packed, activity-filled two days. We saw the sights, did the clubs and even went on a trip to another famous resort an hour away. It was beautifully planned and executed. A few months later I went on another stag week-end in which the same number of people went into the mountains to stay in a hut, with an ample supply of food and beer. We simply hung out together and did a little walking. The question is, which one was better? Unreservedly, the second weekend was better: we had more time to simply be together. All the activity of the first weekend got in the way of simply enjoying our time together. We were acquiring stories to tell on our return, satisfying our narrative selves rather than focusing on the present. The fact is, nearly every (positive) thing we do is better if we give it a bit more time, a bit more attention.

Attention is limited at any given point. When we switch activities or transit between activities, the brain needs to give a certain amount of attention to figuring out what it should do now. This is called the *task switching cost*, which we discussed in Chapter 5 with regard to multitasking. On the first stag weekend, our attention was focused much of the time on figuring out the latest activity, or even how to get there; there wasn't much time left to simply have a good time. We lost a lot of our time preparing to be happy, rather than being happy.

Sometimes deeper enjoyment starts with something as simple as deliberately doing less. How could you do less to enjoy the experience more?

The big messages in 'From buzz to joy'

There are two types of happiness: **narrative happiness and experiencing happiness.** Narrative happiness involves our assessment of our life satisfaction, including assessments of success, like those addressed in Chapter 8. **Experiencing happiness is concerned with engagement** – our depth of immersion in our present. This chapter calls for **focus over distraction, joy over buzz** and **engagement over busyness.**

BEAT YOUR ADDICTION TO THE BUZZ

- **Busyness is addictive,** rewarding us with a small **dopamine squirt** – like that released by cocaine – each time we jump to a new task.
- The growth of addiction isn't just about the buzz, though; **it's about emptiness** and a lack of meaning.

THE JOY OF ENGAGEMENT

- **Flow moments are states of optimal experience** in which we are totally engaged with what we're doing, losing all sense of ourselves and of time.
- Flow experiences motivate us to follow **the path of engagement**; we naturally go deeper into activities that are uniquely aligned to our strengths and values; we **naturally become more differentiated.**
- **Flow is the antidote** to a life of distraction, to the addiction to buzz.
- **Create flow** by challenging yourself, setting goals, concentrating on experiences, making a determined effort and getting feedback.

INHABIT YOUR THREE SECONDS

- From a psychological perspective, **the present moment lasts three seconds.** All we ever experience is held in those three-second bubbles. To replace buzz with depth, we need to be more engaged within our three seconds.

- **Time management** tends to drive us towards slicing time and splitting attention, and away from engagement. **Focus on managing attention instead.**
- **Savour moments** more fully by noticing **'happy attacks'**, **sharpening your perceptions** and increasing your capability to **get absorbed** in the moment.

Go-Do

INCREASE YOUR JOY

Identify when you experience flow in your typical week and increase the amount of time you spend doing the most flow-inducing activities.

TRIGGER FLOW

Identify one important activity or piece of work you are currently spending a lot of time on. Increase either the intellectual or physical challenge either by making the task harder (drying three plates at once) or by setting yourself a tough goal. By doing this you are likely to concentrate harder and experience more flow.

Experiments

DO LESS

Try, for the next week, to do fewer things, both at work and in your personal life. This doesn't mean you work or play less hard, it's just the overall number of things you are doing is lower, so you spend longer on each activity.

HAPPY ATTACKS

When you are in a moment of true joy, don't let it pass unnoticed. Give it your full attention by calling out that you're having a happy attack.

Chapter 9

Reconnect

In 1990, British school teacher-turned-aid worker, Monica McDaid, walked into a drab grey building at the heart of the medieval town of Siret, Romania. What she saw in that building was, in her words, 'beyond belief'. She found children listlessly lying three or four to a bed, starved of attention, filthy and ill due to a lack of medicines or washing facilities. In that year, aid workers such as Ms McDaid discovered similar scenes repeatedly across Romania. Cighid Orphanage, a 19th-century manor house housing 300 children, was one such place in which children were isolated from human and physical warmth. Ill-trained and overwhelmed staff numbed themselves to the horror, distancing themselves from the orphans: children got minimal treatment, and next to no care. They even gave drugs to the children so they would sleep and allow the staff some respite. These places were worse than kennels for babies: harsh, cold and loveless. Between 1987 and 1989, in Cighid Orphanage alone, 137 of the 300 children died.

How did this happen? Were the orphanage employees evil and cold to treat young children in this way? Possibly, but I suspect the major fault lies with the policy makers, with the Ceaușescu. Nicola Ceaușescu, egged on by his wife Elena, had had a vision. He wanted to double his population in a decade and raise a great Romanian Workers Army. He banned contraceptives and taxed all families with fewer than five children. Unfortunately food and heating oil were scarce. Families started dumping their children on the doorsteps of the state-run orphanages; some were even paid to leave their children in state care. Orphanages would be the training ground of a new population, a new army. His plan didn't work. On the surface it might seem like his plan failed because his country ran out of money when he started to try and repay foreign debt. However, even if the money had been in place, his orphanages were founded on a faulty assumption: that all a child needs is food and shelter to grow and flourish.

This assumption was also dominant in the UK following the Second World War. At that time, thousands of children across the world were growing up as orphans while their home countries struggled to recover from the ravages of that terrible conflict. Orphanages around Britain were designed to offer the very best in physical care. These children grew up in safe, clean, warm environments where they were well-fed and watered. Yet paediatricians started becoming alarmed at the high death rates in these places, and began to wonder whether priorities were in the right place. One paediatrician even went so far as to replace a sign saying 'Wash your hands twice before entering this ward' with one saying 'Do not enter this nursery without picking up a baby'. As we now know, touch, attention and time – love – are not just helpful in a child's development; they are critical. Without it, many of these well-fed, warm children just couldn't prosper, couldn't develop, and died.

Many years later, studies of the survivors of the Romanian orphanages show that the biggest long-term damage to these children was caused by the lack of attention, stimulation or affection. Those children fortunate enough to be adopted and raised in loving, supportive environments still showed wide-ranging damage: they were more likely to be smaller; have lower IQs; significant behavioural problems; have more depression and anxiety; suffer schizophrenia and autism; and even demonstrate clumsiness and poor motor skills. In fact, brain scans by neuroscientist Charles Nelson of Boston Children's Hospital show quite how fundamental the effects of such a horrible upbringing can be. He found that children raised in Romanian orphanages had less electrical activity (or 'alpha power') in their brain. In his words, 'If a normal kid is like a 100-watt light bulb, these kids were a 40-watt light bulb'.

Doctors started recognising that some children would simply give up living because of a lack of attention, or would develop long-term

physical, neurological and psychological problems. This phenomenon gained a name: *failure to thrive.*

What these examples demonstrate is the centrality of relationships,
the necessity of touch and the lasting consequences of loneliness.
My contention is that it isn't just infants that *fail to thrive* if their relationships are impoverished; lives of isolation diminish all of us. No
one can thrive unless nourished by giving and receiving love and
attention by those they cherish.

This chapter is the third part in the section on engagement. It
looks at the value of deep engagement in our important relationships, and at some technologically enabled social trends affecting our
relationships. It suggests how to focus our attention on the relationships that will enrich our lives most, and provides some practical
ideas and reflections on how to deepen your most valuable relationships. The world of too much is a demanding, stressful place. It
is easy and natural to respond by becoming busy, but in doing so we
undermine our happiness, our wellbeing and our resilience. As you
face the torrent of demands, don't do it alone. Hold fast to your priorities, stay close to your loved ones, cherish the inconsequential
moments . . . and reconnect. Because relationships matter.

Everyone needs relationships

Lisa Berkman is an internationally respected expert on the effects of
social and public policy on health. Over her years of experiments and
careful statistical analysis of populations, she has become clearer on
what drives health and wellbeing: quality relationships, or, in her
terms, 'social connectedness'[1]. In one study of 7,000 adults, those
with fewer social ties at the beginning of the study were two to three
times more likely to die during the nine years of her study than those
who had plentiful relationships[2]. On a cultural level, she suggests that
this is the reason that the United States, despite spending more than
any other OECD country on health (about twice its nearest competitor per head of population), ranks in the bottom third of those
countries in longevity: other countries have stronger social connectedness. Jonathan Haidt, the brilliant professor of psychology and

author of *The Happiness Hypothesis*[3] summarises the research by saying that good relationships strengthen the immune system, speed up recovery from surgery, sustain mental functioning in old age and minimise the risk of anxiety and depression. Relationships even boost the mood and wellbeing of introverts who don't feel they want more relationships[4]. In fact, loneliness and isolation have been shown to be bigger health risk factors than smoking![5] This isn't simply because of the support we receive: research suggests that giving support is even more beneficial than receiving it[6].

We're not just healthier as a result of better relationships; we're also happier. Ed Diener, a senior scientist for Gallup, and Martin Seligman studied very happy people to see what we can learn from them[7]. They found that the common factor linking the happiest people was 'their strong ties to friends and family and commitment to spending time with them'. Other research shows that the single best way of having more in-the-moment *experiences of happiness* is to spend more quality time with loved ones, and that people are most happy when spending time with friends and family, and are least happy on their own.

On the more romantic side of relationships, Diener and Seligman also found that almost every person in the top 10 per cent of happiness was involved in a romantic relationship. It appears that one of the best decisions you can ever make, from a happiness perspective, is to get (and stay) married. Married adults are happier than anyone else: 40 per cent call themselves very happy – nearly twice as many as never-married people – and they are the least depressed.

Relationships and busyness

If we have a high level of engagement with those who are important to us, our lives are good. If we don't, our lives are bad. It's pretty much as simple as that. We cannot thrive without great relationships, and relationships cannot thrive without time and attention.

Despite their importance, our most important relationships are in the front line in the war with busyness. Our nearest and dearest are the first to suffer and are injured most by our physical or psychological absence. We pillage and plunder those relationships for the time, attention and energy to devote to email, Facebook and that report that has to be done for Monday. We steal attention from those relationships because we can. We feel confident they 'understand' that we 'have to' do this work; that we need to answer that call. We trust them to deal with the scraps of us: serving them only what's left of us after we've spent all our energy, creativity and focus in dopamine-fuelled activity binges.

Unbridled busyness destroys our relationships from the inside out – slowly, imperceptibly, but surely. In doing so it erodes the foundation of our lives, the only thing that really matters in life. In siphoning attention away from those that are closest to us, we don't end those relationships, but we do suck the richness and colour out of them. We impoverish them and consequently they nourish us and fulfil us less, which means we thrive less (and so do our loved ones). This is where we tip back into the busyness cycle: as our relationships nourish us less, we feel more isolated and alone.

Busyness is a gentle poison whose effects will be seen, not in a year, but over a decade as the tell-tale cancers take hold. Unfortunately for many people, by the time the symptoms have become visible, it is already too late.

The future of relationships

As I discussed in Chapter 5, amazing technological advances are driving changes in working practices without regard for how the brain works. The same is true of relationships: technology is enabling different forms of communication that are wonderful and exciting. However, just because we *can* do these things, *should* we? What are the effects of our new technological capabilities on our relationships?

Sherry Turkle, Professor of the Social Studies of Science and Technology at Massachusetts Institute of Technology, is a psychologist, sociologist and psychoanalyst, and she studies our experience of technology and how it is changing us. Her most recent book *Alone Together* has been the guide and inspiration for this section[8], in which I want to reflect on the changing nature of relationships as a result of technology. Turkle set out to write a book about how parents are being driven crazy by their children's over-use of technology (games, SMS, Facebook etc.). During her research she uncovered a much more significant issue: parents were driving their children crazy through *their* overuse of technology!

This section will focus on two areas: how we 'connect' with each other, and how we pay attention to each other. I have selected these areas because technology, as well as technologically enabled *busyness*, has significantly impacted on how we relate to each other. Since relationships are so fundamental to our wellbeing, it's useful to pause and think about what technology is doing to them.

Connected but isolated

It was all a little awkward. A large man, in height and in width, sat down opposite me on the train and started talking at me, very animatedly. He was clearly cross about something. What he was saying didn't make a lot of sense, as though I was missing a big chunk of the full picture, like there were gaps in his story. Suddenly, with no apparent warning, his whole body relaxed; he sat back, smiled, then started laughing – great shoulder-shaking guffaws. After regaining his composure he was silent for a long time, or so it seemed; in reality, it was probably no more than a couple of minutes. He looked variously placated, anxious and then affectionate. Finally, in a tender voice, looking at me, but not directly in the eye, he said, 'Okay. I'll speak to you later. Love you. Bye', and he hung up his phone. After a moment's pause and reflection, his picked up his phone and made another call.

This odd behaviour made me reflect on the weirdness of our private bubbles these days. While technology has, superficially at least, helped us to connect, it has also isolated us. Before the advent of the mobile phone, such behaviour would have been correctly diagnosed as psychotic, or, at the very least, impolite. This man exposed an incredibly private conversation to a group of strangers, without a thought. He appeared to feel no embarrassment, no desire to keep his intimacies private and no concern for our feelings. He was in his head, completely isolated from us. Our technology, in allowing us to connect with people in different places, sucks our presence away from the here, splitting us not simply between tasks, but also between locations.

Meeting people is hard and messy; we are busy, so we revert to the safety and certainty of our electronic bubble. At conferences, parties and public places around the world, people aren't quite meeting. Increasingly, we pass each other, like ships in the night, because in our pockets are all the people we need; why try to connect with the people in our current location? We 'phub' each other constantly (Tom Chatfield's brilliant term to mean snubbing people by using your phone)[9].

I can't help feeling, as I look around a conference coffee room filled with people not-meeting, not-chatting and not-present, that we're missing something of the serendipity of unexpected encounters. I can't help wondering whether our communities and lives are the worse for the ease at which we transport ourselves elsewhere, for the fact that we're less and less inclined to step out of our isolation.

We feel this isolation in our interactions even with those we know well. While it feels okay to text or email someone, we increasingly shy away from calling them. A phone conversation is too demanding; it is asking too much from the recipient. We are expecting them to commit their precious attention, fully, to us at the moment of our choosing. The same can be true in our offices: we IM, text or email to gain permission for a conversation; we don't want to intrude into others' bubbles – after all, they're busy. We do this, of course, because we don't want anyone to intrude on ours. Calls, or real meetings, will take too much of our precious time and attention, and place too much pressure on us to perform. Tara, a 55-year-old lawyer, explained, 'When you ask for a call, the expectation is that you have pumped it up a level'. Or, as Randolph, a 42-year-old architect, explained, 'Now we have email, when you ask for a call the stakes are raised; people expect a call to be a fuller thing, more complicated. It asks more, it creates higher expectations, and you had better deliver'[10].

So, busy and stretched we decide to revert to our comfortable-but-frenetic, hyper-connected isolation. The fact is, people are complex and we are each different; proper, meaningful interactions are always going to be messy. In fact, a new app is now available, called 'Hell is other people' after Jean-Paul Sartre's famous moan; this actually helps you avoid bumping into your friends and having to actually socialise with real people. It uses the app Foursquare to track where all your 'friends' are, and directs you away from those places. You could argue that this antisocial media app is following our technologically driven, connected isolation to its natural conclusion: in helping us connect to lots of people, conveniently and superficially, it also helps us to disconnect. Our social media makes us connected but antisocial. Our smartphone allows us to avoid committing fully to our present location, to our present time, and to being present with others. It's much simpler and more efficient if we can just be 'left to our own devices' (pun intended): connected to millions, but isolated from the world.

Social multitasking

At the forefront of technological boundaries are our teens. Many teens say that they prefer to communicate via IM and text rather than in person, because it allows them to multitask their interactions. 'Personally, I like talking to a lot of people at a time', a Pittsburgh-area teen told researchers. 'It kind of keeps you busy. It's kind of boring just talking to one person, cause then like ... you can't talk to anyone else.'

I've talked a number of times about the dangers of thin-slicing our attention. Nowhere is this more corrosive than when we thin-slice our relationships and are only partly present with those who are important to us. When Sherry Turkle started working on her book, she found children and teens driven to exasperation by call-interrupted dinners, by email-perforated conversations, and by parents too distracted to notice the important 'unimportants' of growing up: the proudly shown stick rocket, the new skateboard trick, the disappearance of the first 'moustache'. She chronicled mothers who used breastfeeding time to catch up on their texts, missing the subtle flickers of emotion across their baby's face. And fathers who are barely present with their children at the park, playing with their iPhones rather than playing ball. She met Audrey, a teen who fantasised about the day when her mother would greet her from school, expectant and focused. Instead, her reality involved arriving at the car to find her mum head down over her phone, too busy to acknowledge Audrey. Her daily reunion with her mum passed in silence, bar the tap, tap, tap on the touchscreen – the chance to reconnect with warmth, relish and attention spurned.

Audrey simply wanted the opportunity to share the ups and downs of her day, but she had to accept that her mum was focused on more 'important' things; she had to accept that her ups and downs were trivial; she was learning to accept that she too was trivial.

Of course we know that those we love are more important than the inbox. Of course we realise that we care less about keeping up to date with texts or WhatsApp than we do about our family and friends. It's just we have a lot on, and we are sure, if they love us, they'll understand this. Next year should be a little quieter ... There is also a sense in which busyness can become an excuse: a way to get out of everyday routines, difficult conversations or boring chores. The trouble is, when we allow 'important' busyness to drive out the small, inconsequential moments, the casual chitchats and the micro-kindnesses, we lose something deeper. Paying attention to the small things is our entrance ticket into the larger. We earn the right and the trust to be a confidant through persistent demonstration of care in the little things. Showing interest in the day to day makes our nearest and dearest believe we will also be interested in their deeper fears and their higher dreams.

If we do allow busyness to steal the micro-moments, we disembowel relationships. All relationships are composed of two elements: being together and doing things together. If we remove the 'being together', we are left with relationships that are focused around activity, tasks or even chores. It is in the 'being together' that most of the happiness comes and from where most of the emotional connectedness comes: the sense of deep connectedness and unity, of joyful banter or heartfelt outpouring. If we strip the 'being together' component into simple physical presence in the same location, our attention consumed in other orbits, we downgrade relationships into activity or transactions. Relationships become less rewarding, so they attract less of our attention and buffer us less and less against the tides of busyness.

In a world of too much, which scatters our attention and is superficial and shallow, we need to take a stand for depth in all things, but especially in relationships. We need to practise and relearn how to be together, unaided and uninterrupted by devices, because that is where trust is built, where joy comes from; that is the source of lasting love. And without love, we may as well sink back into the barren immediacy of busyness.

Focus on fewer people: less is more

In earlier chapters I discussed how one of the underlying causes of busyness is the constant striving for 'More': we attempt to succeed through doing *more*; we fuel our desire for busyness through striving for *more* stuff; we cope with the emptiness by stimulating ourselves *more*, and get more buzz, but less joy.

'More' spills over into our relationships too. We want *more* relationships, *more* connectivity and to be *more* popular. There appears to be an insecurity that propels many of us to seek affirmation of our value in the size of our social networks, in the number of 'likes' we achieve, or in our Klout (a website calculating online social influence) rating. There is an acquisitiveness in gaining Facebook friends and Twitter followers: whatever the number, we want more.

Social media scholar danah boyd (who spells her name in lower case) was interested in how connected we are. She persuaded a fellow undergraduate at the University of California, Mike, to allow her to analyse his email archive[11]. Even though this study was done a number of years ago, she found an astonishing level of connectivity: over the previous five years he had sent and received 80,941 messages with 15,537 unique people. boyd calculated that this meant Mike had ties with 662,078 people in the world, if you count the effect of messages being forwarded etc.; rising up to 11.7 million, if you count all the messages he sent or received which had more than 50 recipients. Whichever way you slice it, that's a lot of people. This analysis was published in 2006. I'm guessing if you analysed Mike's inbox – as well as his social media activity – today, you would find his connections would be a very large multiple of the above number.

Undeniably email, Facebook, Twitter, LinkedIn, WhatsApp, text and IM help us to connect to more people, more easily. In particular, aided by our technologically enhanced memory, we lose contact with people less frequently, and we can find them again in a Google search. Who hasn't thrilled at the rekindling of friendships with very old school friends or acquaintances, glad that, in a very small way, they have re-entered your life? Technological tools of communication make mass broadcasting or brief messaging easy, so old connections no longer need prohibitively time-consuming phone calls to bring them back into the realms of active contacts (and what would I say anyway?); just a couple of words on their Facebook wall and you're back up and running. Who hasn't been pleased to improve their publically acknowledged popularity score: their number of Facebook friends, Twitter followers or LinkedIn connections. Social media and electronic communication have extended our reach across the planet, and back in time; we are potent and omnipotent.

But ease and scale of connectivity come with a catch: when you send messages out and connect, people are likely to respond – lots of them, and often. Very soon, keeping up with all the messages, maintaining all those relationships, becomes exhausting. In fear that our popularity score may drop, we set about managing the electronic stream of updates, pictures and messages. We talk of getting rid of emails, cleaning our text inbox. Even outside of work, these social 'relationships' can soon become tasks to be executed. It can all become something of a burden. Where is the nourishing, life-enriching joy of connecting in this mass of electronic jabber? Our friends, family and acquaintances can become just one more job to add to the list, one more thing to increase your busyness.

When Sherry Turkle, author of *Alone Together*, interviewed 16-year-old Sanjay he explained how much pressure he felt in trying to keep up with all the texts he received. As he finished the interview he commented, 'I can't imagine doing this when I'm older', and then more quietly, 'How long do I have to continue doing this?'

Affinity vs popularity

One of the things that I find most interesting about Tim Kasser's research is the distinction he finds between affinity and popularity. Affinity means 'being together' and deepening key relationships. This stands in contrast to the attempt to be popular across the larger population. When I came across this research it got me thinking. I guess I had always lumped all kinds of socialising together, regarding intimacy with close friends and family as the same thing, albeit on a different scale, to banter and friendliness at a party. His research made me question this.

Kasser's research relates to the values, the motivations of people.

Are they aspiring to have deeper relationships with close friends and family, or to become more popular and have more friends? His findings indicate that those with a powerful focus on 'affinity' tend to enjoy happiness, health and mental wellbeing. On the other hand, the reverse was found with those who strove for popularity: they were less happy, more depressed and more anxious. It seems that striving to deepen and strengthen important relationships is nourishing, fulfilling and life-enhancing. Going for 'More' is a great way to increase your likelihood of having a miserable life.

Despite all the TV images and social-networking norms to the contrary, joy is not to be found in *more*, but in *less*. If we want to be happier we should shift our attention to those special people, many of whom are probably not anywhere in your social network, but who are central to your existence. I personally believe this has always been the case, but I think the argument for a greater focus on our central relationships has never been stronger. We have limited time and attention, so we have to decide where to place it. We should shift more of our energy away from the many and onto the few. We should focus, unremittingly, on deepening, strengthening and nurturing important relationships, and cease trying to become important through our relationships. As in so many aspects of busyness, if we focus more and scatter our attention less, we will start to thrive again.

Who are your 15?

Primates have complex social groups. The maintenance of these groups takes effort, often termed 'social grooming'. As a group gets larger, the grooming required increases, as does the effort to know everyone and understand how they relate to everyone else. British anthropologist Robin Dunbar strengthened this theory when he found a strong correlation between primate brain size and average group size[12]. It appears that when groupings of apes and monkeys get too big, they start to fall apart: they are just too difficult to maintain. On the basis of his work with other primates, Dunbar calculated the size of social groupings that humans could manage based on their cognitive capacity. His answer was 150. This has become known as 'Dunbar's number'. He then went a step further and started analysing historical records to see if social groupings, across cultures, tended to conform to his theory. He found that Neolithic villages tended to average at around 150 people; evidence suggested Hutterite settlements split up when they reached 150; and 150 was often the basic unit size of armies, and remains the size of a company in the modern military.

Dunbar goes on to say that, as 150 is an absolute maximum, most societies wouldn't have clustered into such large groups. As groups get larger the effort to maintain them grows, so that only those societies under intense survival pressure would have been willing to invest the necessary effort. So, a first question to ask would be, how large is your social grouping? If it's larger than 150, it's unlikely that you have the intellectual capacity or energy to manage all of those relationships properly.

Dunbar's analysis went a little deeper: through careful study of social groupings he found remarkable consistency in the shape of social structures. He identified that our level of relationships can be thought of as concentric circles. We tend to have five people who are closest to us, who will often be immediate family and our partner. The next circle contains 15 people, the next 50, then 150. If you combine Dunbar's findings with those of Tim Kasser, the implication for me is that wellbeing, satisfaction and joy come from the 15. It is these magic 15 people, your closest friends and family, who will trigger more flow experiences, who will make you assess your life as better and who will reduce your depression. The juice of life isn't in the 500 Facebook friends; it's in the 15. I'm not suggesting there isn't fun to be found in larger, more disparate, weak ties through social media; it's just that this activity can in no way replace the deeper meaning that comes from the 15.

If you remember nothing else from this chapter, remember this: overinvest your time and attention in your 15; revel in being together with them, support them and understand them. Any increase in the quality of these relationships, in the quality of your time together with your 15, will be an increase in your overall life satisfaction. You can be disastrous on social media; you can fail to develop a large network of acquaintances, and it will have little impact on the quality of your life, but unless you get the 15 right, you will not be happy; you will not thrive.

So, who are your 15?

Your support network

We all have a range of psychological and emotional needs. When we get busy, we can close off from our friends, from our 15, because we are too drained to devote the time to them. This is the opposite of the 'More' problem I discussed above, but just as real. As our sense of busyness increases, so our active support network can diminish as we cancel nights out with friends, as we exit quietly from the football team. We can end up, at our busiest times, with an active support system of only one or two people just at the time when our need for support is greatest. These needs are unlikely to be met by the superficiality of social media relationships. They need something more meaningful, more present.

We've probably all had the experience of meeting an old school or college friend who has become a little hollow, who speaks without energy about their lives and has lost their vitality. We all become hollow when we don't have our needs met. When we close off from the 15, we close off from the possibility of having some of those needs met. In doing so, we close off part of ourselves. We become a little narrower; a little drier. This can put pressure on our very closest relationship – the one with our partner. We start depending on them to meet a much wider range of our needs, resenting the fact they cannot meet all our complexities. The reality is that no single person will be able to support you across all facets of your personality and aspirations.

One way to help to motivate you to put the time into your full 15 is to think which aspects of you are supported by each person. The experience most people have when doing this is twofold: firstly, it makes them realise how over reliant they are on their partner to support them in areas they are not equipped or inclined to do; secondly, they realise that, painted across the 15, is their full personality. Collectively, their 15 support the vast majority of all their needs, aspirations and passions. Take Mary, for example, a hardworking lawyer married to another lawyer. She loves Joe dearly, and he understands her really well, but there are times she wants to howl with laughter and gossip. Joe doesn't do that for Mary, but Helen and Eva do. There are times Mary wants to create: she loves art and poetry – both doing them and debating them; Joe doesn't, but Bill and Asiya do. At times she wants the unquestioning maternal love of her mum; or to be with Lucy, her running and weight-loss partner. Engagement across the full 15, in Mary's case, makes her more complete and fulfilled. With the best will in the world, and a bucket load of love, Joe can't do all this for Mary; nor should she expect him to.

Your 15 should not be trimmed back as you get busy; cut back the 50, the 150 and the 500, but don't cut back the 15. Your 15 can support you, in all those deep and meaningful ways, through your darkest periods of workload and demand.

Copy the table below and fill in the names of your 15. Next, ask yourself how each person meets a need for you in a unique way, addressing a part of you that nobody else can, or doing so better than anyone else.

Name	Support this person provides

Giving more

About three million years ago, early hominids split off from the apes and something strange and wonderful started happening. The hominids started rapidly developing bigger brains, which allowed more complex social interactions (or vice versa). This posed an evolutionary problem: how to give birth to a baby with such a big head and still retain a pelvis that would allow vertical walking. The solution was to give birth to babies way before they are fully developed. Brain growth and development continues well after birth in humans. Humans are the only species on earth whose offspring are helpless for the first few years of their life. Jonathan Haidt believes this could be the origin of love. If we were going to evolve to give birth to helpless children, we would have to evolve emotions to ensure our species would care for its offspring.

Neuroscientists Jorge Moll and Jordan Grafman have shown a neurological basis for the human tendency to care[13]. Specifically, they looked at what happens in the brain when we are altruistic. Using functional magnetic resonance imaging they showed that both receiving money and giving it away to charity activated the mesolimbic pathway, a part of the brain that is involved in rewards for things such as food and sex. However, in addition, when subjects gave to charity they also activated another brain circuit (the subgenual cortex), which is related to social attachment. There are two implications of this. Firstly, it appears that altruism isn't simply a higher moral act, but a basic human function that we're hardwired to do. Secondly, more importantly, altruism gives you more bang for your buck than receiving.

If, on reflection, you are not giving enough, here's a thought: the old adage that it's better to give than receive turns out to be supported by the evidence. Research into altruism has persistently shown benefits to health, happiness and psychological wellbeing. One study into sufferers of multiple sclerosis, for example, found that patients who offered support to other MS patients actually experienced more benefits than those they helped – in terms of confidence, self-esteem, depression and daily functioning[14]. Giving also helps protect us from the stress of 'too much' by building our resilience[15].

How could you give more to feel better? Specifically, how could you give more to your 15?

Obligations

Emile Durkheim, the 19th-century French academic and father of sociology, carried out an interesting analysis. He collected data related to suicide rates from across Europe. He was interested in whether he could isolate a common factor to explain differences between communities and countries. What he found can be summed up in a single word: constraints[16]. He found Protestant communities, who lived the least socially demanding lives at the time, had the highest rates of suicide. The rate was lower in Catholic communities, where the obligations were greater. The lowest rates of all were found in Jewish communities, where the dense network of social ties and commitments was strongest. In addition, single people were more likely to kill themselves than married people without children, and both these groups were a lot more likely to commit suicide than married people with children. Obligations, commitments and 'degree of social integration' all appeared, to Durkheim, powerful predictors of happiness and wellbeing (or at least of not killing yourself!). In a curious modern signal of the evolutionary benefits of commitment, studies have shown that women in stable sexual relationships ovulate more regularly, and continue ovulating longer into middle age than those in unstable relationships[17].

A friend of mine was afraid of commitment. He wanted to keep his options open. Even though he had a wonderful girlfriend who he claimed to love – a girlfriend who unquestionably loved him – he was unable to commit. For years he had an on/off relationship with this girl, breaking up for a series of unfulfilling dalliances with other women, but always returning to her. Amazingly, she remained loyal, even though she became increasingly frustrated (as did her parents). In the end I'm not sure what triggered his decision, but he decided to propose and get married. This isn't an unusual story, especially in these days of maximum choice and minimum commitment. The point of the story is the conversation I had with him a few years after the wedding. I was reflecting on his history and asking him, rather intrusively perhaps (but then I am a psychologist!), how a life of committed monogamy compared with his premarital life of variety and choice. He explained how happy he was now, and that his level of satisfaction was way beyond anything he had previously experienced. He said that prior to marrying he used to spend a great deal of time and energy worrying about whether he was making the right choice, whether his girlfriend really was right for him and searching for something better. Once he had made his choice, this time and energy was suddenly released for him to get on with enjoying life. In taking up the 'burden' of commitment, he had shed a much bigger burden, and so became happier. He, of course, felt he *had* made the right choice, but I was struck by the fact that he felt the commitment itself was such a major component of his happiness.

This takes us right back to Dan Gilbert's photography class, and the students' preference for the picture when they were stuck with it. When we commit, we free up the brain to go about synthesising happiness, becoming happy with the choice we made. Clearly this doesn't mean that we can choose to commit to anyone and will always be happy. It does, however, mean that when we keep our options open, when our relationships are disposable, we cast away a lot of the joy and wellbeing we could have gained in favour of the illusion of freedom. This applies to friendships just as much as to romantic couplings. Even at a trivial level, we can shy away from tying ourselves down to particular dates or regular meetings in case something else comes up.

How could you commit yourself more completely and unreservedly to your 15?

Deepening relationships

So far in this chapter we have discussed the importance of relationships; how relationships are the first thing to get damaged by busyness; how technologically enabled busyness is changing the way we connect and pay attention to each other; and, finally, that we should focus our resources more strongly on the relationships which will nourish us the most: our closest 15 people.

The rest of this chapter will devote itself to sharing ideas on how to deepen those relationships. I included this section, not because you don't know how to build and deepen relationships, but because so many of us need reminding to prioritise time for our loved ones. In the craziness of our lives today, we can let relationships slip. I find, unless I deliberately and intentionally give attention to my important relationships, days, weeks or months slip by without meaningful interaction. So don't see this as a toolkit, so much as a collection of reflections and calls to action. Integrate them with what you already do.

Being together (or the mindfulness of interactions)

As I mentioned earlier, what matters isn't being together geographically, but attentionally; the starting point for deepening any relationship is getting better at your part of the 'being together' experience. Like my comments on mindfulness, this starts with practice. So many of us have got out of the habit of being fully present with others; we are more comfortable with the intellectual bubble gum of partial attention. So 'being together' isn't as easy as it sounds. Here are three suggestions on how to practise becoming more fully present with that other person, whether they are a child, a partner, a sibling, a parent or a friend. If these sound a little intense, don't worry – I'm not suggesting you do it all the time. However, like meditation, when we practise deep attention at certain times, the abilities we develop spill outside of our 'practice' times. We become more attentive.

Avoid distractions

This first strategy is fairly straightforward. If you want to deepen relationships with a person, show them you care by giving them your full and undivided attention. Ask yourself what distracts your attention away from the other person. The most obvious first step is making sure your phone is switched off, and not visible, during times when you want to be present with the other person: for example, my friend who transformed his meals out with his wife, simply by removing his smartphone from the dinner table.

Clearly, in a family, having phones off all the time may not be an option, but it is absolutely essential that protected, technology-free time is built into the daily rhythm. It might be a decision to reduce the stimulation in the environment: watching TV together is hardly 'being together', for example. Likewise, a walk together might be a richer experience than a drink in a loud and busy bar. When there is less to see and hear, our attention naturally zeroes in more actively on the other person; we are then more likely to properly engage in a conversation and enter a flow experience together.

Get in the zone

Using the principles from sports psychology and flow research, focus on something in the moment to help you immerse yourself in that encounter. You might do this by focusing on something physical: take a leaf from the mindfulness comments earlier and notice the other person's breathing, trying to get in sync. You might, alternatively, practise your empathy skills: as you talk try and fully understand how the other person might be responding to your actions, what they might be thinking. Finally, you might simply set yourself a goal for the conversation: 'I want X to leave this conversation happier than they were when we started'. A simple goal like this can help you to strain harder to pay attention; you dive deeper into the interaction and you are more likely to get into flow.

Turn off the autopilot

A lot of our behaviour is on autopilot as we recognise patterns and automatically engage our standard response. This tendency is extremely helpful in making our thought processes more efficient, but less helpful for things like creativity when we want to see the problem anew. Autopilot can also be unhelpful in our relationships. Every relationship develops patterns, and we can get hooked by these patterns, responding automatically. In doing so, we fail to be fully present in two ways: we are responding instinctively, rather than with a clear, conscious choice; our behaviour is driven by the past interactions which developed these patterns, rather than the current context.

Eckhart Tolle, author of the *Power of Now* and influential spiritual thinker, tells a story of his return home to his parents[18]. His father asks him, 'So, what are you doing now? Are you still messing about with that spiritual nonsense? When are you going to get a real job?' Such comments draw us powerfully into familiar patterns and spirals of conversation. Choosing to respond to someone in the now, without drawing on the past, is pretty hard but can be really interesting. It often sparks conversations that go in directions never explored before. Together you step off the well-trodden routines and into deeper, newer fields.

'Wait a minute'

If you're a parent to young children, let me ask you this: how many times a week do you say, 'Wait a minute' in response to a request for attention from a child? Every single time we say that, we signal our priorities and our child's lack of importance. Pause for a moment and reflect on how you would feel if your nearest and dearest persistently said, 'Wait a minute' to almost every request for a few moments of attention. Pretty irritated or deflated, I imagine. My wife and I caught ourselves (and still catch ourselves) doing this regularly as we rushed around the house in our oh-so-important daily busyness. We wondered what would happen if we didn't say 'Wait a minute'. What would happen if we paused our busyness instead of pausing our child? I found I started entering a lot more of these random little moments. One minute I'd be tidying the kitchen, the next I'd be helping my eldest son Jack with a tricky instruction model he was building, or playing football with my seven-year-old,

Ben. I'd be plunged into special moments of togetherness that were light and trivial, and in that triviality I found myself smiling more, connecting more. These were sublime distractions. I was shocked by how quickly the children could drag me into joy if I didn't pause them. I was even more shocked by how brief these moments were.

Yesterday, my daughter Seren asked my wife and me to dance with her. We, of course, were involved in something terribly important, though I'm struggling to remember what it was. We put our thing on pause, and got up to dance. We danced and laughed for about 20 seconds. After that, my daughter was done; satisfied, she moved onto the next thing. I don't say this to suggest those 20 seconds weren't important to her, or great moments for us; it's just her attention, as a four-year-old, had scuttled on to something new. I had been assuming that the requests my children make for my attention are adult-sized requests. In most cases, it turns out, they aren't. They are tiny fragments of joy, brief beautiful butterflies, asking for little effort – just a moment to pause and enjoy and, in this joy, to deepen our relationship.

I am trying to pause my busyness more often.

Creating rituals

When I was at university I had a theory. This theory sprang from the responses I would get from people when you asked them 'What are you doing for Christmas?' If we put aside for a moment the fact that many people don't recognise Christmas for religious and cultural reasons, I was struck by the vast difference in the answers. Some would light up as they recounted, in great depth, the family traditions they had. Others would talk vaguely about turkey and knitted jumpers. My theory went like this: you could use the depth and quantity of family rituals and traditions as a proxy for how happy that person's childhood was. I appreciate this is a fairly flaky theory, but I have been left with a belief that there is something potent, symbolic and binding in rituals and traditions within families and relationships.

I can't remember where I first heard the term, but I'm a big fan of 'date nights'. This is the practice of putting a regular night aside, often once a week, for a nice, one-on-one meal with your partner. I'm told even Barack Obama and David Cameron have date nights with their wives. If your schedules are crammed with activity, it can become easy to pass like ships in the night for weeks. Scheduling time for each other can be a way of managing this. Dulcie and I have our own spin on this. We like our food, so every now and then (certainly not weekly) we have our own date night. We have rules for this. These meals are four courses. She cooks two and I cook the other two. Neither of us knows what the other is cooking (apart from the main ingredients), and every course has to be something we have never cooked before. The anticipation, the planning and the cooking are every bit as much part of the experience as the meal itself.

However, date nights are nowhere as important as another ritual that developed by chance: our 'three-cups-of-tea mornings'. At least once a week, more if we can make it, we sit down for a tea-drinking, conversational marathon. We cover more ground in those three teas, conversationally, than we might do in days otherwise. We plan our finances, we discuss the children, we look ahead and dream. We are seldom more together than over those cups of tea. So we stretch out the moment. We stay for three cups.

Rituals work on two principles: the activity is extremely specific and repeatable; there is a rhythm with which they happen, which is normally daily, weekly or monthly.

Think about your 15: what rituals could you start to deepen those relationships?

The power of positive emotions

'What did he say? I can't believe it! I'm furious!' When we are over-taken by negative emotions, all our evolutionary heritage kicks in: our attention zooms in to the subject at hand, our adrenaline starts flowing, and we start getting ready for a fight or planning our escape. Negative emotions have been critical for survival, short-circuiting complex decision-making to allow rapid response times in the face of threat, uncertainty and danger.

But what about positive feelings? From an evolutionary per-spective, how could joy help? Positive emotions were considered an evolutionary anomaly, albeit a pleasurable one, until Barbara Fredrickson, Professor of Psychology at the University of North Carolina, started her work. She randomly assigned people to watch movies eliciting either positive or negative emotions. Afterwards, she put people through tests and exercises. She found that people in the grip of positive emotions such as amusement or contentment were more creative and had more of a 'big picture' focus. Further work showed that these emotions undo the cardiovascular effects of negative emotions, helping us to relax us quicker and, over time, dissipating the effects of stress. In addition, these positive emotions seem to help build resources and develop capability.

Through her work, Fredrickson developed the 'broaden and build' theory for positive emotions[19]. Positive emotions broaden our attention, helping us to learn and lay down the resources and psychological capital which will be used for the rest of our lives. In summary, negative emotions are about short-term survival; positive emotions are about long-term growth and capability.

The same applies to our emotions in relationships. When we're in the grip of anger or anxiety, we focus on ourselves, on winning or getting out of the situation; all attention is focused on the short term with no regard to long-term damage. All that matters is what's happening at that time. In the context of all the comments I have made about attention and being present in the moment, some of this may sound a good thing. However, in our anger or anxiety-driven outbursts, we seldom do much good; more often than not, we have to recover and repair damage when the red mist dissipates.

Positive emotions, on the other hand, broaden and build our relationships in a couple of ways. Firstly, they broaden your attention, making you more likely to notice subtle signals from the other person, which helps you to navigate the dance better. When our attention is broadened we are also more likely to 'get out of our heads' and more readily appreciate and empathise with the other person's viewpoint and feelings. By increasing our powers of observation and understanding we also learn more about that person and ourselves. We grow, and in so doing, help the relationship to grow.

In addition, positive emotions are typically shared. So while the 'broaden and build' effect influences your behaviour and growth, which indirectly helps relationships, it also has a more direct effect. When we're enjoying positive times with a friend, family member or partner, our *mutual* attention broadens. I often think that a simple gauge of the strength of a relationship is the range and depth of things you are able to discuss together. As relationships develop we go through a process called *social penetration*[20] (a horrible term, I know) where we increasingly know, understand and can talk about more things. In less positive moments our mutual attention is focused on the bare minimum required to complete the interaction; we are transacting in the narrowest sense. As our joint mood improves, conversations open up, the things we choose together widen and our relationship unfolds. Positive emotions enlarge our moments together, they expand our interactions and deepen the relationship. The relationship builds trust and resilience through these interactions. They simultaneously become stronger and more fun.

Positive to negative ratios

The 'broaden and build' theory was reinforced in private relationships and in business through further work by Marcel Losada, a Brazilian colleague of Fredrickson. Losada went into 60 companies and started transcribing every word that was said in their business meetings. One third of those companies were flourishing economically, a third were doing okay, and a third were failing. Losada looked at the ratio of positive to negative comments and found a clear link to performance. Companies where the ratio was higher than 2.9 positive comments for every one negative remark were doing well. Any companies with a worse than 2.9:1 ratio were doing badly. This has become known as the Losada Ratio[21]. John Gottman used the same principle to calculate optimum ratios with married couples. He found the benchmark was higher in couples: a 2.9:1 ratio predicted divorce; you need a ratio of 5:1 to predict strong, healthy marriages[22].

The principle of the ratio has been applied to numerous aspects of positive emotions. People whose ratios of positive to negative emotions are out of balance suffer less wellbeing and poorer life outcomes. Now, a recent article has challenged the accuracy of the Losada Ratio, questioning the differential equations and the nonlinear dynamics used. All very clever stuff, but I say blah, blah. In the end, what matters is not the exact ratio, but the principle that the proportion of positive to negative emotions and comments has a lasting impact on the health and strength of those relationships.

Think of a key relationship – one of your 15 (or even one of your five). What's your ratio?

Celebrate better

What do you think is a better predictor of a strong relationship: the way you argue or the way you celebrate? I don't know about you, but I would have thought the answer was obvious: it is how we act in the heat of battle when the unspeakables are spoken, when we put aside our respect of the other person in favour of a victory. I was wrong. Shelly Gable, Professor of Psychology at the University of California, has demonstrated that how we celebrate is a better predictor of relationship strength[23]. It appears that how we behave in those moments of triumph and joy makes a huge difference; it can either build or undermine the relationship.

So what is the secret of a great celebration? A bottle of champagne, flowers with a funny greeting card, or a hearty slap on the back? Seligman suggests that there are four basic types of response when you hear some great news (unfortunately none of them involves Moët and Chandon!). In the table below, the four types are shown with an example of each response.

News: 'I've been asked to be on the regional gymnastics team. The team is going to compete in Paris, France next month in an International Competition.'

Response:

	Passive	Active
Constructive	'That's great news. You deserve it. They should have selected you ages ago.'	'That's amazing. How do you feel? How did they tell you? How did you react? Tell me more about the trip.'
Destructive	'Oh. Can you pass the salt?'	'Ahh. Paris is a long way away. Will the trip be expensive? Will you still have enough time for your homework?'

It isn't hard to see the strongest approach. Yet after I came across this distinction I became painfully aware how often I reverted to passive constructive. We may be willing to focus more energy on the right response for the really big occasions, but what I realised was how I was missing so many micro-celebrations with my children: the news of a rare and long-awaited soccer victory; the unexpected school 'diploma'; and the proud display of a sculpture that Granny had said was fabulous were all greeted with well-meaning comments like 'Brilliant. I'm so proud of you'. My responses were heartfelt and true, and they were well received, but they were unsubstantial. They weren't just driven from an ignorance, but also from being in a rush, always; too busy to stop and drop into a celebration. Passive constructive is quicker, and slots into rushing, busy lifestyles more comfortably than a more active celebration. Pausing to listen, to be curious, can interrupt our rapid motion between tasks.

I now celebrate better. Real celebration, for the small and big stuff, isn't about verbal pats on the back; it's not even about my thoughts and feelings, thrown at them like so many flowers to the victor; it's about helping them to revel in their emotions. When, instead of responding automatically in our busy lives, we take the time to help people to celebrate the big or the small, we join them in their emotions; we urge them to relive the experience so we too can share their moment of triumph, which helps them to expand and extend their exultation.

I can't pretend I always celebrate brilliantly. I can't pretend that, at times I don't revert to drive-by congratulations (pat, pat). However, at least now I realise *they're* missing out; *I'm* missing out; and therefore *we're* missing out. I'm not perfect, but I do sit down a little more often, ask a few more questions and revel a bit more. This is my favourite kind of psychology: simple, blinking obvious (once explained) and life-enhancing.

Go celebrate.

Better than Prozac

If I told you I could prescribe something for you that would make you happier than Prozac, would cost you nothing, was very simple and would have no negative side effects, would you be interested? The following is an exercise developed by Martin Seligman and his team called Three Good Things[24]. It has been tested using random controls. It works, and what is more, it is a practice that many find to be sticky: a new behaviour that can rapidly become a habit. In fact, it works so well that those people tested with deep, dark, can-hardly-get-out-of-bed depression, in just a few weeks had improved to a state of mild depression (like when we're watching TV).

Here's how it goes. Every night, write down three things about the day that went well, or you are happy about. Write a little bit of detail, but you don't need to go overboard. That's it!

Why does it work? We tend to over-focus on the negative, we ruminate, worry about and remember the mistakes, the problems and the fears. A simple activity like this can help to rebalance our focus. It can help to reframe your memory to be more positive; or in the language of Chapter 7, it builds a more positive narrative. I don't mean you fake it or try and fool yourself into thinking what was bad is good: I'm not a believer in unbridled, exaggerated positivity. I simply mean trying to balance your memory to be more accurate. This helps because, in recalling more of the positive, you start to shift your narrative in a positive direction, and so judge yourself to be more satisfied with your overall life.

All this works well, and would have been appropriate in Chapter 7. However, I have included it here because I've adapted it with my children. For years I would ask, on the drive home from school or at bedtime, 'How was your day?' It was a boring question, and I got depressingly bored, perfunctory answers. One day I asked instead, 'What were three things that went well today?' The conversation was infinitely richer; the children started thinking and vying with each other to come up with the best answers. It has become a regular and brilliant conversation for the children and me, and has helped to strengthen our relationship. I also like to think that it might make a small impact on their developing narrative happiness, though of course that's only conjecture.

The big messages in 'Reconnect'

Relationships are not 'nice to haves': they are central to our lives and wellbeing. Strong relationships help us to **live longer and to be happier and healthier**, physically and mentally. **We cannot thrive unless we have strong relationships.**

The **first victims of busyness are often those that are closest to us**. We siphon our attention away from these relationships, trusting our loved ones will 'understand', and in doing this we are diminished.

THE FUTURE OF RELATIONSHIPS

- Technology has enabled us to connect to more people, but due to the demand all those relationships place on us, we have more shallow interactions; we shy away from the intrusiveness of the phone call or the face-to-face; we are **more connected but more isolated**.
- Our mania for speed, stimulation and multitasking means we dive less deeply into conversations; **we are less present and so we build less fulfilling relationships**.

FOCUS ON FEWER PEOPLE: LESS IS MORE

- Research shows we are better off **focusing on fewer close, deep relationships** than lots of (shallower) relationships.
- Using Robin Dunbar's research, perhaps the people to **focus on are your closest 15** relationships.
- Think about how your 15 support you. **Could you spread the support role** more evenly across your 15 to improve your wellbeing?
- **Giving is good for you**: it makes you healthier, happier and more resilient to stress; so think about how you can give more to your 15.

DEEPENING RELATIONSHIPS

- In a world in which **attention is at an absolute premium**, you can get better at being fully present by putting your busyness on pause more often. **Avoid distractions, get in the zone** and **turn off the autopilot**.
- **Positive emotions** help to broaden and build your relationships, so make an effort to generate these emotions. Consider the **ratio of positive to negative comments** in your relationships and how you can **improve this balance**.

- Relationships deepen not just as a result of getting through tough times, but also in how good times are **celebrated**. Make an effort to celebrate positive moments in an **active and constructive** manner.
- Engage with the positive moments in the lives of your loved ones by asking: **what three things went well today?** It will build your relationships and might also improve their personal narrative.

Go-Do

YOUR 15

In one respect, happiness is very simple. Identify the 15 people in the world who you cherish the most, and spend as much quality time as you can with them.

RITUALS

Rituals can be powerful and sticky. Start a new one this week with one or more of your 15. Make it really specific, and create a regular rhythm for its occurrence (daily, weekly, monthly).

Experiment

PHONE-FREE MOMENTS

Forget the phone when you're with important people. Practise prioritising them over your calls or emails. At the very least, don't put your phone on the table when you're talking or eating!

GET MESSY

Speaking to people and meeting them face to face is more messy and involved than texting and IM-ing; so get messy! Try increasing the percentage of calls and face-to-face time you have with your 15; for those outside your 15, text and IMs might be just the ticket!

CELEBRATE BETTER

When someone important has good news, stop and ask them how it feels and what happened; don't default to a drive-by pat of con-gratulation.

Section Four

MOMENTUM

This section will discuss how to develop the momentum to move beyond busy – to a life of mastery, focus and engagement. There are two big factors which can kill off any momentum: the first is fear and the second is inertia. Fear can immobilise us into busyness. To achieve the momentum necessary to move towards what's really important to us, we need to get on the front foot; to have the confidence to move beyond defensive busyness, to take more positive and individual steps towards a better and more effective life. The section also addresses how to overcome inertia, explaining in concrete terms how to convert good intentions into action; to start making sustainable changes in your lifestyle and habits so you can begin to thrive.

The magic of momentum

Clive Wearing is an accomplished British musician. He sang for the Westminster Choir, acted as chorus master at Covent Garden and arranged choral scenes for operas to be performed at Sadler's Wells. In 1981 he was given responsibility for Radio 3's musical content on the wedding day of Prince Charles and Lady Diana. He continued to work successfully on the BBC until he contracted a *herpes simplex* virus in 1985.

The disease attacked his nervous system and caused irreparable damage, leaving Clive with amnesia. He is unable to store or retrieve new memories for more than 20 seconds, meaning Clive is no longer creating a history for himself. Living with amnesia is like waking up from a 10-year sleep, three times a minute. Clive can remember the word 'chicken', but not what it tastes like. He can remember he's married, but not what his wife, Deborah, looks like – though when he does see her, he recognises her and exuberantly embraces her as if he hasn't seen her for years. He can't maintain a conversational thread. Deborah tells of the time in July 1985 when he asked how long he had been ill. She replied, 'Four months'. He instantly joked, 'Four months? Is that F-O-R or F-O-U-R (ha ha!)?' After reflecting briefly on that fact, he asked again how long he'd been ill, got the same reply, and made exactly the same quip. After two weeks of this circular conversation, Deborah decided it was legitimate to start saying 'Nearly five months' in order to avoid the joke.

Clive is a changed man, except for one thing: his ability to play music. Even though he cannot remember his musical training, when the music starts, he can play. Deborah discovered this by chance one day. She picked up some choral music and began to sing. Clive joined in with the tenor line. She realised he could still read music. Following further experiments, they discovered Clive could play the choir organ and even conduct music. In those moments, Clive appears to be Clive again; he is carried along by the momentum of the music. The rhythm creates the tempo that allows him to flow back to his former self; engrossed in the music he becomes animated and energised – until the music stops. When it does, so does Clive. When the music stops, he loses momentum – and without momentum he is lost.

Keeping momentum

Over years of working with individuals and organisations, I have become convinced of the importance of momentum. I have seen people make dramatic shifts in their lifestyles, and others who, despite repeated efforts, fail to make anything other than the most temporary progress. I have seen huge efforts in organisational change come to nothing, and seen other movements take hold of businesses and transform them effortlessly. The difference between success and failure is often about the degree to which we are able to build momentum. Successful changes build on momentum; the unsuccessful ones flounder in the force of the oncoming stream. Put simply, our progress towards change will be in one of three states at any time: it's moving in the wrong direction; it's not moving; or it's moving in the right direction.Building sustainable momentum is more important than the speed at which change happens. Once you're moving in the right direction, once you have momentum – whether you are an individual or an organisation – your task becomes infinitely easier. The starting point is always to get momentum working in your favour.

Chapter 10

On the front foot

Richard Feynman became one of the greatest theoretical physicists of the 20th century and won the Nobel Prize. As a boy, he liked to play with radios. As a 12-year-old he set up a little lab in his room, bought his first radio, and rather than listening to it, he took it apart. He soon became quite good at fixing radios. This was in the early 1930s, during the Great Depression, so a boy who could fix radios cheaply was useful. On one occasion, he was picked up by a client who seemed convinced that this boy would be a waste of his time and money. He kept on asking Feynman how a boy could know anything useful about radios until they arrived at the client's house. Feeling pressurised, Feynman turned the radio on. It started wobbling, then gave out a terrifically loud roar for a few minutes before quieting and playing correctly. Feynman was confused. He had never encountered this before. He shut the radio off, began pacing around the room and thinking. The client was entirely unimpressed. He wanted action; he wanted to see the boy working; he wanted to know Feynman knew what he was doing. He started protesting to Feynman, asking him to stop wasting his time and get on with fixing the radio, or leave[1].

Despite the heckling, Feynman kept on thinking. He wondered how any radio could make such a noise. Most radios failed because of faulty equipment or loose wiring; he wasn't convinced it would be either. After a while, he came up with a theory: radio sets in those days were made from a series of tubes; if he took them out and reversed the order the vibration and noise might disappear. Now, at last, Feynman was ready to act. He changed the tubes and turned the radio on. It worked perfectly. The man was astonished. He became one of Feynman's biggest advocates, telling everyone he knew of the boy who 'fixes radios by thinking'.

Under pressure to perform, most of us would have dived into activity to demonstrate how hard we are working and that we know what we're doing. We would have prioritised action over thought and in doing this we might have got so caught in the detail of the wiring that we missed the bigger possibilities. Feynman had the confidence to do his own thing. He recognised playing around with wires would look right to the client, but everything he knew about radios told him that the wiring wasn't the problem; he needed to think about other options. He gave himself the time to think in the face of pressure to conform and, in doing so, he succeeded.

Uncertainty

To walk our own path and create our own possibilities takes the confidence to resist the pressure to conform and get busy. It means doing things that may fly in the face of people's expectations. This can be challenging in today's working climate because the world of too much is not just a place of too much demand, too much information and too much distraction; it is also a place of too much uncertainty. As markets become increasingly fast, unpredictable and innovative, our organisations have less and less ability to plan for the future. They need more flexibility, and the first place they tend to look for this is their employee pool. This makes us all expendable; and this has shaken our confidence, introducing fear and insecurity into our working lives.

I do, however, think there is an entirely different way to look at the employment market today. In some ways, I don't think there has ever been a better time to be employed. The lack of predictability means organisations have to move from hierarchical command-and-control styles to a situation that allows, and even encourages, autonomy and innovation. Technology has enabled entirely new ways of working and communicating. The need to retain flexibility means that employers are more open to alternative contractual relationships than ever before, allowing a real portfolio lifestyle. There is more freedom, opportunity and excitement in work today than there has ever been. We have never had so many options for the way we live our lives, so much capability to achieve great things and so many ways to connect and have rich relationships. There has never been a better time to live. Whether you experience your career as one of insecurity and fear, or one of boundless opportunity depends on your approach.

You can fritter away the opportunities available to you on ten thousand things; on the endless stream of micro-tasks and urgent inconsequentials; and on the vacuous buzz of stimulation and reactivity. You can persuade yourself that you have no choice, that other options would be dangerous, that it's what you need to do to succeed, or that it's okay to disconnect from everyone and everything because of a goal that will never satisfy you.

Or you can walk a different path. You can shift your energy from prevention to promotion and start learning your way to a life beyond busyness. We can bring real focus to what will make the biggest difference at work; we can make an impact; we can shape our organisations and in so doing, shape our careers. You can re-engage with the sources of our energy and our joy, reconnecting with your core values and diving deep into your most cherished relationships. As you increasingly recognise busy as the refuge of the unimaginative and start grappling with the big problems in life; you start to step ever more confidently into who you could become, and you start learning how to live again. This chapter will show you how.

On the front foot

The term 'on the front foot' comes from cricket (of course, as an Englishman, I feel I had to squeeze some reference to cricket in the book at some point!). When someone is throwing (or 'bowling') a hard ball at you at 70 miles per hour, the natural temptation is defend yourself; to use your bat to block or divert the ball. Also, when you step forward to strike a ball, you leave your 'crease', which is a bit like taking your foot off a base in baseball, you are no longer safe. If your swing misses the ball, the wicket keeper behind the 'stumps' (the three sticks in the ground you have to guard) can catch the ball, knock your stumps down and your innings is over. When you step forward, you are taking a risk. However, the best, most attacking shots are played not off the back foot, but off the front. Stepping forward gives you more momentum, and so more power. Truly great batsmen dominate the bowlers by regularly stepping forward onto their front foot and hitting the ball out of the ground.

Busyness is like playing defensively off the back foot. When we are on the front foot, we have the advantage, we are acting positively, creating the momentum necessary to become the masters of our environment and our lives. There might be fear and anxiety aroused by playing off the front foot, by not engaging in defensive busyness, but we should not let that anxiety drive the way we lead our lives or our careers. The fear and anxiety we should pay attention to is the quieter, deeper angst that we're not living in line with our values; the anxiety we're letting our loved ones down; the concern that your addiction to the white noise of organisational uber-communication is getting in the way of your ability to make a difference. This deep fear speaks without the shriek of the immediate; but when the dust settles it will be the only voice still speaking. Your only question will be whether or not you listened. Whether or not you had the courage to play off the front foot.

Self-regulation: prevention vs promotion

To achieve mastery over our lives, to play off the front foot, we need to manage our emotions and behaviour. In psychological terms this is called self-regulation: the conscious control over our activities in order to achieve our goals. For example, we need to go to the library rather than the pub in order to prepare for exams; we need to actually listen to the other person in order for them to be interested in us. The ability to self-regulate has been shown to significantly affect all kinds of things, including job performance and life satisfaction.

In 1997 Edward Tory Higgins, a Psychology Professor at Columbia University wrote an article for the *American Psychologist* called 'Beyond pleasure and pain'[2]. In it he argued that we need to be a little more sophisticated in our understanding of how our goals affect our self-regulation and motivation. He developed a concept he called Regulatory Focus Theory to describe two fundamentally different forms of self-regulation. Our motivation and the way we control our behaviour varies according to which fundamental needs are being served. The first set of needs is that of safety and survival; the second set involves growth and achievement. Higgins suggested that each set was driven by different forms of regulation, which he called a *prevention focus* and *promotion focus* respectively.

Our prevention focus is all about avoiding negative outcomes: when we are performing tasks we might have to avoid obstacles that could cause us to fail. The promotion focus is all about positive outcomes: striving to achieve goals that are important to us. For example, imagine you were studying for a professional exam: you would want to study hard, read around the subject etc. These activities are regulated by a promotion focus. In order to do well you will also have to abstain from going to the movies rather than studying, or from staying out too late the night before the exam. The regulation of our behaviour that stops us failing the exam has a prevention focus.

It's pretty clear how both these regulatory mechanisms work in tandem: no matter how hard you study, if you don't abstain from a heavy drinking session and turn up to the exam with a stinking hangover, your good work may have been in vain. When it comes to work performance, the assumption has been that both promotion and prevention were important in achieving success. Some people would lean more towards one than the other, on the basis of personality differences, but this difference was more about preferred style, and had little impact on actual performance. That assumption held true until 2012.

In 2012, researchers at Michigan University carried out a thorough review of all the studies in this area[3]. Using a clever statistical technique called meta-analysis, they analysed studies involving over 25,000 people. Their interest lay in the relationship between regulatory focus and performance. What they found was that a promotion focus was strongly related to task and job performance. It was also positively related to other good things like openness, innovation, helpfulness, job satisfaction and organisational commitment. Prevention, on the other hand, was not related to job performance. It is likely that a strong prevention focus stops bad performance, because it drives a concern to avoid negative consequences, but it does little to improve performance above average. Interestingly, prevention-focused people, possibly because of their greater fear of bad outcomes, and the desire to play it safe, tended to be less open, less innovative, less helpful, less satisfied with their job and less committed to the organisation. To me it sounds like a preventative strategy is a great way to make sure you don't thrive.

It's the easiest thing in the world to hunker down and play defensively. For me, busyness is defensiveness. Busyness is all about avoidance. Busyness is a prevention strategy. Yet, in the organisations I work with I see too much prevention and not enough promotion. What worries me is that most of these people aren't the kind of folk who you'd typically expect to be defensive. They are aspirational, career-minded people. Driven by uncertainty in the job market and overwhelming demands, they are choosing the safer of the two paths; they are choosing the reassurance of immediate safety over the prospect of flourishing in the longer term.

I accept prevention is a valid goal, and busyness is a natural preventative strategy in a world of too much. However, let's not fool ourselves. If you decide to be busy, be clear it will not move your career forward, or your life, or your happiness, or your relationships. At best, it might stop bad things happening (in the short term). If you want to thrive, you will need to focus more on goal attainment, on your values and ideals, than on prevention. You will need to take some risks, confident in the knowledge that you'll be able to cope with the consequences. Finding your own path is harder, but a lot more satisfying and, as the evidence above re-affirms, a lot more successful.

Manage negative emotions

Organisations are emotion-soaked places these days. The ambient levels of angst are at record highs: fear, stress and uncertainty course through the corridors. Emotion fuels activity but deadens performance: it drives unnaturally high states of perpetual alertness and endless activity, but also reduces our ability to think, create and prioritise. We do more, but it's less thoughtful, dumbed down. Emotion-fuelled activity is great if what's needed is repetitive, low-level task execution. Unfortunately we live in a different world now, and just when the complexity and speed of global markets require more complex and creative thinking than ever before, we've contrived to create a working environment psychologically guaranteed to reduce our intellectual performance, not to mention our physical and mental wellbeing.

Emotions such as stress and anxiety can be helpful to some aspects of performance in the short term. Unfortunately, we can get used to the expectation that more stress will lead to more urgency and energy, resulting in heightened performance and start relying on this stress to propel us, super-charged, through our daily demands. However, more stress reduces the effectiveness with which we think, learn and remember. When we're anxious we make worse decisions and prioritise badly. So in the interests of our wellbeing and performance, it's time to turn down the emotion, and tune in the thinking. To help us to get on the front foot, I want to turn to the high-pressure world of sports.

Chimp vs Human

Steve Peters is a psychiatrist with a history of working with the worst offenders in maximum security prisons. In 2001 he became friends with Dave Brailsford, now the British Cycling Performance Director, and began working with elite cyclists including Sir Chris Hoy, Victoria Pendleton and Bradley Wiggins to help them to manage their emotions better, and in so doing to help them focus, engage and win. In the years following, British cycling moved from a marginal sport, with next to no recent track record of success, to the dominant country in Olympic cycling, winning nine medals at the 2012 Olympic Games. Sir Chris Hoy claimed it was Steve Peters that helped him win the Olympics; Pendleton said 'Steve Peters is the most important person in my career'.

Peters has learned a lot about emotions through his work with offenders who seemed serially unable to control their emotions, and his work with elite athletes where the smallest loss of focus will cost you dearly. He has learned a lot about how anxiety, fear and anger can derail us. In what he accepts is a massive over-simplification, he has developed a working model of emotion[4]. I love it, because, with simplicity and a bit of humour, it describes something very complex, based on extensive scientific research. Peters describes the psychological mind as having three brains, the frontal, the limbic and the parietal. The frontal brain he calls the Human; the limbic brain he calls the Chimp; the parietal brain he calls the Computer. The Computer is the memory of responses, it's important but for this chapter I want to focus on the other two brains.

The Human is rational and logical. When we think about ourselves, it is the Human we are thinking of. Theoretically, since it is the Human that plans and makes the ultimate decisions, it is the Human that is in charge. In reality, this is often not the case. The Chimp thinks emotionally and, in the same way that a real chimp would be five times stronger than a person, the Chimp can easily overpower the Human. Also, information is sent first to the Chimp, and the Chimp is fast, so it always gets its response in first. This is one of the biggest reasons that so much of our behaviour isn't in line with what we know is the right thing to do, or with our good intentions: if something is bothering the Chimp, the Human can lose any semblance of control.

The Chimp thinks emotionally and independently of the Human. Peters' characterisation of the Chimp has elements of the rapid, automatic System One thinking that we discussed in Chapter 2: it jumps to conclusions, can be irrational and thinks in a simplistic, binary way – black and white, good and bad. However, Peters' description of the Chimp is broader; it has more purely emotional parts, which I'm interested in here. The Chimp thinks catastrophically, worrying about the worst possible consequences; it is also paranoid, continually scanning for threats to safety or status.

Part of what fuels our wild bouts of busyness, or stops us pursuing the areas we know will make a difference or help us re-engage, is the fear and anxiety resulting from the Chimp's catastrophic and paranoid thinking: the terrible consequences of not submitting that summary or the earth-shatteringly important email we'll miss if we don't get to the bottom of our inbox. We fear that others will judge us badly if we don't appear stretched to the limit, or that we may

somehow fall behind in the perpetual race for recognition and promotion if we're not always on, always doing. When we hear news
of organisational changes, job losses or economic crises, we can't
help but see the most catastrophic outcome for ourselves, or fear the
consequences of a lack of effort. The Chimp won't be settled unless
we work harder; churn out more and more stuff. Like in feudal days
when nobles would erect wood or stone walls to protect them from
threat, so the Chimp prompts us to build up barriers to keep it safe:
the quantity of things we produce, our willingness to work through
weekends and holidays and our visible exhaustion. To the Chimp,
each one of those activities is our badge of commitment to the
cause, our guarantee of safe passage through troubled times. It's all
a form of defensive, protective busyness – a prevention mindset.

The Human recognises it should prioritise important things over
the electronic white noise; that thinking and creating aren't done
best in thin slices or at 100 miles per hour; and that a lack of attention is damaging its most life-affirming relationships. However, the
Human can do little until the Chimp is settled. These days, with all
the pressure and competition, the Chimp hardly ever relaxes. So we
often wait 'until things settle down' and, year after year, they don't.
We soldier on, expending all our energy on maintaining our force-
field of certifiable busyness, and have little left for what's important
to us. As we flop onto the sofa and dull our pain with wine and TV,
the Chimp is satisfied but the Human in us knows it's all wrong.

Fear worsens performance

Imagine you are looking at a picture of a maze. At the centre of
the maze is a little mouse, representing you. Your task is to find the
route out of the maze. Some mazes have a picture of cheese near
the exit. Some mazes have a picture of an owl in flight on the opposite side of the maze from the entrance. Do you think you'd solve
the maze faster to get to the cheese, or to get away from the owl,
or neither? I suspect you'd say neither. After all, it's just a paper maze
with black and white pictures of a mouse, cheese and an owl. But
when this experiment was carried out by psychology professors
Ronald Friedman and Jens Förster, they found people generated 50
per cent more ideas after they had completed the 'get to the cheese'
mazes, than when they were the 'get away from the owl' type[5].

We have known for a long time that anxiety and fear reduce performance, but what this experiment shows is that this occurs even
when we're not even aware of it. I don't imagine those people completing the 'get away from the owl' mazes were thinking 'I must
hurry, the owl will eat me, oh no . . .'. Yet, somehow, the Chimp
was activated and unsettled. As a result, energy was sucked away
from the player's prefrontal cortex; their attention was narrowed,
reducing their ability to see the whole problem, and thus the solution took longer to find.

If we translate this into the workplace, so much of what we do
is visible to the 'owls' of our organisations. Whether we realise it or
not, this is likely to make us act protectively; for most of us, that
means doing it all, by keeping everyone happy (even if that means
not doing what's important). As well as causing us to default to
busyness, this ever-present threat is also likely to have two additional
effects, which in their turn cause more frenetic activity.

Firstly, our raised anxiety levels take resources from working
memory, which reduces our intellectual processing power, making
us think slower. Our effective IQ actually drops when in the grip of
powerful emotions[6]. In slowing down, we take longer to do what we
need to do; we have to work longer, with fewer breaks to keep up.

Secondly, threats and worries also narrow and weaken our attention. When our Chimp is agitated, what we notice and what we
think about become very narrow, as do the memories that are triggered[7]. We notice only what's immediately in front of us and rely
on the Chimp's emotional instincts to help us to decide whether to
fight or run. However, the sheer quantity of stuff we notice is
reduced, not just the breadth.

In addition, when our attention narrows we are less able to see
the 'big picture'. We lose awareness of what's important, and even
of the relative priority of things. We are less equipped to sit back and
make tough priority decisions; so we accelerate, pedal to the floor,
trying to do it all. I'm sure you can think of times when, flustered
with a deadline approaching, you simply gave up trying to think,
prioritise or plan, and just dived into wild activity. In those moments
of emotion it's really hard to think clearly and make choices.

The shame of it is, while reckless busyness might temporarily quieten the Chimp, it does nothing to address the underlying causes of
your fear and nervousness: busyness does little to differentiate you, it

prevents you from having the impact you would like to have, and it gets in the way of your becoming the person you want to be. Busyness as an approach to calming the Chimp is like taking Prozac in an attempt to be happier: it is simply treating the symptom, not the cause of the emotion. In fact, busyness is probably making the fear, insecurity and anxiety worse in the long run by preventing you from taking the kind of focused action on important areas that will genuinely move you forward in your career and your life. For example, in the American Psychological Association's 'Stress in America' report in 2010 they found that people 'report being too busy as a primary barrier preventing them from better managing their stress'[8]. Whether we focus just on stress or widen it out to fear, anxiety, worry, nervousness, concern and tension, the same holds true: being busy prevents us from addressing the underlying causes of our angst.

Calming the Chimp

The first thing to do if you want to allow the Human in you to make good, logical choices about how you use your time and live your life is to quieten the Chimp. You will remember that I mentioned it is the Human who ultimately makes decisions; the Chimp only suggests. Although it may be difficult to overpower these suggestions, the Human still retains the power to choose. The Chimp will never change: its drives and instincts are what they are. The Human, to learn to live the life it wants, needs to work out how to operate despite these drives so that it is in the position to make rational choices.

It is difficult to overpower the Chimp's drives through willpower alone – as Steve Peters puts it, attempting to control the Chimp this way is an arm wrestle you will always lose. Instead, you need to nurture the Chimp by recognising the Chimp's drives, and that when these are not met, it becomes more agitated. Chimps are driven to gain more power and status; to achieve security and protect themselves; to gain ample food (translate this, for us, into money); to belong to a troop and be one of the gang; and to have a territory which they protect from invasions or turf wars.

Early in my career I was working with those facing potential redundancy. In one case, staff at a manufacturing plant had been told that, in 18 months, 50 per cent of all staff would be made redundant.

This was in the context of a sluggish job market and the employees' recognition that they were significantly overpaid for their skills in comparison to equivalent jobs locally. In addition, labour relations were poor at the best of times in that company, and the communication of the plans had been communicated badly: most employees had learned of the impending job cuts through the media. Emotions ran high. In fact, at my first session I was mistaken for 'management' and someone took it upon themselves to throw a chair at me! Over the course of the project I was struck by how long some people clung onto their anger; in fact, I came to realise that, for many, anger was simply the public face people were putting on their fear. While people were 'angry', they could not move forward. They were stuck in blaming 'them'.

On the other hand, there were others who took a totally different approach. I remember one man called Dave. At our first meeting he had been petrified. He had a wife who wasn't working, a mother-in-law who lived with them; three children; and he had bought a new house six months prior to this announcement on the strength of his current salary. He couldn't afford to be unemployed. He also didn't trust management enough to leave the fate of his family in their hands. Unlike many people who simply waited for the fateful day in 18 months' time, he took action. When he wasn't on shift, he trained to be a driving instructor. It wasn't this that impressed me about Dave's story – it was what happened at work. He was satisfying his Chimp's fear, so it allowed him to get on with work free of the burden of anger, fear and anxiety. At a time when everyone else seemed to be falling apart (it was a tough time) he stood out as a beacon of calm effectiveness. He had never really been noticed before, but six months before the decision day he was asked to play a role in the transition process since he was 'so good at change'. Not only was he retained, but he was promoted. He told me later he framed his driving instructor certificate and hung it on a wall at home as a reminder to stay prepared.

Reappraisal: techniques to soothe the Chimp
When we suppress emotions, and try to bottle them up, we do little to calm our Chimp. In fact, some studies show that suppression makes emotions more potent, more debilitating. James Gross, Professor of Psychology at Stamford University, had two people

watch an upsetting film together to compare their responses. One person, in advance, had been told to suppress their emotions, not showing any reaction during or after the film. After the film, the two subjects had a conversation. The person who was acting naturally was emotionally expressive as a result of the upsetting nature of the film. The other person kept their face neutral and their voice more monotonous. When Gross analysed the effect of this, he found three effects of this suppression. First, the person suppressing their emotion felt distracted, because they were trying to do two things at once, which took resources away from the working memory. Secondly, the suppressed person experienced an increase in blood pressure. Finally, the other person was slightly repulsed by the obvious suppression by their partner. They experienced that person's suppression as some kind of threat (since they weren't being more natural) and their blood pressure also increased. It seems that, not only does suppression not work very well, it also bothers those around us[9]. Clearly a better tactic is needed to satisfy the Chimp.

'Reappraisal', on the other hand, works much better. It involves changing our interpretation of an event, thought or experience – like the prisoners in the concentration camp, who were able to find the freedom to find some happiness despite the most horrific situation. We don't feel fear or anxiety because of events in themselves, but because of the meaning we give to them. Change our meanings and we change our emotions.

When Gross measured the brain activity of those watching these movies, he noticed that the subjects who were trying to suppress exhibited a large increase in limbic activity; those who were reappraising (acting naturally) had a reduced amount of limbic activity, as if, through reappraisal, the brain no longer 'saw' a threat, and so the Chimp calmed down[10]. In addition, those who were reappraising had activated the ventrolateral prefrontal cortex – thought to be the brain's braking system. This suggests that reappraising puts the brakes on emotion. Going further, Gross collected data on hundreds of people and grouped them according to whether they tended to use suppression or reappraisal to manage their emotions. He then tested them for optimism, life satisfaction, environmental mastery and the quality of their relationships. Reappraisers were significantly better on all these measures: they thrived more.

Reappraisal takes cognitive effort, but it is absolutely critical in a world abounding with novelty, uncertainty, competition and expectations – all of which can be experienced as threats, causing our Chimp to get agitated. Unless we can control this through re-appraisal, we will suffer from persistent anxiety and stress. More importantly, we will be unable to think clearly about our priorities and will revert to the 'safe' option of busyness. Busyness might feel safe in the short term, but it is a certain path to reduced wellbeing, lower performance and damaged relationships. As Kevin Ochsner, Head of Social Cognitive Neuroscience at Columbia University said in conversation with David Rock, 'If our emotional responses fundamentally flow out of interpretations, or appraisals, of the world, and we can change those appraisals, then we have to try to do so. And to not do so, at some level, is rather irresponsible.'[11]

Reinterpretation

One of the most common ways to reappraise, is to give different interpretations to either our internal emotions or external behaviours. When I started public speaking I found myself getting scared. My stomach would tie up in knots, my mouth would go dry and my heart would start pounding so strongly I could feel it in my neck. More importantly, when I was in the grip of these emotions, I'd mumble and rush my words, and fail to connect with the audience. But I was keen to develop the capability to present and facilitate, so I needed to find a solution. At that time in my life I was also a wannabe adrenaline junkie: I had taken up surfing, was listening to grunge music and had been paragliding. My goatee beard and long hair did little to disguise the fact that it was all image, but it was an important image to me at the time. It was also an image that helped me totally change my relationship with presenting. I'm not sure how it occurred to me, but I told myself, as I started to feel the tension rising, 'Wow! I'd pay a lot of money to jump out of a plane and get a rush like this!' It worked like magic. I had reinterpreted nerves as the very thing I craved: adrenaline and experience.

I think reinterpretation is the most common and most useful of the reappraisal techniques. We have all had experience of someone who upsets or irritates us, only to walk away and find out that their mother just passed away. It puts a whole new perspective on what happened. It doesn't change the events, it doesn't take away the words they said, but it makes them okay somehow.

In charting a new path through too much you will need to find ways of reinterpreting a lot of experiences to allow you to think clearly and avoid the default response of busyness. As well as learning to reinterpret your silent panic at the sight of 171 unread emails, you may also have to help others to reinterpret your behaviour. I found a while ago that when I didn't respond immediately to email, it caused irritation to a particular client until I explained I only checked email once a day to allow me to think, create and focus on the important. Once he knew that, rather than being annoyed, he was a little inspired.

Regaining perspective

Have you ever had a moment you wanted to shout, to cry, to punch the wall and to crawl into a corner and hide . . . all at the same time? A few months ago I was in exactly that state. Work was piling up, deadlines loomed, an unexpected and urgent issue had arisen and I had a big event the next day that I was worried about. I needed more time. I didn't have more time. Help!

In a mad fluster of activity I tried to work through it all, but I made next to no progress. Fortunately, I had a flight to catch and had to drag myself from my desk for the 65-minute drive to the airport. There is no way on earth, at that point, that I would have voluntarily taken a break. I was in it up to my armpits, Chimp jumping all over the place, unable to think properly, unable to work, but also unable to realise how rubbish I was being. My forced break turned out to be miraculous. Somehow, the drive allowed me to step back, to allow my attention to broaden again, to allow me to gain perspective. The low-level distraction of driving made the anxieties and fears feel less overwhelming – the raging of the Chimp was no longer so deafening. It allowed me to see the priorities more clearly. I could think again. By the time I had arrived at the airport, I had not only calmed the Chimp, I had formulated a plan. I was ready to engage in purposeful, focused activity.

When those moments hit us, we feel entirely compelled to put our heads down and do stuff. Two things are almost certain: in the grip of those emotions your decision-making and priorities will be hopeless, and the last thing you will want to do is take a break – but it is what you need.

Confidence

Learning to manage our emotions is a critical first step in the progression from rampant busyness to a more positive approach; from prevention to promotion. However, to move to a more promotion-focused, positive strategy in the face of too much, we need to do more than just control our negative emotions; we need to feel confident. Specifically we need to believe more strongly in our capability, our ability to deliver value in ways other than busyness. When we feel confident in our ability, we are more likely to make our own choices, walk our own path. Since moving beyond busyness means taking a stance against the social norm, confidence enables us to do what it takes to thrive. To tread a different path it helps to build your confidence.

The next step is, in many cases, the big one: to step into the hazard. This involves choosing not to respond in the default way to the demand and communication assault; to choose a different path. In an insecure world, that involves taking a few risks.

The fear that causes us to default to frenetic activity doesn't just come from big risks, like job loss, but also more mundane, daily risks: we need to have the confidence to accept the risk of choosing to miss a few 'important' emails; to say 'no' at times; and to give up delivering on everything, always. Busyness, in many respects, is easier because it avoids these risks.

However, let's be clear, busyness itself is not without risk; it's just that those risks are more easily discounted. In choosing busyness we risk our impact and fulfilment, willingly accepting the massive, career-decelerating, life-diminishing risks because we want to manage the more immediate micro-risks. We forgo opportunities to make a real difference to our organisations because we want to keep our inbox safely empty. We allow ourselves to become absent in our own homes in order to be present at all the endless work meetings.

We need the confidence to shift our gaze from the pressing flurry of micro-demand onto the more important, more rewarding and more differentiating big stuff. We need the confidence to move beyond busy.

What 'confidence' really means

The term 'confidence' is one of those words that mean too many things to too many people. It has been hijacked by the 'gurus' peddling an endless diet of positive thinking and affirmations: if we think only positive, confident thoughts, the universe will deliver us all kinds of good things – which is clearly rubbish. In fact, one study showed that positive affirmations only increase the confidence of already confident people. If you lack confidence, affirmations actually make you feel a lot worse.

Although the term 'confidence' is a little vague scientifically, I have used it because the more accurate psychological terms (which I'll introduce shortly) are ugly and forgettable. I will refer to them only to demonstrate the different aspects of what we would conversationally call confidence. This greater clarity on the meaning of 'confidence' will make it easier to identify how to build it. After that, forget the scientific labels and get on with feeling more confident.

Psychologists have identified a number of different measures of what you and I would call confidence. These have been combined into something called Core Self-Evaluation (CSE) by Timothy A. Judge, Professor of Management at Notre Dame University[12]. Core self-evaluations are our overall assessment of our capability and worth – our self-confidence – and have been shown to be a strong and reliable predictor of successful careers and life satisfaction. CSE comprises four aspects (again with equally catchy names): locus of control, self-efficacy, self-esteem and neuroticism. Chapter 1 addressed how we can feel more in control (locus of control), and the beginning of this chapter explained how we can manage our emotions (neuroticism) better. So, in this section, I'll focus on the missing elements: self-efficacy and self-esteem.

Building self-esteem

If self-efficacy is all about a person's belief in their ability to do things, self-esteem is their evaluation of themselves. Self-esteem is pretty judgemental. Our self-esteem is based on purely emotive, positive and negative assessments of our value; are we good or bad, worthy or worthless?

Self-esteem is really important in the fight against busy. People with a strong self-esteem are more comfortable charting their own course, confident in their convictions and trusting their own judgement. As a result they are more able to sit back from the flurry and ask the question 'What is the best thing to focus on right now?' rather than 'What are all the things I need to do now?' In addition, they are more likely to stand up for their beliefs, such as the need for thinking time, or that holidays are sacred, email-free periods. People with strong self-esteem expend less energy and intellectual horsepower worrying and feeling guilty, leaving them able to think better and do faster. Finally, those with strong self-esteem tend to suffer less from constantly trying to keep others happy. The ability to feel good about yourself, independent of constant reassurance, makes it a lot easier to disengage from the treadmill of reactivity in which we seek constant reassurance of our worth by keeping everyone happy. Keeping everyone happy comes at a cost: you never do anything of import, never bring your values to life, never really succeed. Without self-esteem it's hard to move beyond a preventative mindset.

Feeling you are 'enough'

We don't build self-esteem by becoming some kind of superhuman, perfect being. In fact, self-esteem normally builds by loosening the image of the ideal self a bit. Brené Brown, the Social Work Research Professor at the University of Houston, has spent the past decade studying vulnerability, courage, worthiness and shame. She was intrigued by the difference between people with low feelings of worth and those with strong self-esteem. One of the big factors she found was courage, but not in the traditional sense. Courage, as she defines it, is closer to the original meaning when the word entered the English language. Then, it meant the ability to tell your story with your whole heart, warts and all. In Brown's definition it means the willingness to be imperfect, and the ability to accept one's own imperfection as being enough[13].

Brené Brown, in her wonderful TED talk, explains that there are three behaviours that result from a lack of self-worth. While she applies this to our relationships, I think all three are also directly relevant to busyness.

1. Perfection
When we don't feel worthy we strive for perfection. We try to perfect our children, we try to perfect our bodies, we try and perfect our lives. In the working world, we place unrealistic expectations of perfection on ourselves. Since perfection isn't possible, something has to give. For the unworthy person, the biggest fear is the shame of being found out by another person. As a result, they are driven to build an appearance of perfection through doing everything, for everyone. What has to give is everything behind the scenes: everything we hold to be dear ourselves, everything we believe will make the biggest impact on our organisations.

2. Pretending
We pretend our actions don't impact on others too much. We actively blind ourselves to the influence of our busyness on those around us, on our loved ones. We wrap ourselves in stories about how 'It will be better when . . . ', but even if we fool ourselves, those we cherish remain unconvinced.

3. Invulnerability
We numb ourselves to feelings of vulnerability to protect our unworthy selves from shame and harm. We close off feelings of vulnerability, and we avoid situations where we are vulnerable. We put on our armour to defend ourselves. We adopt a prevention strategy. The problem is, from an emotional point of view, Brown found that when we numb ourselves to vulnerability, we also numb all other emotions. In other words, without the willingness to be imperfect and vulnerable, we cannot fully experience joy and love. In the workplace, without the willingness to be vulnerable, we cannot go beyond the mundane by taking risks and differentiating ourselves. We fade to grey.

It's a funny thing to think that we build self-esteem, not by becoming perfect, but by accepting our imperfection; by accepting our failings, and by opening ourselves to risk. We don't have to lose 20lbs or gain that Master's degree or be promoted to boost our self-worth.

In fact, those things are unlikely to cause much more than a temporary boost to our self-esteem. We are flawed, all of us. Confidence stems not from fixing the flaws, but from accepting them, recognising that they are an essential aspect of your 'you-ness'.

What are your flaws? How can you be okay with them? How can you genuinely feel you are 'enough'?

Disorder: a little experiment

Think how many times you were told to eat all your dinner or put all your toys away as a child. We learn empty plate and tidy room equals good; dirty plate, messy room equals bad. We learn to protect ourselves through displays of perfection. By getting to zero emails, zero tasks in the to-do list and a tidy desk we show the world how perfect we are (so they don't notice our inner sense of imperfection).

In attempting to build your self-esteem, how about some playful experiments to see how it feels, and to see if the sky falls down? How about playing with being imperfect and vulnerable; with not getting to zero? How about practising being deliberately imperfect in all walks of life? Why not start leaving food on your plate? Or play a game to see how many unopened emails you can have at the end of each day, or how many meetings you can miss a week? Or throw away the to-do list, on the basis that you'll remember the important stuff anyway? Let go of some of your 'essential tools' that help you get to zero: 'forget' your smartphone for a week and leave your laptop at work. I'm not necessarily suggesting these are the right strategies in the long term, but if you're addicted to displays of perfection, a bit of playful detoxing might help you to recognise that your self-esteem can survive in the face of your imperfection.

How could you practise disorder today?

Identify core beliefs to change them

Imagine how confusing the world must be to a baby. In fact, babies don't even know where they stop and the world starts when they are very young. It's only after lots of flapping and lots of bangs that they realise that that thing down there is their leg, and that it continues all the way down to somewhere around their big toe. You might think of babies and young children as scientists. They are constantly coming up with hypotheses for why things happen and testing them. Slowly, over time, their theories for why things happen become more sophisticated and accurate. As they do, the child can start becoming ever more effective and independent.

Now stop and think for a moment about how many theories a baby needs to develop in order to understand our world: everything from why some things hurt when we kick them through to why does their mother sometimes come as soon as they start crying, but takes ages to come at other times (I must have been bad). Over time these theories are buried deep in our heads; we don't really talk about them; in fact, most of the time we're not even aware of them. But whether or not we are aware of them, we operate as though they are truths.

Cognitive behaviourists call these theories 'schemas'. This all works well as long as our schemas are pretty accurate and helpful. However, not surprisingly, most of us have some pretty unhelpful schemas which contribute to feelings of low self-esteem. These schemas explain to ourselves why we are not enough. For most of us, these can just lead to a little anxiety or ineffectiveness; but unhelpful schemas can also lead to severe anxiety and depression. Cognitive behavioural therapy (CBT) helps people to identify and reframe their unhelpful schemas so they feel more worthy; they can then begin to merge their ideal and real selves – and it works.

The following exercise is based on CBT. It's called a thought diary[14].

> *Over the period of a couple of weeks, capture your thoughts about sig-nificant experiences. Firstly, write the details of a situation, describing what happened. Next, describe honestly your reactions, your feelings and your response to the situation. Finally, identify why you felt and acted that way. What were your underlying beliefs and assumptions?*

What you will notice is that patterns will start to appear among your reactions and the core beliefs (or schemas) that drive them. Your job is not to change these schemas fundamentally, just to loosen their grip on you, to make them less disruptive. A classic example of this would be a belief that 'to be a good person, I should keep everyone happy'. You can imagine how unhelpful this belief can be (especially in a world of too much). If you had such a schema, you wouldn't want to move to 'I do my own thing no matter what other people want from me'; more probably you'd try to soften it to 'It's important to be nice to people, but I can't and shouldn't try to always keep everyone happy'. If we can loosen our schemas to allow for our imperfections, we can start to build our self-esteem.

Three good things

In Chapter 9 I introduced Seligman's 'Three Good Things' exercise. A slightly adapted version works really well for building self-esteem too. This shouldn't be a surprise since the activity is designed to improve our internal stories, and self-esteem is all about the stories we tell ourselves about our actions, our abilities and our worth. What does the adapted version look like?

Again, each night before you go to bed, take a notebook and write three things. This time, though, ask a more specific question. Instead of asking 'What went well today?' you ask 'What did I do well today?', or, if you're feeling a little wild, 'How was I great today?'. Repeat this exercise daily for 30 days, and you'll experience a tangible shift in your self-esteem.

Self-efficacy

In the last three lines of a poem called 'The Road Not Taken', the author Robert Frost writes about reaching a fork in the road and choosing to take the path 'less travelled' with profound consequences. I love this poem. It speaks to me of moments clothed in deep contemplation of the inconsequential; bent grass, untrodden leaves and two paths. I reflect on the choice of roads: trivial, yet, through sequence and consequence, momentous. It makes me pause in wonder at the infinite possibilities I decline each day, and the freak of fate that led me here: the one path I actually chose. It makes me ask myself how often I take the one less travelled by ... because I know it will make all the difference.

Frost's poem could be considered to be a meditation on living life on the front foot; on choosing paths less trodden, knowing they will make a difference rather than following the norm. To have the confidence to step out on different paths takes self-efficacy; without it, our good intentions may gain no momentum at all, as the next experiment shows.

At a university 155 undergraduates who were all regular smokers were given four short academic papers[15]. Each one contained a convincing argument backed up with evidence and research citations. These four papers were on the following topics:

1　Just how bad is it if you develop lung cancer? (Severity)
2　What are the risks of developing lung cancer if you're a smoker? (Probability)
3　What does it do to your risk if you give up smoking while still young? (Effectiveness)
4　How successful are most students at giving up smoking? (Self-efficacy)

Each person was given one of two possible versions of each paper. So, for example, in the case of paper number one, a person could receive a version giving a fairly unpleasant and graphic account of the disease, or one (based on fabricated evidence) that explained that lung cancer wasn't so bad really.

The same options were available for each of the four papers. This allowed the psychologists to assess which factors would most influence people's intention to act. The experiment was designed to test something called Protection Motivation Theory, which states that we are motivated to adopt protective behaviours when we know a consequence of our actions is bad (severity), that this bad outcome is quite likely (probability), and that the protective or coping behaviour will be effective at reducing the risk (effectiveness). The first three academic papers were designed to influence people's views on each of these factors: severity, probability and effectiveness. The final paper was designed to influence judgements of self-efficacy: whether they would succeed on quitting smoking if they chose to.

What was interesting in this study was that, though each of those factors influenced the intention to act, none had so strong an effect as the one on how successful students tend to be at giving up smoking. Those who read the paper explaining that most students were successful, had a boost to their self-efficacy. Even when the papers painted a much less threatening picture, or described the benefits of giving up smoking as marginal, if the person believed they'd be capable of making a change, their intention was influenced. It's as if they thought, 'It might not be that important, but what the heck, I can do it, so why don't I?'.

Self-efficacy increases our likelihood of doing new things – difficult things[16]. Since nearly everything we need to do to move beyond busy will be new and difficult, self-efficacy is critical. Think of your typical day. I'm sure you're working terribly hard. I'm sure you're under a lot of pressure. I'm also sure a bunch of the stuff you fill your day with is probably pretty mundane and unimportant (even though it may be terribly urgent). If, by contrast, you were to start thinking of something you would do if you were to truly focus on what was important to you, which could bring real value to your organisation and really differentiate you, it would almost certainly be 'one less travelled'. When we start to work on the basis of our ideals, when we follow hunches that we feel could drive real innovation, when we do what we feel uniquely positioned to do, we are going off-road. If you want to do something fresh, if you have turned off your autopilot, there is no map: you just have your values as a compass, and your dreams as the stars to guide you.

To step off the path takes a leap of faith. It takes a belief that, even though you don't yet know what challenges you'll face, you hold one thing to be true: you will be able to cope with whatever you encounter. That step takes courage, that step requires belief, and the name of that belief is 'self-efficacy'.

High self-efficacy makes people more willing to take action, especially on new activities. It also has two other relevant benefits in combating busyness. Firstly, those with higher self-efficacy persist longer in the face of difficulties[17]; they fight harder for what they believe to be right. Since busyness is the norm, a healthy dose of self-efficacy can help fight off the forces of frenetic mediocrity. Secondly, those with higher levels of self-efficacy tend to get more engrossed and immersed in their chosen activity and are more likely to experience flow. Experience of deep joy and engagement, as I discussed earlier, is one of the most powerful antidotes to the buzz of busyness.

So, if self-efficacy is so good, how do you go about building it?

Aim at the right goal

If you follow football, more particularly if you have any interest in the English Premier League, you will know of the great history of Liverpool Football Club. Liverpool have won the European Cup (now called the Champions' League) five times (more than any other British club); they won the English League title 18 times, and the FA Cup seven times. Under legendary managers such as Bill Shankly and Bob Paisley in the 1970s and 1980s they were seemingly unbeatable. A few years ago, their previously unassailable record of 18 league titles was overhauled by arch rivals Manchester United.

Speak to any Liverpool fan, and the thing they yearn for, more than Champions' League titles or the FA Cup, is the league title. They want to be dominant domestically again.

Liverpool reached out to our old friend Steve Peters, following his success in cycling, rugby and snooker, to help them regain their former glory[18]. He recognised the burden of history the players and coaching staff were carrying and the weight of expectation from fans, for whom anything less than a league title was disappointing. He realised that the whole organisation was struggling with fear: that it would never live up to its glorious past; that this generation would always be seen as failures. Specifically, Peters realised that the perennial goal of the team, to win the league, was the wrong goal. No matter how hard they tried, how much they developed, the league might still remain out of the team's reach because they had no control over the preparation or spending of their rivals. It was a goal for which they would always be victims (or occasional victors) of circumstance. As a result, year by year, their confidence – and with it their chance of winning the league – was steadily eroding.

Peters realised from his work with other elite athletes that confidence-building goals have to be within the control of the team. Self-efficacy builds via the experience of goal achievement, so goals must be achievable. Peters differentiates dreams from goals. It is okay to work towards, and dream about, winning the league title, but Liverpool shouldn't make it their concrete goal. Instead, they should build their goals around their own performance levels, their own fitness levels. They should simply identify goals that push them, plan how they will deliver them, expect to achieve them, and build confidence in their achievement.

It's your performance that matters, not the outcome

Build your sense of self-efficacy around the quality of your performance, not around the final outcome. I remember, about 12 years ago I had a rude awakening. At the time, I'd been facilitating events for about four years and had a pretty good track record. I was getting good results, people laughed at my jokes and the evaluations were great. Then I did a series of events with a big insurance company. I bombed! Nothing I did seemed to work. The groups didn't want to engage, the conversations were turgid and all my best exercises and gags fell flat. I talked this through with a friend of mine, Andrew Jones, who is also a great coach. He listened to my woeful moans, my excuses and my disappointment. He recognised that, under it all, I'd had my confidence knocked. His advice, which has helped me many times over the years, was to loosen my attachment to the outcomes. As he rightly said, my job was to provide a great content, a great design and great facilitation. However, participants had a role too. It was their choice, as adults, whether they wished to engage or not. This doesn't mean I should let myself 'off the hook'; it simply means, whether an event goes brilliantly or less well I should judge myself and build my confidence around my personal performance.

In what aspects of your life are you basing your confidence around the outcomes, or things beyond your control? How could you refocus on aiming to do a brilliant job yourself, rather than getting a great result?

Confidence to cope with failure

It might feel hard to separate your own performance from the result. If you give a presentation, for example, and people are on their email, bored and unconvinced, it's tough to try to stay positive before your next one! How do we feel confident when we know, no how matter how hard we try, we might fail? The answer is simple, but profound: build your confidence around your ability to cope with whatever happens. As I mentioned earlier, we are remarkable at synthesising happiness no matter what, we are great at coping with reality (but terrible at churning over future possibilities and risks). So trust in your capacity to deal with whatever happens; you will be okay. If you walk into a presentation, confident that you are prepared, confident that you will do your best and confident that, no matter what response you get you will be able to cope; you have developed strong self-efficacy.

Modelling

Around 75,000 years ago something dramatic happened. All of a sudden, human cultural evolution started developing rapidly and it has been accelerating ever since. Neuroscientist Vilayanur Ramachandran believes the explanation for this transformation is the arrival of 'mirror' neurons[19].

Mirror neurons were discovered in a lab in Parma, Italy, when Giacomo Rizzolatti and his colleagues were studying macaque monkeys. They happened to have a monkey wired to electrodes (poor thing) when someone in the lab shelled a nut. The electrodes fired. On further study, they realised that when a monkey watched someone else shell a nut, parts of its brain were firing just as if the monkey had shelled the nut itself.

It turns out that when I watch you do something, my neurons fire as if I were doing that thing myself. They don't fire to quite the same intensity as when I do it myself – only 20 per cent of the intensity, in fact – but they fire up. It's as if I'm mentally imitating you. This is the work of the mirror neurons, and they are believed to help us get better at predicting the intentions of others, almost to get inside their minds and bodies, to rapidly identify if they were friend or foe.

One of the huge benefits of mirror neurons is that we can learn really well through observation. Our ancestors, 75,000 years ago, suddenly realised they didn't have to work out every action, every skill, from base principles via trial and error. If someone learned something, it could be efficiently copied by others and therefore saved, culturally.

We can build self-efficacy in a similar manner, through observation. We do know, however, that learning is more effective when the person being observed is similar to the observer. For example, in one study of people with a phobia, subjects' self-efficacy improved most when they observed a fellow phobic struggle with, and overcome their phobia. If the observed person succeeded too easily, or they had no phobia in the first place, there was much less of an impact on the self-efficacy of the observer.

Who could you observe and learn from? Who would be a great role model for you – someone who is still grappling with busyness, but seems to have more confidence in how they respond?

Practice makes perfect

The most reliable and powerful way to build self-efficacy is through doing things, and through succeeding (which also builds self-esteem). When we achieve things and overcome obstacles we build an enhanced sense of capability, a feeling of mastery which increases our self-efficacy. It has been shown that self-efficacy on specific tasks tends to spread out and boost confidence in other areas of your life too, especially those that have some similarity to the task you nailed.

Start small: experiment with an activity that is meaningful to you. It may be something which you have been putting off (because you're terribly busy); or it may be a change in habit, such as only checking email periodically, which you feel is a risk. Whatever it is, start small with little experiments. As you start to achieve success, you'll start to feel your commitment and your self-efficacy grow.

What small step could you take to start building self-efficacy?

Push the edge

Much of our busy behaviour is about filling the gaps left from not doing the things that daunt you. We carry big, impactful things that we know we should or could do; they would give us pride and deliver lasting value, but they're hard and a little scary. I mentioned one of the things holding us back is our obsession with immediate outcomes such as achievement and success. Maybe, in some areas, we need to accept that we will be rubbish at first; we have to start some-where after all. It is only through repeated practice that we'll learn and develop confidence. If we approach some of these tasks with the mindset that we are just 'practising', we can suddenly feel liberated to try new things, big things. When we practise, we learn; we grow.

As we practise and learn, our self-efficacy grows and we build momentum. In very specific tasks, the more we practise, the more confidence we build. When it comes to self-efficacy around busyness – the confidence to be different and to differentiate ourselves through high-level impact and insight, rather than low-level activity – we build that sense of confidence through pushing ourselves, and deliberately and intentionally stretching our capabilities. This is what George Leonard the aikido expert calls 'playing the edge' or testing where the edges of your capability are. As Peter Drucker, the management guru, once said, 'The better a man is, the more mistakes he will make, for the more new things he will try'[20]. If you're not making enough mistakes then you're not trying enough new things which means you're not going to differentiate yourself and you're ultimately not growing your self-efficacy.

What could you practice today?

The big messages in 'On the front foot'

Our world of too much isn't just about too much demand and too much information; it's also about **too much uncertainty. This insecurity can breed fear and anxiety.**

There are two broad strategies we adopt to manage our emotions and behaviour: **prevention** and **promotion** – avoiding bad things happening; or making good things happen.

To create momentum, we need to adopt a **promotion strategy** which will allow us to become **masters of our busy environment.**

MANAGE NEGATIVE EMOTIONS

- Learning to manage our emotions is a critical first step in moving to a **promotion strategy.**
- Our emotions are like an **unruly Chimp. You can't change the Chimp,** but you are **responsible for managing it.**

- **Reappraisal** is a powerful way to manage your emotions. You can reappraise by reinterpreting events or deliberately regaining perspective.

CONFIDENCE

- To move to a less defensive, more positive approach requires confidence. To build confidence you need to work on your **self-esteem** and **self-efficacy**.
- **Low self-esteem** makes us poorer judges of the best focus of our attention, focusing on keeping everyone happy all of the time, and **trapping us in a prevention mindset**.
- According to Brené Brown, we mask low self-esteem with **perfection, pretend** our actions don't really affect others and build up our **defences** – all three of which perpetuate busyness.
- Have the **courage to be imperfect, vulnerable**, and to make **mistakes** – all three things we need to move beyond busyness.
- High self-efficacy makes you more able to take the '**road less travelled**' – it increases your belief, lets you persist longer in the face of challenges, and you experience more flow.
- We build self-efficacy through '**mastery' experiences**, so practise trying things and succeeding.
- Build your **confidence based on personal performance**, not on outcomes.
- When you're **confident you will be able to cope no matter what**; you will have self-efficacy.
- We learn through observation, so pick a busy-busting **role model**.

Go-Do

KEEP A DIARY

Develop a habit of capturing reflections at the end of your day to boost your self-esteem. Use a version of Seligman's 'Three Good Things' by writing about three things you did really well that day.

THE RIGHT GOALS

Set yourself goals for things that are important to you; but make sure they are concrete goals that are within your control, more focused on how you perform than the uncontrollable outcome.

Experiment

REAPPRAISE

Practise dealing with negative emotions by reinterpreting their meaning. Notice when your emotions fire up and deliberately re-interpret the situation.

DISORDER

Play with being deliberately imperfect, get comfortable with imperfection as a way of building self-esteem by recognising that your worth isn't dependent on perfection.

PUSH THE EDGE

Deliberately adopt a practice and learning mentality in the way you attempt to move beyond busy: try new things, see what works and move forward.

Chapter 11

Make good intentions stick

On a bitterly cold morning in 1916, Floyd and Glenn Cunningham arrived at their schoolhouse in rural Kansas. There was no one at school yet so, like most days, the two boys went to the stove, soaked the wood in kerosene (so it caught more easily) and lit the fire. Unfortunately, by mistake, someone had put gasoline in the can rather than kerosene. The resulting explosion and fire killed 13-year-old Floyd. His younger brother, Glenn, woke up in the hospital a few days later, screaming in pain: his lower body had been ravaged by flames. At first the doctors believed he would die. He survived, but needed to have his legs amputated: his skin had been burned away, he had lost all his toes on his left foot and his right leg was so deformed by the fire it had become two inches shorter. Glenn, however, had other ideas. He screamed so loud and so persistently, they decided to let him try to cope with his tattered legs[1].

Bringing life back into his legs would not be easy. He needed horrific stretching exercises and massages, which in his words 'Hurt like hell'. Most young children would have given up, but he was determined to walk again. When his father grew tired from administering the painful stretches and massages, he asked his mother to take over, then when she tired, he continued himself.

In 1919 his mother wheeled him outside only to return and find him on his knees. She rushed to help, assuming a problem, but was brushed aside as he crawled to the picket fence. Stake by stake he clambered along the wall, willing his legs to move. Over the coming months, he worked so hard along that fence that he wore a path in the grass.

After many months of this self-inflicted ordeal, to the astonishment of everyone, Glenn took his first unaided steps for years. He recalls how painful it was. Bizarrely he found it hurt less if he did a kind of hopping and running step. So that's what he did. For the next six years pretty much every step he took was running.

Six years after the accident, not only was he running, he was outrunning everyone in the town (even though it was still uncomfortable to walk). True to form, though, Glenn didn't stop there, he continued pushing himself. Over the following years he became one of the greatest middle-distance American runners of all time, setting the world record for the mile, 800m and the indoor mile.

Glenn Cunningham achieved amazing things because he persisted. He knew what he wanted and he kept pushing for it. It was hard; his injuries bothered him for a decade, but he willed his body back onto its feet, he willed himself to become the best. I like this story because teaching himself to walk again wasn't a one-off challenge he faced. It was a long-term struggle. I can only imagine how many days he woke up not in the mood for the difficulties facing him that day. At so many points in his journey he could have settled for something less than he dreamed of, but much easier to achieve. At many points those around him believed he should accept his lot. Yet he pushed on.

The challenge with busy is not a one-off change either, it's a long-term struggle. There is nothing in this book that, if you do it, will flick the switch onto a better life. It takes work, persistence and, at time, defying those around you. To walk, or run, your own path, to move beyond busy is most certainly not the easy route. You could settle for less, you could accept busy; I just encourage you not to.

The truth is that, each and every day, we mess our lives up a little bit by not making the changes we know will make a difference to us, our businesses and our loved ones. We have good intentions, but, somehow, we fail to follow through on them. Think about your own life for a second: how many times have you 'decided' to do something different? How many New Year's resolutions have you broken? In his book, *Change Anything*, Kerry Patterson claims that 98 per cent of us fail to break bad habits despite wanting to; and 95 per cent of our attempts to diet are unsuccessful[2]. What I find curious is not that we don't follow through on our intentions; it's that we don't *learn*. We still seem to believe that if we know something, and decide something, and are sufficiently motivated, we will change.

We are wrong.

It is certainly possible to modify behaviour; it just takes more than good intentions. Fortunately, we now know a lot about how people respond to change, and what those who are successful at making alterations do differently to us mere mortals. This chapter will share that knowledge; it will share practical and efficient strategies –'tricks of the trade' – for building the momentum to get you started on the path to changing your behaviour. It will then explore willpower – how it works, how it is affected by busyness, and how to strengthen it. Finally, it will look at how to make deep change to those areas of our behaviour which, despite repeated efforts, stubbornly resist change.

This chapter is devoted to one thing and one thing only: helping you to do what you want to do. You may have enjoyed this book; it may even have inspired you to make changes; all that means little, unless you actually change something as a result.

So the question is . . .

What are you going to change?

Given the challenges of making changes, I suggest that you only choose one thing to focus on at a time, one big change you want to make to give your efforts a focus. You can then use all the suggestions in this chapter to increase your chances of success.

So, **STOP!** Pause from ploughing on with your reading.

Take a break from being the audience; get out of the role of the person being stimulated with ideas – and into a more active state, of someone with agency who will make things happen.

Get a pen and paper and spend a few minutes reflecting on what you really want to change. Is your priority to regain a sense of mastery over your life again? Do you want to build a feeling of control; be more effective at prioritising and making choices (and especially at un-choosing things); overcome the fear and anxiety that is holding you captive to busyness; or build the self-efficacy and self-esteem to have the confidence to chart your own path?

Alternatively it may be more about your performance at work. You may recognise that you have been using busyness as a brand, and acknowledge that you are rapidly heading towards the background, fading to grey – one of the crowd. You may want to develop a coherent and differentiating strategy and bring real focus to bear on key business challenges. You may recognise that you could think a lot better, and want to build working disciplines to allow you to get more out of the couple of pounds of blobby matter between your ears. Or you may be determined to make more of an impact, delivering real change and, in the process, capturing the attention of the business.

Then again, you may want to reconnect with your personal life, to dive back into those things and relationships that will nourish you most. You may want to reframe how you think about success, redefining it in a way that drives you towards what really matters to you, not towards a barren and vacuous goal. You may want to smile again, to feel more joyous and present. Or you may want to re-engage with those people whose love and wellbeing are most important to you.

Whatever you want to focus on, you will find this chapter infinitely more useful if you read it with a clear idea of the specific behaviour you want to change.

Building momentum

How long do your good intentions last? Whenever we go on a training course, or read a book and finish with good intentions, how long will those intentions remain strong – awaiting some action or impetus? Over my career I have worked with tens of thousands of people, thousands of teams, hundreds of organisations, and I see a clear pattern. Unless action rapidly follows good intention, the intention quickly dissipates. I have come to call this the half-life of change. The way I explain it on events is that the likelihood of anyone following through on the good intentions they currently have will drop by 50 per cent within seven days. It will drop by a further 50 per cent over the following week, and so on. I have never empirically established these statistics; they just seem descriptive of my own observations. Whatever the exact figures, the principle certainly holds true: if you genuinely intend to do things as a result of reading this book, if you intend to move your life beyond the psychic prison of busyness, then act quickly – even do something today; if you don't build the momentum of change, your resolve will dissipate fast, blown away on the winds of too much.

This section will give you the practical and efficient suggestions you need to help you build the momentum to move beyond good intentions, and make changes. It's all about initiating forward motion. It doesn't matter how fast you go at first; just get going and keep that momentum.

Make your goals clear

One way to avoid the inertia that follows good intentions is to make your goals for change as clear as possible. The benefits of doing this were demonstrated by Steve Booth-Butterfield and Bill Reger, professors at West Virginia University, when they were thinking of an effective way to persuade people to eat more healthily. They looked at how they might simplify and clarify the message. They identified that if the average American switched from whole milk to 1 per cent milk, their diet would immediately attain the USDA recommended levels for saturated fats. So they focused on creating a single, specific behavioural shift in a specific context: they told people that when they were in the grocery store, they should buy 1 per cent milk rather than whole milk. The clarity of this message worked like magic: market share for 1 per cent milk doubled and, as a result, people dramatically changed their saturated fat consumption[3].

The principle of clarity works on ourselves too. Saying we want to have more impact at work is like saying we want to eat more healthily. It's a broad and relatively ill-defined goal. To move forward you have to get to the clarity of the 1 per cent milk example. What is the specific behaviour that you feel, if adopted regularly, will drive this change? What is the context in which that behaviour will happen? Is it switching off your email notifier all morning at work; is it persistently practising Plan-B thinking on all projects; or is it 'thin-slicing' the big stuff at work first thing each day? Getting clear about the specific behaviour, and the context required, to achieve your goal makes it a lot more likely you'll be successful.

Writing the goal

I do this exercise with clients to help them get really clear about their core goal, and I suggest you do this too. Firstly, take a blank sheet of paper and start writing about your goal. Make no attempt to be succinct, inspirational or even clear. Do not edit yourself as you do this, just write and try to be complete. Capture all aspects of the goal that spring to mind. Once you are confident you have captured it all, stop and reread it.

Now rewrite your goal a second time in a more focused manner. Be more succinct in your language and more focused on the key areas. Importantly, also be explicit about the context in which this change will happen. This is your goal.

Once you have done this, do it a third time. This time, write it in less than nine words. Capture the very essence of the change you want to make. Use words that resonate with you, that mean something. When you have this, it will become your mantra, the thing that you can hold easily in mind. The longer goal that you wrote is still useful and you can refer to it regularly, but it is the mantra that will really shift your attention onto your change efforts. Find ways of reminding yourself of your mantra regularly.

What's your '1 per cent milk'?

Keep it really small

Sometimes it can help to start really small. Robert Cialdini, the leading expert in the psychology of influence, had his researchers go door to door to collect money for the American Cancer Society. One group of researchers asked 'Would you be willing to help by making a donation?' The other researchers asked the same question, but followed their request with 'Even a penny will help'. Of those asked by the first group of researchers, 29 per cent donated money. Of the latter group, 50 per cent donated. The extra 'Even a penny . . .' almost doubled the likelihood of donating, but made no change to the average size of the donation as compared to those who donated without the 'Even a penny . . .' addition. It simply increased the likelihood of triggering action[4].

The first step towards change can often be the most important, so take that step, even if it's really small. It will help you build momentum.

Plan your next step

So, what next? How do you turn the first step into momentum? The clue comes from Howard Leventhal's seminal study into mobilising action. Leventhal and his colleagues wanted to persuade more students to go and get vaccinated for tetanus. They showed graphic pictures and lectured students on the consequences of tetanus and how easily it could be contracted. Their efforts had a powerful effect on the beliefs of the students: most were totally sold on the danger of tetanus and the value of getting vaccination, but only 3 per cent actually got that vaccination.

In a follow-up, Leventhal added something to the persuasion tactics: he included a simple map of the campus, with the health clinic and its opening hours highlighted, and the recommendation that they make an appointment[5]. The lectures and pictures were the same. However, the addition of this simple map, explaining the next step, increased the number of students getting vaccinated by more than nine times to 28 per cent. This was despite the fact that all the students knew very well where the clinic was!

The fact is that, especially when we're busy, if we have to do more than one thing at a time we can get distracted away from our intention. In this case, those without the map had to decide if they wanted to go, and what to do next. Those with the map only had to decide if they wanted the vaccination; the next step was super clear. David Allen suggests that a goal isn't enough for any project, or, in this case, change intention: what we need to do is identify the very next step. Mostly these next steps will be incredibly small and easy, but cumulatively they can add up to a huge change. So, no matter how big the change, to turn movement into momentum we must always be clear of the very next step.

Willpower

Surely all these steps to build momentum aren't necessary, you may be thinking; all I need is my willpower. Wrong. The more psychologists explore the topic of willpower, the more we realise how weak most of us are at resisting temptation. This is a problem, since we are exposed to a lot of temptations in a world of too much; each and every one of those could throw you off track from your desired change.

Wilhelm Hofmann and colleagues monitored a group of more than 200 men and women in Germany[6]. They all wore beepers which went off at random. On hearing the beep, each participant had to record whether or not they were in the grip of a desire or temptation at that precise moment or not. They found that these people spent about 25 per cent of their waking hours actively resisting temptations. These temptations ranged from desires for food, sleep or sex to more modern desires such as checking email, surfing the web, watching TV etc. On the whole, they were pretty good at resisting the temptations for sex or food. They were less successful when it came to the internet, TV or checking in on email: they failed to resist 50 per cent of all desires in those areas. It turns out that the attractions of busyness – the appeal of too much information, stimulation and communication – are very hard for us to resist; against our will we succumb to our desire for a quick fix of stimulation, a quick glance at the phone.

Self-control, our ability to resist temptation, has been shown consistently to be one of the biggest predictors of success at school and at work, in sport and in marriage, and in life satisfaction. People with higher levels of willpower achieve more, connect more and live more. I would argue that people with stronger willpower will be more able to make the right choices when faced with information overload, will resist the multitude of technological temptations, and focus on delivering real value. People with strong willpower will be able to make the changes to move beyond busyness.

Willpower is worth building. Here's how.

What reduces willpower?

Before starting work on building willpower, it's necessary to understand what reduces it. Imagine you have been fasting and you walk into a room full of the smell of freshly baked chocolate-chip cookies. This was the situation facing subjects at the start of Baumeister's 'Cookies and Radishes' study; one of the classic psychology experiments of all time. Participants sat at a table containing cookies, chocolate and radishes. Some students were invited to eat the chocolate and cookies; the others were told they must eat the radishes[7].

The experimenter left the room, leaving the students to their treats and temptation. The radish subjects were clearly tempted, but none succumbed; they dutifully ate the radishes. When the experimenter returned, everyone was told they would now do a second, unrelated activity. They were given logical problems to solve – with a wicked twist: the problems were unsolvable. What Baumeister was interested in was how long the participants would persist in trying to solve these problems. Those in the radishes group lasted about nine minutes before giving up. Those who had eaten cookies lasted 19 minutes!

This study was one of the first to demonstrate *ego depletion*. Those who had resisted the cookies had used up a lot of their willpower already, so they had smaller reserves to draw on to persist with the logic challenges. The cookies group, on the other hand, had resisted no temptation, so were fresh to face the puzzles and lasted longer. What this experiment shows, as do numerous others, is that we have only a finite amount of willpower, and we use this same stock of willpower for lots of stuff. We are said to be 'ego depleted' when we have used a substantial amount of our willpower, and become more vulnerable to new temptations.

However, ego depletion doesn't just reduce your ability to *resist* temptation; it also increases the degree to which you *feel* temptation. Working with Kathleen Vohs, Baumeister showed that ego-depleted people reacted more strongly to all kinds of things: sad movies made them extra sad; happy pictures made them unusually happy; cold water felt more painful to them than normal; they felt stronger cravings for cookies; they were sparked to extreme emotion more readily. Ego depletion then is double-trouble: you experience stronger urges, and you have less strength to resist.

Ego depletion and busyness

Modern organisations take ego depletion to the next level. We have to do more thinking, make more decisions, cope with more pressure and maintain a superhuman work rate. Work approaches us from every direction, all the time. There is little time when we are not at full-speed ahead. Even when we do have time, we fill it with more activity, which does little to restore the brain's cognitive capacities or fire up the default network, as we discussed earlier. We become tired, stretched and ego depleted. In fact, I think ego depletion is pretty much the default state in most organisations; busy means ego depleted.

So, while in a calm moment, we might agree that we spend too much time playing about on Facebook, or sending IMs, we may still fail to resist the pull of the ping. When we try to work on the bigger, more important areas, we have less willpower to persist, so we distract ourselves or allow ourselves to be interrupted (and tell ourselves that this is okay because we're being available and responsive). Ego depletion stops us from achieving what we're capable of, and it prevents us from living up to our expectations and dreams. When we're ego depleted we don't have the strength to bring the full force of our attention and willpower to bear where it will make the most difference.

Willpower strengthening

Australian psychologists Meg Oaten and Ken Cheng were interested in what might help strengthen people's willpower. They recruited people who desired to make a change in an aspect of their lives: getting fit[8], improving study habits[9] or managing their money better[10]. In each case they had some input from an instructor; they had to complete certain tasks (such as going to the gym); and they had to maintain a log to track their progress.

At various points in the process, participants had to come into the lab for some seemingly irrelevant tests. They had a visual test of attention to perform. The challenge was that, while doing the test, a video of a stand-up comic routine was playing on TV. If participants got distracted by the TV, they would perform less well in the test. Each time they came to the lab, they did this test twice. After the first test, the subjects performed a variety of activities designed to exercise willpower and result in ego depletion before performing the second visual test.

As the weeks went by, the people who were regularly exercising their self-control through exercise, studying or money management got better at resisting the temptation of the comedy routine. In particular, their performance in the second (ego-depleted) test got much better. There was an additional, and welcome, surprise from this study. The improvement in willpower started spreading to other areas of the participants' lives: those on the exercise programme, for example, started spending less, studying better, smoking less, keeping their homes cleaner and procrastinating less.

This study shows three things:

- Even though willpower is finite and reduces as we use it each day, deliberately practising willpower can strengthen it over time.
- There are two aspects of willpower: strength and stamina. Strength is the absolute ability to resist temptation. Stamina is our ability to withstand the effects of ego depletion: we can experience more temptation before we become depleted. Exercises in willpower are particularly effective at increasing our stamina (not our strength).
- Working on our willpower in one aspect of our lives will positively affect other areas of our lives; in the same way, ego depletion in one area infects other areas too.

A programme to strengthen willpower

So, all is not lost! Our willpower is horribly weak, but we can strengthen it, support it and cajole it to help us make sustainable changes. The rest of this chapter will outline research-based techniques to help you do exactly that in order to makes the changes you want and move beyond busyness.

Use social influence

I talked in Chapter 6 about the power of social influence on our decisions; we can use this to good effect to keep us focused on our efforts to change. In a lovely little study at Newcastle University[11], researchers demonstrated how feeling that you are being watched can influence behaviour for the good. In the campus kitchen they had tea and coffee available. Employees were expected to pay for their drinks, and so an honesty box was left, clearly labelled, with recommended prices listed. For 10 weeks, researchers placed images above the prices, giving no explanation. Every week the image changed. The images were either of eyes, which appeared to be looking at the person making their drink, or of flowers. No one commented on the images; no one asked about their significance. When the money in the honesty box was counted at the end of each week, the difference was dramatic. In the weeks when flowers were shown, the average contribution made per litre of milk was 15p. In the weeks that the eyes were displayed, that figure more than quadrupled to 70p.

Many studies have shown that we are more likely to act in a desirable manner when we are being watched, and we can harness this fact to increase our willpower. Choose an area of your life that matters to you. I would suggest that, in the context of this chapter, you pick the change you identified at the start of the chapter. What's most important is that you are intentional, not just about making progress on your change, but also about building the strength and stamina of your willpower. You will find, even though you are focused on just one area, that your ability to resist ego depletion, and therefore to resist temptation, will spread to other areas of your life.

Step One

- Speak about your change with someone you respect. Depending on the topic, this may be a trained instructor, a work mentor or a friend. Get their advice and support, but, importantly, have them help you to develop a schedule of activity.

Step Two

- Follow the plan, diligently.

Step Three

- Keep a log of your progress, recording what you did when, any challenges to willpower you faced, and how you fared. Also record any observations about your willpower's improvement in other areas of your life.

Step Four

- Review progress regularly with the person you identified in Step One and others who will support you and push you to continue.

It's not rocket science! But it works. In doing this you'll improve in your chosen project, and you'll also increase your general willpower and ability to resist all kinds of temptations and distractions; you'll stay focused better and you'll engage better.

I unwittingly walked into this type of support myself. My sister-in-law Shiv and I had both been talking about writing, and 'working' on our books for ages. At a certain point I started recognising Shiv's excuses for a lack of progress and challenged her, explaining that I thought she was letting herself off too lightly for not progressing with something that was important. Anyway, she finished soon afterwards, and made a reciprocal offer to me: to hold me to account for allowing my 'busyness' to distract me from writing. She asked me to draw up a timetable for chapter completion and if I slipped from my schedule, which I did at times, she came down on me like a ton of bricks. I can't pretend I wasn't irked by some of her chasing, even though I knew it was what we agreed and that she was going out of her way to help me. However, there is no doubt I made a lot more progress as a direct result of trying not to let Shiv down, trying to deliver on my commitments. Shiv, thanks for nagging, it made all of the difference (and I look forward to getting my own back when you start your next book!).

Monitor yourself

Why do male prisoners get fatter in jail? It's unlikely to be because of the rich food, and options for exercise are normally available. Brian Wansink believes it's because they don't wear belts![12] Since they don't have belts or tight-fitting clothes, they are not getting regular feedback on the growth of their girths. One of the simplest and most effective ways we can improve our ability to resist temptation is through regular monitoring.

It appears that one of the purposes of self-awareness is to boost our self-control. Even putting a mirror in front of people changes their behaviour; they tend to act more honestly and diligently. The Quantified Self movement builds on the recognition that monitoring our behaviour helps us to improve. A typical Quantified Self tool will be an app or other piece of software which helps you to monitor and track your behaviour in some way (see a useful list of apps in the Appendix on p.312). RescueTime, for example, is a program that tracks your computer usage. The program has turned up data that the average person uses 16 different computer programs, visits 40 websites and is interrupted every 5.2 minutes by a message every day. The founder, Tony Wright, was depressed to find he spent nearly a third of his day on 'the long tail of information porn' (his words, not mine!): visits to sites not related to his chief work.

There are some brilliant apps out there for monitoring your behaviour, so don't go it alone. Once you are clear on the change you want to make, find an app that will help you track your progress. This can add a bit of fun and gamification to your change efforts, and a number of apps have a social support and peer pressure aspect too. Get measuring; get changing; develop the willpower to move beyond busy.

Develop better habits

In an analysis of many studies into willpower, researchers were interested in determining when self-control was most impactful. They grouped the behaviours recorded in these studies into mainly automatic behaviours and those requiring self-control[13]. They assumed that those with strong willpower would excel in the behaviours needing control, at resisting temptation. Yet, that wasn't what they found. Those with strong willpower had more self-control because of the strength and effectiveness of their automatic behaviours. In other words, strong willpower helps you to set up good habits; it helps you avoid temptation not resist it. Those with a lot of self-control used it to structure their lives in such a way that the automatic behaviour was in line with their goals. They didn't eat healthily by resisting plates of chocolate cake when offered, but by making sure their fridge was only full of healthy, low-fat foods.

This is very true for busyness and the distractions that pull us back into its embrace. These habits are often obvious; the trick is to identify the obvious temptations that are likely to lure you away from your change, and to develop preventative habits. For example, if you want to be more focused, switch off your email pop-up notifier: it's incredibly hard to resist, especially when you are doing hard thinking. Or, if you want to be more present at home, leave your work phone in your work bag. If you must work at night, do it in specific bursts, rather than letting it infect your whole evening and undermine precious time with the family. What you need is not iron willpower, but great habits.

Build new habits

What happens when you get hot? You start sweating and your bloods rushes to the surface of the skin to cool. When you are cold, you start shivering, and your blood is withdrawn from areas where it is likely to lose a lot of heat, such as your skin and toes. The body has an incredibly effective thermostat that regulates our temperature within a very small range. The word for this process of maintaining stability is 'homeostasis'. It's critical for our survival to keep all kinds of internal processes in balance and prevent them from changing.

Habits are great, but they are hard to break. There is a kind of homeostasis that kicks in whenever we try to change our behaviour. We may be able to do things differently, with conscious thought and willpower; this change may last for a few days, even a few weeks, but as soon as our guard slips, as soon as our willpower softens, the forces of homeostasis kick in and we revert to the old path. More than that, homeostasis can be active in pulling us back to normality: the body doesn't just sit and wait for your temperature to drop; it does something: it sweats. So it can be with behaviours too. Take the common example of getting fit. How many of us have tried to get fit, fuelled by loads of great intentions? It could just be me, but it seems as if your brain, your body, and even those around you, actively resist this endeavour. You get aches and pains; you feel old and ridiculous as you lumber down the street; you get an injury; your mates say 'Fancy a pint?' just at the point you decide to go to the gym; your partner starts grumbling at the amount of time you are spending running, or the money the gym membership is costing. These are all the homeostatic forces that seem to appear from nowhere to batter you back into your place.

But homeostasis doesn't always work against you. You only need to fight against homeostasis until you have built a new habit. Once a habit is established you can relax a lot more because homeostasis will help to ensure that this habit continues to happen.

The usual rule of thumb is that new habits take 30–60 days to become established. Clearly this is strongly affected by how frequently the new behaviour is performed; for example, establishing a new habit over email usage, performed daily, would become engrained more quickly than a behaviour that is only going to be performed once a week. However, as a broad principle, for regular, busy-related behaviour, we need to consider investing significant effort in this behaviour change for at least a month.

Slipstreaming habits

If you've ever cycled long distances with a group of people, you'll realise the massive benefit of tucking into the slipstream of the cyclist in front. You seem to get sucked along, facing less resistance and using less effort. We can apply the same principle to establishing new habits. It's much, much easier to build a new habit on the back of an old one, than in isolation. In doing this, the new behaviour seems to get swept along more easily by the automatic motion of the established habit.

This is one of the reasons I think Brian Tracy's simple idea of 'Eat that frog' – which I discussed in Chapter 2 – works so powerfully. This is the idea that, first thing in the morning, before we open email or voicemail, we attack the big and important work that otherwise might get squeezed out by the flurry of too much. In eating frogs, we build on the established rituals that we perform at the start of our day – often some of the strongest in a working day. The early morning rituals have more than strength; they are pure: unbattered by the flak of daily office life. It is much easier to retain choice before formally opening up for business. So, if you make it part of your morning ritual that – along with unpacking your laptop, grabbing a coffee and chatting with Maria – you will spend 30 minutes on big stuff, you can benefit from the morning routine's slipstream.

The slipstream effect works for most new behaviours. If you want to have better conversations with your son, why not build a post-football match routine, or a pre-bedtime chat? If you want to create more time for your default network to be active, don't just think 'I'll create more task-free, stimulation-free time'; rather decide, for example, to do your commute device-free.

Think of the behaviour you want to change; which of your current habits or routines could you slipstream?

(Pre)Commit

In July 1519, the *conquistador* Hernán Cortés landed in Veracruz with 11 ships and 500 men on his mission to conquer the Aztecs. However, Cortés had a problem. A number of years before he had developed romantic relations with Catalina Xuárez, the sister-in-law of Diego Velázquez, the Spanish Governor of Cuba. At the same time, Cortés had also supposedly flirted with Catalina's sister, and Velázquez had been unimpressed. Over the years the relationship between Velázquez and Cortés had soured, despite that fact that Cortés ultimately married Catalina. The problem now facing Cortés was that Velázquez was the ruler in these parts, and, at the last minute, had revoked Cortés's charter. When Cortés set sail he was in open revolt against Velázquez – and Cortés's men knew it.

Cortés was concerned that his men, especially those loyal to the Governor, would be easily persuaded to mutiny against Cortés and return to Cuba. This would be disastrous for Cortés, his mission and, probably, his life. So he strengthened his men's commitment; he sank all of his ships on arrival. Retreat was no longer an option. It left his expeditionary force with only one option: to conquer the Aztecs and return home victorious.

Hernán Cortés's actions are an extreme example of pre-commitment. A pre-commitment recognises the human tendency to make good decisions in a cold, rational state, but in the heat of the moment (or height of battle) to give in to temptation. When faced with the chocolate cake, even though we have good intentions to eat more healthily, we choose instant gratification over our long-term goals. This is a real challenge when trying to overcome busyness, because the instant gratification of opening those emails will overcome your good intentions.

This is true, and you will not be able to change that tendency in yourself. So what can you do?

Reward good behaviour

A starting point to pre-commitment is to use simple behaviourism: our choices are significantly influenced by the rewards we get immediately. When it comes to busyness, even though our long-term rewards are a life of focus and engagement, the immediate rewards of this goal may seem less compelling than the relief of an empty inbox. One client dealt with this head-on. He wanted to bring real focus to a project he was passionate about – one he thought could make a big impact on the business – but which no-one was shouting for. Persistently he would get lured into reactivity by the reward of the ping. He decided to fight fire with fire. Around the corner from his office was his favourite coffee shop, which had a lovely vibe and served a vanilla latte he loved. Instead of going straight to the office he 'treated' himself to 45 minutes every morning in this coffee shop on the condition that he was working on his project. He also never signed up for their Wi-Fi, so he was 'dark' during his time in the coffee shop. After a while he didn't stick to doing this first thing every day; at times he went there at other points in the day, but he always saw it as his project place – a place which rewarded him into change.

Punish yourself

Behaviourism has a flip side: punishment. The principle of immediacy applies here too; again there will be very obvious and pressing negative consequences of not acting on your impulse to be busy: the angst of not completing that report in the evening is enough to prevent you from playing hide and seek with the children; the pressure of a mounting inbox is enough to cause your attention to drift away from the conversation. So how can you counter these immediate short-term consequences with some creative consequences for not completing your long-term goals?

Earlier I mentioned Ian Ayres' StickK.com, where you can sign a contract to pay a forfeit if you slip on your good intentions[14]. I have known families which agreed beforehand to forfeits for not following through on promises. How about this: any time you are seen glancing at your phone during a conversation, it will cost you the washing up! Or fail to 'get around to' that important work, and you'll have to do it during your favourite TV programme, or, of course, donate money to charity. You can be creative with these, but increasing the deterrent might help to keep you on the straight and narrow.

Get back in the saddle

Participants in a study were asked to turn up to a laboratory hungry. On arrival, some people were given nothing; others were give two very large milkshakes, enough to make a person feel very full. They were then taken to the experiment, which they were told was a taste test. They were put in private rooms in front of big plates of cookies and crackers, and asked to rate the flavours. Those who were still hungry ate quite a lot; those who had been filled with the milkshakes nibbled a bit, assessed the taste and left. This is what everyone did – apart from those on diets. They did the opposite! Those who had drunk the giant milkshakes actually ate *more* cookies and crackers than those who hadn't eaten for many hours!

Why? This pattern showed up in repeated experiments and Peter Herman and his colleagues eventually called it 'counterregulatory eating'. I, however, prefer Baumeister's term – the 'what the hell' effect[15]. The dieters, once they'd already blown their diet for the day with the massive milkshakes, lost any willpower. They thought 'What the hell; I've ruined the diet today, so I may as well have fun and start again tomorrow'. The risk is that, tomorrow, the 'what the hell' feeling may be extended a little longer, and a little longer . . . and then the diet is over.

'What the hell' is a dangerous moment for any change effort. Any change involves resisting some form of temptation. We will almost always slip at times, or be 'forced' to act counter to our change plans, like the dieters who were asked to drink the milkshakes. There will always be that urgent call that derails your best intentions, or the project crisis which has you jabbing away at your keyboard through the night. The issue that will determine your long-term success is not whether or not you were 100 per cent true to your change plan, but how quickly and persistently you got back onto the horse after you fell off.

So, don't just choose the change you want to make; come up with a plan for how you will get back on the horse immediately after you fall off.

Imagine you are committed to switching your smartphone off at night, so you can be more present with your family. Accept, right from the start, that you may not be able to follow through on this every night, and prevent the odd slip from killing your momentum by any, or all of the following:

- Every time you do use your phone, send yourself an email, which reminds you to re-commit to your goal, to read in the cold light of the morning.
- Ask your partner to challenge you when they see you using your phone at night. In particular, their job is to ask you this question: 'Okay, so you are letting your goal slip tonight. Will you restart your commitment to phone-free nights tomorrow?'

- Give yourself phone 'jokers'. The idea is to acknowledge in advance that, a few evenings a month, you will want to use the phone. For each of those nights you can play the 'joker' as your permit for a phone night. This tactic builds exceptions into your change effort: the odd night doesn't break momentum – it's part of the pattern.

Deep change

There are times when, despite using what research tells us about change and willpower, certain aspects of our behaviour stubbornly resist our best efforts to make progress. The gravitational pull of homeostasis in these areas is just too strong. I think a lot of us, when it comes to the way we live our lives, might be there right now: we've tried loads of tips and techniques, but remain hopelessly distracted, stretched and disconnected. If you recognise this situation, if the techniques and the reminders aren't working but you remain keen to change, we will have to go deeper. To succeed, it will not be enough to *make* a change; *you* will have to change.

Technical and adaptive problems

There are two fundamentally different kinds of changes we might try to make, or problems we might face. Some of those changes require information, practice and skill development. Ronald Heifetz, a leadership expert, calls these types of changes 'technical problems'[16]. These are not necessarily simple, or unimportant, but there are recognised ways to address them; there are standard routines and processes. Examples of technical problems might range from organising your Outlook better using colour coding and subfolders; completing the Rubik's cube in under a minute; or landing a fighter jet on an aircraft carrier. They might be tough, but with enough learning and practice, you could succeed.

Adaptive problems are a different matter. A problem is considered adaptive if there isn't a correct way to solve it or a proven solution; there isn't an instruction manual. A problem is adaptive if the only way to resolve it is through changing the person with the problem:

their mindset, beliefs and assumptions. Time and again, I see people endlessly seeking 'the solution' to problems they have had for years. They misdiagnose their problem as being a technical one, seek technical solutions, and fail – repeatedly. They don't need to solve the *problem*; they need to change *themselves* in order to progress. A classic example of this is losing weight. On one level it appears to be a straightforward technical problem: just eat less food and exercise more. However, anyone who has persistently grappled with this problem knows the repeated cycle of excitement and despair as they go from diet to diet. The technical solutions seldom work sustainably. What is normally needed is a more adaptive response: a fundamental change to their relationships with food and exercise.

If you think your change is an adaptive challenge (and there is a very good chance it will be), the following section is for you.

Immunity to change

A lot of my work involves helping people to make changes – as individuals, teams or organisations. Technical challenges are easy: you can share tips and techniques with people, and help them to plan a way forward. However, when it becomes clear that deep change is required, this doesn't work. For adaptive challenges, you need to help the problem-owners to get under the surface of the problem and gain real insight into their underlying assumptions and fears.

Now imagine you're coming to meet me in the middle of a busy working day. You've just come out of a bruising forecasting meeting with the director, you've already responded to 212 emails today and you have a big deadline looming tomorrow; then I start asking you about your fears and assumptions! I knew for years I needed to get people talking about the underlying stuff, but not every busy business person wants therapy. Quite frankly, it was often a struggle to get anywhere near people's core issues to help them gain the insights to learn, grow and change. We often ended up identifying superficial, technical plans to address much deeper challenges.

Then I came across the work of Robert Kegan. In his fantastic book *Immunity to Change*[17] he describes a simple process of analysis that gets deep very quickly. I have used it with hundreds and hundreds of people and groups. Whenever I have used it, people are able to get under the surface of their change rapidly to identify hidden assumptions and conflicts; it seems to help even those who are unused to introspection and self-analysis. More importantly, once people have this understanding, they change.

Competing commitments

Before I go on to explain how the process works, I want to explain a core principle of Kegan's thinking: that of 'competing commitments'. There are often very good reasons why we do things as we do today – very compelling reasons for us not to make the change. These reasons don't disappear when we decide we want to make a change. These are our competing commitments. So when we try and make a change, those commitments actively fight against the thing we want to do. Even though the change we want to make will meet certain desires or needs we have, our competing commitments are also servicing needs – often quite deep needs; they will not give up the fight easily. Unless we unearth these competing commitments, we will be fighting blind and, more often than not, our attempts to change will stall.

To bring this to life, I'll share something of my own experience. I mentioned earlier how I procrastinated about writing this book for years, but I didn't tell the whole story. Ever since I left university I talked about writing a book. At various points I have played with getting started, but never made much progress. All this time, I would happily tell people 'I'm going to write a book'. Finally I started researching in earnest about six years ago, but failed to put pen to paper for about four years. During this time I promoted my story to 'I'm working on a book'.

Naturally, when people met up with me they would often ask how my 'book' was coming on. It started to get a little embarrassing! However, I had a story. I explained how I was very 'busy' (yes, I did use *that* word) and I was travelling a lot. So it was simple: if I was to start writing a book, the time to work on the book would come directly out of precious family time. People accepted this; I believed it too. Until one day I decided to take my own medicine: I decided to really think about why I wasn't making any progress on something I'd been talking about for years. I started working through Kegan's process of analysis and quickly realised that my 'story' was an excuse, not a reason. I had a big fear, an unspoken fear, which was fighting against any moves I might make to write. I was scared I might have nothing to say. I was fearful that I might not be able to write. I was petrified I might fail, and as a result, lose my identity as a 'bright bloke who is going to write a book'.

As you might imagine, any of the *technical* solutions I might have tried to help me to manage my time better or prioritise would have had little effect. Until I named my fear and grappled with it directly, I would make little progress. The solutions that put me onto the path to writing this book were not technical. I did nothing to clear my diary, or free up space to write. In fact, the year in which I wrote this book has been the one with the highest workload of my career (independent of the book). The big solution for me was to start writing – publically – and actively seek feedback. I started blogging. By blogging I was practising and experimenting: I was practising writing and getting feedback to see what worked and what didn't; I was experimenting with the possibility that I might be a rubbish writer and have little to say, and that might be okay.

My point in sharing this story is not to pat myself on the back, or make some trite motivational point the way contestants on reality shows do: 'I did it. You can too if you only believe!' My point is far more humble. I'm a psychologist; I do this stuff for a living, and I fooled myself for over a decade over why I wasn't writing. I was convincing myself with half-truths and excuses. Yet, once I had finally accepted that I wanted to understand why I wasn't changing, once I was determined to get under the surface, the truth wasn't that hard to unearth – and the truth changed everything.

Unearthing competing commitments

The heart of Kegan's process for unearthing commitments is very simple. First you identify, at length, the specific things you are doing, or *not* doing, instead of your stated change commitment. So, for example, if your commitment is to focus more on work that you value, you might identify things like 'I say yes to everything'; 'I have my email on all the time'; 'I prioritise on the basis of urgency, not importance', etc. Or, in my case, the list would have started 'I am not writing anything'. Make a list of these. You don't have to interpret anything at this stage, just identify what else you are doing and not doing.

It's the next stage that gets interesting. Go through each of the negative items and imagine what it would feel like if you did the exact opposite – the thing that you are supposed to be doing. Some of the items will elicit little reaction; others will trigger a pronounced feeling – a 'Yuck' effect. When you trigger that worry or discomfort, you're often onto something. Ask yourself 'What is the worry or fear that's causing me to feel this way?' and put a name to it. Then ask 'Therefore, what is the competing commitment I am holding onto which prevents me making the change I am striving for?'

This process can be powerful. A friend of mine went through this exercise. His commitment was to get 'race fit' again, so he could start competing in marathons like he used to. For years he had been frustrated by his lack of progress. Sure, he exercised at times, but it was fairly light and patchy, and he was putting on weight. The items he went through on the list, when he thought about doing the opposite, caused no emotional reaction until he reached 'Go out for gentle runs, not pushing myself'. When he thought about doing the opposite – pushing himself really hard – he felt uncomfortable. Even a day later, when he told me the story, his eyes filled with tears. His deep fear, the fear that was stopping him training, was a fear of getting old. The realisation that had hit him like a sledgehammer was that he was committed to feeling young and vital. Whenever he pushed himself, his body ached and felt old; these times highlighted his physical decline. The very act of doing the thing that would make him feel younger in the long term, made him feel old – and feeling old disgusted him. I am happy to say that he is now running and is also slimmer; he is also competing again.

From my own experience, and from watching others go through this, it is the brutal clarity that this process gives that makes the difference. Once the underlying causes of the lack of progress are laid clear, the path towards your goals can be fairly obvious. It typically involves a process of learning and experimentation, where you play with alternative behaviours. Effectively, you are testing and reframing your catastrophic fears. You are creating different, healthier and more nuanced interpretations of the world. To change you are not simply doing stuff; you are growing and becoming more self-aware.

We all need to do a lot more of this to thrive.

The big messages in 'Make good intentions stick'

Change is hard. All the research shows that **good intentions are not enough**; nor is being motivated to change.

You need to **build the momentum** that will get you started on your path to change, **strengthen your willpower** and address the areas of your behaviour that stubbornly resist change.

BUILDING MOMENTUM

- **Good intentions don't last long**; if you intend to do something, **take action quickly**! It's all about momentum.
- It's easy to get overwhelmed and lapse into inertia. So start building momentum by getting **really clear** about the behaviour you want to change, and the **context** you'll make that change in.
- **Start really small,** build on the fact that we like to be consistent and make the next step for yourself obvious.

WILLPOWER

- To make lasting changes you need willpower. But one thing is almost certain: your **willpower is weaker** than you think it is.
- **Willpower is limited**; it gets used up, leaving us ego depleted and less able to resist further temptations.
- The good news is that you can **strengthen your willpower**. A strengthening of willpower in one area spreads to other aspects of your life.

DEEP CHANGE

- Problems can be **technical or adaptive.** Technical problems have known solutions that require knowledge, skill and practice. **Adaptive problems** don't have known solutions; they involve **personal change**, learning and growth.
- When people are **struggling to change**, after persistent efforts,

it is often because the **problem is adaptive** and they are using technical methods to change.

- To solve an adaptive problem and move forward we have to unearth our **competing commitments**, the behaviours we currently exhibit, which are blocking our change.

Go-Do

START IMMEDIATELY

If you've been inspired to make changes through reading this book, start immediately. What can you do today?

SET A CLEAR GOAL

If you want to change, set a really specific goal. Work on one thing at a time until it is built into your habits

PLAN YOUR NEXT STEP

Always know your next step in the change you are making. Take some time to plan ahead so that you're really clear about what to do next.

CHANGE YOUR ENVIRONMENT

Willpower is weak. Make changes to your physical, social and technological environments to reduce the temptation to stray from your goal.

Experiment

STICKK.COM

Try using this website as a way of establishing pre-commitments.

IMMUNITY TO CHANGE

If you are persistently failing to change in a particular area, buy *Immunity to Change*, a great book by Robert Kegan.

Appendix

Planning for change

In the previous chapter, you worked on setting a clear goal for change. You now have loads of ideas and intentions and you also have a number of change strategies up your sleeve, but how do you bring it all together to drive and direct your attention towards making this change happen?

The best way to do this is by writing a clear plan of action. I find that setting a timeframe of 30 days works best for two reasons:

1 Most new habits can be formed in 30 days
2 You'll learn such a lot during the first 30 days, you will want to write a fresh plan for the next 30 days which incorporates these new discoveries.

The right kit

Remember the study in Chapter 11 about prisoners getting fat because they didn't wear belts? The reason they put on weight in jail was because without belts the prisoners had no way to monitor their expanding waistlines. The same goes for making change happen – by monitoring your behaviour and tracking your progress you increase your chances of achieving your goal. If you prefer to do this with paper and a pen, treat yourself to a lovely new notebook. You'll write down your plan in this, but, importantly, you'll also use it to review your progress towards your change goal on a daily, weekly and monthly basis. Alternatively there are some great apps available to download, many of which take what you can do on paper to another level. Some apps automatically monitor your activity, others incorporate analytical and visual tools to present your progress in a compelling manner, or provide you with support by connecting you with other users who share similar goals. The type of app you require to monitor your progress will vary depending on the goal you have set, but I have included a list of the self-monitoring apps I find most useful below. If you want to explore more options visit www.quantifiedself.com/guide which provides an overview of most of the self-monitoring apps available.

RescueTime	This app will be useful if your goal is to cut down the time you spend surfing the internet or on email. It automatically tracks the time you spend online so that you can easily monitor your progress.
Daytum	This app is useful for measuring progress against almost any change goal as it lets you track pretty much any quantifiable behaviour.
Momento	This nice and simple journal-keeping app will be useful if you like the idea of making your own notes about your progress but would prefer not to carry a notebook around with you.
Goal-Buddy	This app helps you to set goals, identify habits and track activity. It also includes a social support feature which allows others see your progress against your goals and encourage you to keep going.
MoodScope	This app has been designed to track and manage your mood. If your challenge with busy is more emotive, it could be useful in helping you to change your mood and identify the events that influence it.
Equanimity	This app will be useful if your goal is to build your mindfulness as it helps you to time and track your meditation practice.

A daily discipline

As well as consistently monitoring your progress via an app or journal, I also find that a person's progress against a plan is accelerated if they build a time to review their progress against their goal into their daily routine.

A lot of research has shown the value of setting aside a time to reflect at the end of the day and if you're worried about delaying your bedtime, don't be – it doesn't need to be a complicated or lengthy process. All you need is about five minutes at the end of the day to sit, quietly, with your notebook and answer the same three questions:

- What went well today in progressing me towards my goal?
- What can I learn from the day that will be useful to help me achieve my goal?
- What is the next step towards my goal? (Be really specific.)

You should set aside a little longer at the end of the first seven days for a more thorough review of progress. After 30 days, review and realign your plan. This isn't a one-off activity, but a process of learning your way to a better life.

That's really all there is to it; but don't underestimate the power of this simple discipline.

The big mistake

If you saw a man collapse in front of you, in a clearly distressed state, would you stop and help? The answer is that it depends. In a famous experiment, social psychologists John Darley and Daniel Batson ran an experiment with people who might be expected to help: trainee priests. Just before leaving for a lecture, some trainee priests were told they were late, others were told they had plenty of time. The effects were dramatic. Only 10 per cent of the trainee priests who believed they were late stopped to help the collapsed man (who they had no way of knowing was an actor). Of those with more time, 63 per cent stopped!

This is an example of what has become known as the fundamental attribution error. We massively over-estimate the degree to which our behaviour, or that of others, is driven by our values or personality; and we massively underestimate how much it is affected by the environment. The big mistake most people make when putting a change plan together is that they focus a lot on the behaviour or the habit they want to change, but not on the environment that will support their change.

With this in mind, I encourage you to build the following elements into your plan:

- **Social norms**: We are heavily influenced by the behaviour of others, so think about how you can find a way to spend more time with people whose behaviour is aligned to your goal.
- **Context**: Think about how you could change your physical environment to help you support your progress. For example, you could work from a coffee shop instead of the office when you want to concentrate on big problems, undisturbed.
- **Reducing temptation**: Think about how you could structure your environment to reduce the temptations that will derail your progress. For example, putting your mobile phone away when you get home, or turning off your email notifier so you don't get distracted from important tasks.

Conversations to have

It's hard this change stuff. It's far easier to succeed, to maintain your motivation and to overcome the challenges you face if you have support from others. To establish this support, there are two types of conversations you need to build into your change plan: the coaching conversation and the negotiation.

- **Coaching**: Identify at least one person to coach you through your change plan. They don't need to be able to answer all your questions, they just need to be willing to give you time and be able to help you work through the challenges you face.
- **Negotiation**: Every change impacts on other people so you also need to think about realigning others' expectations of you. Think about the conversations you need to have. Whether you

want to change your working patterns or have the flexibility
to concentrate on creative projects during your working day,
it's always better to proactively address and build these changes
into your plan, rather than waiting until the issue comes to the
surface and derails your progress.

Experiment

The final element of a great change plan includes experiments (like
the ones I've included at the end of each chapter). These experiments can be one-off activities or new habits you are testing. In
most cases, they will be things you are unsure about, but feel are
worth a try. The experiments may or may not work, but either way
you'll learn something. Let's say, for example, you like the idea of
looking at email only twice a day, but you're not sure whether it will
be tolerated in your organisation. You could ask a few people what
they think, but all you will get is opinion. What you really need to
do is try out this new behaviour for a limited period of time and
assess how it works. For example, you might operate this way for a
week and measure your progress at the end of the week against criteria such as: did you get more important work done? Did you get
into trouble?

The most important thing here is the willingness to try it out,
assess how well it went, then try other stuff – and keep learning
your way forward.

Your change plan

Now it's time to write your plan of action. No one can write it for
you – the writing of the plan is part of the process – but here's a
template to get you started:

Goal
What is my specific change goal?

Preparation
What practical preparations do I need to make? (Notebook, apps.)

Social norms	**Context**	**Temptation**
Whose behaviour is aligned to my goal and how can I spend more time with them?	*How could I use my physical environment to support this change?*	*What could I do to reduce temptation to stray away from this change?*

Conversations
Who could coach me through this change? When should I speak with them?
Who do I need to negotiate with to set boundaries and realign expectations?

Experiments
Which aspects of my goal am I not sure about, but would like to experiment with?
How will I assess these experiments?

Change review
When will I hold my change review each day?
How will I ensure I stick to it?

What have I learned?

If learning to thrive is an adaptive challenge, what have I learned? Firstly, I don't pretend to have 'busy' cracked. It is a work in progress for me; but I have made big progress through the process of writing this book. I have learned some stuff about myself, and I have learned some stuff about how to respond to a world of too much. Some of those lessons have been hard-won, but they have all been valuable. I don't pretend all these will work for you; it is after all an individual journey we must all make, but I share them in the same spirit that a fellow traveller would recommend a restaurant here, or a venue there. It is just my experience; you decide if it's useful to you.

Tough choices

I have taken on too much this year. I have worked too hard. I am exhausted. I didn't need to organise myself better; I just should have made tougher choices. I have become crystal clear that the next frontier for me to address is my ability to realistically predict how long things will take, and then to decline a lot more opportunities. For a few years, when the global economy was struggling, I had to take on everything I could find. I now realise the legacy of that was more than a little debt, it was a fear that the phone may stop ringing again. This fear has hindered me this year by agreeing to too much. What has been valuable is that this year forced this fear to the surface. I can now name it, and so address it.

Focus

The very positive flip side of taking on too much at the same time as writing this book was that it forced me to focus like I have never done before. I was astonished at how much activity I could either drop altogether, delegate or downscale. I won't pretend it didn't have consequences at times, but the scale of the consequences was dwarfed by what I achieved in their stead.

One example of this is the leadership team sessions I run. These are always bespoke, and so I didn't want to cut back on interviewing folk before the event. However, I used to spend ages designing big proposals, and 'preparing' for these sessions (which included designing beautiful slide decks). I have increasingly switched to 'big idea' proposals, which are much simpler, much shorter and much quicker to write. Clients seem to prefer them to my old Word documents too! I've killed slide decks too. I was getting known for producing great visuals, and I enjoy doing them, but they are non-core to what I do. So I go into most of my sessions now without slides. In doing this I have also realised that, by not distracting myself with slideware, by going into events 'naked', I force myself to be more present with the group, to add value through what I do in the moment. It has triggered me to become braver in my facilitation.

It's not about time

On any scale I could use, this was the worst year of my life to write a book. I had no time. Yet I did it. I paid for it at times, but I did it; and I feel good about that. It has really emphasised to me the order of things. Stephen Covey was right: you choose the big rocks first, the ones you are passionate about, then fit the pebbles in around them. I could never have written this book if I hadn't just made it happen, and then dealt with the consequences. Yes, I should have put fewer pebbles in my jar, but I have no doubt that doing this book was the right thing for me.

Pulsing

For the first few months of this year I was flat-lining. I wasn't doing trivial stuff a lot of the time, I was learning and writing and working; but I was doing it without pause. As an example, I take about 100 flights a year because of work. Between podcasts of recorded lectures, my Kindle, and the odd book, I made sure every second of my travel time, including driving to the airport and going through security, were learning filled. What I became aware of was, in learning and learning and learning, I had no time and space to stand back, to integrate and to make the research and ideas I was reading and hearing into my own. I have started creating space on these trips without input or stimulation; time for intellectual ambling; all the best ideas for the book came from those times.

Big chunks

The principle that made the most dramatic difference for me in writing this book, and in my other work, was big-chunking my time. I hear many authors talk about needing to write every day for momentum, doing a few hours at set time. For me, that doesn't work at all. I work and write best in massive great chunks of time. I learned, to my cost, that a huge percentage of the writing I had done in evenings and on flights, the writing I had done in one-hour lumps, I ended up discarding. I worked best when I could put a whole day aside, and entirely engross myself in the full chapter.

While in my other work I don't need such big chunks, I have pushed to increase pretty much all the working chunks I have, and squeeze email etc. between the gaps. It works brilliantly for me.

Boxing

As a development of the big chunking idea, I have started doing something I call 'boxing' which is working really well for me. It's not rocket science but I allocate slots of time (and even locations) for only one thing. So this evening, for example, I have allocated my flight to designing an event. In doing this, it has a couple of bene-fits: I relax, knowing this particular task will be taken care of in that 'box'; I am primed and ready for the task as I go to the airport so I benefit from the Zeigarnik effect; and I don't have to decide what I'll do when I get there (the decision has been pre-made in a 'cold' state) so I get into it quicker.

Out of sight, out of mind

For me the email and phone thing became very simple; if it was out of sight, it was out of mind. I turned off my Outlook and removed all alerts. I do email in bursts at times when I'm tired through the day. I also set my phone to only download emails on demand. I make sure I can never see the phone at night or the evenings. I still often carry it, and will take calls, but I never charge it, for example, on the kitchen counter . . . it's just too tempting!

Rituals

I mentioned earlier the 'three-cups-of-tea' ritual my wife and I have. In all the craziness of this year, we have maintained rituals such as that. It has seemed that once it's ritualised, once it has a name, it happens more regularly and more often. Our three cups of tea have been critical for easing us both through this year, together.

Presence is more than time

Given how tight time has been, and how much I have travelled or disappeared into my office, I have worked hard at being present with the children. I realise how much time I am in their vicinity in normal life, but not fully present with them. This year, in contrast, some of the 10-minute moments have been rich and energising, for both of us, because I have dived whole-heartedly into that experience.

In my guilt, at one point as I was disappearing into the office for yet another weekend, I told my children I would buy them a big present each when the book was finished. A few days later I realised how wrong that was. What they had missed and what I had missed this year wasn't stuff, it was time, presence and engagement. The following day, over breakfast I announced my new plan. I told the children that, when the book was finished, as a thank you to them all for being so wonderful and patient as I wrote the book, they would all be having a day off school. Each child will do this on a separate day, so they get undiluted attention. The day was theirs to design, to do whatever they wanted. More importantly, it would be spent with Dulcie and myself, totally focused on them. At the time of writing, my daughter wants to go swimming in the morning, to McDonalds for lunch and to the beach for the afternoon. My youngest boy wants to go to a football match and the eldest is keen to try go-carting. They are infinitely more excited about this 'Book Day' than they could ever be about a present.

More me

My last, and biggest, insight builds on the previous. This year has been hard, as I have said; but I have experienced periods of sheer elation, times when I could hardly believe what I was doing and how much joy it gave me. It is the joy of walking my own path. I had the sense, on many occasions, that what I was doing at that moment was absolutely the best thing for me to be doing. At times I was hit with waves of something akin to relief that I was finally writing. More commonly, it just felt *right*.

The consequences of this I have experienced in two ways: I have been buoyed up throughout a torrid year with previously unknown levels of energy and perseverance, because I was tapping into a rich source of motivation for me; I was following my purpose. More than that, though, I feel a little more *me* at this point than I did last year. I have grown into myself more; I feel more grounded and more unique. More like the person I want to be. I'm a long way from becoming individuated in a Jungian sense; but being a bit more like Tony Crabbe feels a good place to start.

With that, I close this book. I'm done with busy. I'm off to join my family for dinner.

Thanks and good luck,

Tony.

Notes

PREFACE

1 Oliver Burkeman (2012), *The Antidote: Happiness for people who can't stand positive thinking*, Canongate Books: Edinburgh.
2 Herbert Benson, MD (1997), 'Role of the mind in physical healing and health', Testimony before the U.S. House of Representatives, published by the American Psychological Association, November.
3 'From distressed to de-stressed', (2012) Regus Media Centre, Reporting a global study of 16,000 workers.
4 The Nielsen Company (2011), 'Women of tomorrow: a study of women around the world'. A white paper reporting the Nielsen 'Women of Tomorrow' survey of 6,500 women across 21 countries.
5 American Psychological Association (2010), 'Stress in America 2010 findings'.
6 Blaine Harden (2008), 'South Koreans abuzz over their obsession with the office', *Washington Post*, 10 May.
7 Early Childhood Association India study (2012), reported by Puja Pednekar (2012), 'Parents too busy to talk to their kids, finds study', www.dnaindia.com, 25 April.
8 K. M. Sheldon and T. Kasser (1998), 'Pursuing personal goals: skills enable progress, but not all progress is beneficial', *Personality and Social Psychology Bulletin*, volume 24, pp. 1319–1331.
9 Tim Kasser (2002), *The High Price of Materialism*, Bradford Books, MIT Press: Cambridge, MA.
10 IBM Corporation (2010), 'Capitalizing on complexity: insights from the global Chief Executive Officer study'.
11 David Foster Wallace (2007), 'Deciderization 2007 – A special report' in *Both Flesh and Not* (2012), Little, Brown and Company: London.

GETTING STARTED

1 E. Langer, A. Blank and B. Chanowitz (1978), 'The mindlessness of ostensibly mindful action: the role of "placebic" information in interpersonal interaction', *Journal of Personality and Social Psychology*, volume 36, pp. 639–642.

2 Glenn Wilson (2005), a private study carried out for Hewlett-Packard, Institute of Psychiatry, University of London. This was not published, and only involved eight subjects. It is included here as being interesting and illustrative, rather than robust and solid science.

3 Gloria Mark, Victor Gonzalez and Justin Harris (2005), 'No task left behind? Examining the nature of fragmented work', *Proceedings of the Conference on Human Factors in Computer Systems*, pp. 321–330.

4 Nicholas C. Romano Jr. and J. F. Nunamaker Jr. (2001), 'Meeting analysis: findings from research and practice', *Proceedings of the 34th Hawaii International Conference on System Sciences*.

5 R. Mosvick and R. Nelson (1987), *We've Got to Start Meeting Like This!: A guide to successful business meeting management*, Scott Foresman: Glenview, IL.

6 3M Meeting Management Team and J. Drew (1994), *Mastering Meetings: Discovering the hidden potential of effective business meetings*, McGraw-Hill: New York.

7 Michael Doyle and David Straus (1996), *How to Make Meetings Work*, Time Warner International, USA.

8 R. Buehler, D. Griffin and M. Ross (1994), 'Exploring the planning fallacy: why people underestimate their task completion times', *Journal of Personality and Social Psychology*, volume 67, pp. 366–381.

9 J. R. Kelly and S. J. Karau (1999), 'Group decision making: the effects of initial preferences and time pressure', *Personality and Social Psychology Bulletin*, volume 25, pp. 1342–1354.

10 John Maeda (2006), *The Laws of Simplicity*, MIT Press: Cambridge, MA.

11 David Allen (2003), *Getting Things Done*, Piatkus: London.

12 Marc G. Berman, John Jonides and Stephen Kaplan (2008), 'The cognitive benefits of interacting with nature', *Psychological Science*, volume 19, number 12, pp. 1207–1212.

13 Ron Gutman (2011), 'The hidden power of smiling', TED talk, www.ted.com/talks/ron_gutman_the_hidden_power_of_smiling.html.

14 Ernest L. Abel and Michael L. Kruger (2010), 'Smile intensity in photographs predicts longevity', *Psychological Science*, volume 21, number 4, pp. 542–544.

SECTION 1: MASTERY

1 M. E. P. Seligman and S. F. Maier (1967), 'Failure to escape traumatic shock', *Journal of Experimental Psychology*, volume 74, pp. 1–9.

CHAPTER 1

1 Robert A. Karasek, Jr. (1979), 'Job demands, job decision latitude, and mental strain: implications for job redesign', *Administrative Science Quarterly*, volume 24, number 2, pp. 285–308.

2 S. F. Maier and M. E. P Seligman (1976), 'Learned helplessness: theory and evidence', *Journal of Experimental Psychology: General*, volume 105, number 1, pp. 3–46.

3 M. E. P. Seligman and S. Nolen-Hoeksema (1987), 'Explanatory style and depression', in D. Magnusson and A. Ohman, *Psychopathology: An Interactional Perspective*, Academic Press: New York, pp. 125–139.

4 D. F. Gucciardi and J. A. Dimmock (2008), 'Choking under pressure in sensorimotor skills: conscious processing or depleted attentional resources?', *Psychology of Sport and Exercise*, volume 9, pp. 45–59.

5 E. J. Masicampo and R. F. Baumeister (2011), 'Consider it done!: Plan making can eliminate the cognitive effects of unfulfilled goals', *Journal of Personality and Social Psychology*, volume 101, pp. 667–683.

6 Jim Loehr and Tony Schwartz (2005), *The Power of Full Engagement: Managing energy, not time, is the key to high performance and personal renewal*, Free Press: New York.

7 Leslie A. Perlow and Jessica L. Porter (2009), 'Making time off predictable—and required', *Harvard Business Review*, October, volume 87, issue 10, pp.102–09, 142.

8 A. F. T. Arnsten (1998), 'The biology of being frazzled', *Science*, 12 June, volume 280, number 5370 pp. 1711–1712.

9 Viktor E. Frankl (1959), *Man's Search for Meaning*. In the 2004 edition published by Rider, Ebury Publishing: London, p. 75.

10 M. D. Lieberman, N. I. Eisenberger, M. J. Crockett, S. M. Tom, J. H. Pfeiffer and B. M. Way (2007), 'Putting feelings into words: affect labelling disrupts amygdala activity in response to affective stimuli', *Psychological Science*, volume 18, number 5, pp. 421–428.

11 Michael J. Apter (1989), 'Reversal theory: motivation, emotion and personality', Taylor & Frances/Routledge: Florence, KY.

CHAPTER 2

1 Barry Schwartz (2005), *The Paradox of Choice: Why more is less*, HarperCollins: New York.

2 Daniel Kahneman (2012), *Thinking, Fast and Slow*, Farrar, Straus and Giroux: New York.

3 G. P. Cipriani and A. Zago (2011), 'Productivity or discrimination? Beauty and the Exams', *Oxford Bulletin of Economics and Statistics*, volume 73, issue 3, pp. 428–447.

4 B. C. Madrian and D. F. Shea (2001), 'The power of suggestion: inertia in 401(k) participation and savings behavior', *Quarterly Journal of Economics*, volume 116, number 4, pp. 1149–1187.

5 N. J. Goldstein, R. B. Cialdini and V. Griskevicius (2008), 'A room with a viewpoint: using social norms to motivate environmental conservation in hotels', *Journal of Consumer Research*, volume 35, pp. 472–482.

6 Solomon Asch (1955), 'Opinions and social pressure', *Scientific American*, volume 193, number 5, pp. 31–35.

7 B. Wansink and J. Sobal (2007), 'Mindless eating: the 200 daily decisions we unknowingly make', *Environment and Behavior*, volume 39, number 1, pp. 106–123.

8 Charles Handy (2002), *The Elephant and the Flea: Looking backwards to the future*, Random House Business: London, new edition.

9 Brian Tracy (2006), *Eat That Frog: Get more of the important things done, today!*, Berrett-Koehler Publishers, Inc.: San Francisco second edition.

10 S. Danziger, J.Levav, and L. Avnaim-Pesso (2011) 'Extraneous factors in judicial judgements'. *Proceedings of the National Academy of Science*, 26 April, volume 108, number 17, pp. 6889–6892.

11 Keith Chen (2012), 'Could your language affect your ability to save money?', TED talk, news.ted.com/talks/keith-chen-could-your-language-affect-your-ability-to-save-money.

CHAPTER 3

1 Brian Wansink (2006), *Mindless Eating: Why we eat more than we think*, Bantam: New York.

2 Nassim Nicholas Taleb (2013), *Antifragile: Things that gain from disorder*, Penguin: London.

3 P. Herriot and C. Pemberton (1995), *New Deals: The revolution in managerial careers*, Wiley: Chichester.

4 R. Fisher and W. Ury (1997), *Getting to Yes: Negotiating an agreement without giving in*, Random House Business: London, revised second edition.

5 I. Simonson (1993), 'Get closer to your customers by understanding how they make choices', *California Management Review*, volume 35, pp. 68–84.

6 A. G. Greenwald, C. G. Carnot, R. Beach and B. Young (1987), 'Increasing voting behaviour by asking people if they expect to vote', *Journal of Applied Psychology*, volume 72, pp. 315–318.

7 Stanley Milgram (1963), 'Behavioral study of obedience', *Journal of Abnormal and Social Psychology*, volume 67, number 4, pp. 371–378.

8 William Ury (2007), *The Power of a Positive No: Save the deal, save the relationship and still say no*, Hodder and Stoughton: London.

SECTION 2: FOCUS

1 Oliver Burkeman (2012), *The Antidote: Happiness for people who can't stand positive thinking*, Canongate Books: Edinburgh.

CHAPTER 4

1 Michael Porter (1996), 'What is strategy?', *Harvard Business Review*, volume 74, number 6, pp. 61–78.

2 Reference to the Nomura Institute in John Kao (1997), *Jamming: The art and discipline of business creativity*, Profile Books: London.

3 Kjell Nordström and Jonas Ridderstrale (2004), *Karaoke Capitalism: Management for mankind*, Pearson Education: UK.

4 Tim Cook quote from an interview at a Goldman Sachs Technology Conference in 2010. Reported by www.businessinsider.com.

5 R. I. M. (1992), 'Neocortex size as a constraint on group size in primates', *Journal of Human Evolution*, volume 22, number 6, pp. 469–984.

6 Broken windows example taken from Malcolm Gladwell (2000), *The Tipping Point: How little things can make a big difference*, Little, Brown: London.

CHAPTER 5

1 A. F. T. Arnsten (2009), 'The emerging neurobiology of attention deficit hyperactivity disorder: the key role of the prefrontal association cortex', *Journal of Pediatrics*, 1 May, volume 154, number 5, pp. 1–43.

2 J. C. Welch (1898), 'On the measurement of mental activity through muscular activity and the determination of a constant attention', *American Journal of Physiology*, volume 1, pp. 283–306.

3 H. Pashler, J. C. Johnston and E. Ruthruff (2001), 'Attention and performance', *Annual Review of Psychology*, volume 52, pp. 629–651.

4 David Allen (2003), *Getting Things Done*, Piatkus: London.

5 D. E. Meyer and D. E. Kieras (1997), 'A computational theory of executive cognitive processes and multiple-task performance: part 1. Basic mechanisms', *Psychological Review*, volume 104, pp. 3–65; D. E. Meyer and D. E. Kieras (1997), 'A computational theory of executive cognitive processes and multiple-task performance: part 2. Accounts of psychological refractory-period phenomena', *Psychological Review*, volume 104, pp. 749–791.

6 Jonathan B. Spira was quoted in an article entitled 'Slow down, brave multitasker, and don't read this in traffic' in the *New York Times* on 25 March 2007. The figure is based on a study carried out by his company, Basex.

7 E. Ophir, C. Nass and A. D. Wagner (2009), 'Cognitive control in media multi-taskers', *Proceedings of the National Academy of Sciences*, volume 106, number 37, pp. 15583–15587.

8 S. Adam Brasel and James Gips (2011), 'Media multitasking behavior: concurrent television and computer usage', *Cyberpsychology, Behavior and Social Networking*, volume 14, number 9, pp. 527–534.

9 Gloria Mark, Victor Gonzalez and Justin Harris (2005), 'No task left behind? Examining the nature of fragmented work', *Proceedings of the Conference on Human Factors in Computer Systems*, pp. 321–330.

10 Ibid.

11 Chip Heath and Dan Heath (2010), *Switch: How to change things when change is hard*, Random House Business: London.

12 A. J. Crum and E. J. Langer (2007), 'Mind-set matters: exercise and the placebo effect'. *Psychological Science*, volume 18, pp. 165–171.

13 Maggie Jackson (2008), *Distracted: The erosion of attention and the coming of the dark age*, Prometheus Books: New York.

14 T. Hedden and J. D. Gabrieli (2006), 'The ebb and flow of attention in the human brain', *Nature Neuroscience*, volume 9, pp. 863–865

15 David Rock (2009), *Your Brain at Work: Strategies for overcoming distraction, regaining focus, and working smarter all day long*, HarperCollins: New York.

16 Marc Berman, Jon Jonides and Stephen Kaplan (2008), 'The cognitive benefits of interacting with nature', *Psychological Science*, volume 19, number 12, pp. 1207–1212.

CHAPTER 6

1 Edward M. Hallowell (2006), *Crazybusy: Overstretched, overbooked and about to snap!*, Ballantine Books: New York, p. 9.

2 M. Baghai, S. Coley and D. White (2000), *The Alchemy of Growth: Practical insights for building the enduring enterprise*, Basic Books: New York.

3 Geoffrey A. Moore (2007), 'To succeed in the long term, focus on the middle term', *Harvard Business Review*, July–August.

4 Robert S. Kaplan and David P. Norton (1992), 'The balanced scorecard – measures that drive performance', *Harvard Business Review*, January–February.

5 Rosabeth Moss Kanter (2011), 'Zoom in, zoom out', *Harvard Business Review*, March.

6 This story is about Brigadier General Rhona Cornum from Martin Seligman (2011), *Flourish: A new understanding of happiness and well-being – and how to achieve them*, Nicholas Brealey Publishing : London.

7 Michael Shermer (2008), 'Patternicity: finding meaningful patterns in meaningless noise', *Scientific American*, 25 November.

8 Daniel T. Gilbert (1991), 'How mental systems believe', *American Psychologist*, volume 46, pp. 107–119.

9 J. Kounios and M. Beeman (2009), 'The *Aha!* moment: the cognitive neuroscience of insight', *Current Directions in Psychological Science*, volume 18, pp. 210–216.

10 Jonah Lehrer (2012), *Imagine: How Creativity Works*, Houghton Mifflin Harcourt: New York.

11 E. Polman and K. J. Emich (2011), 'Decisions for others are more creative than decisions for the self', *Personality and Social Psychology Bulletin*, volume 37, number 4, pp. 492–501.

12 Devi Shetty and Cemex stories in *The Economist* (2010), 'The world turned upside down: a special report on innovation in emerging markets', 17 April.

13 Tim Harford (2012), *Adapt: Why success always starts with failure*, Abacus: London.

14 Mihaly Csikszentmihalyi breakthrough experiment reported in Kevin P. Coyne, Patricia Gorman Clifford, and Renée Dye (2007), 'Breakthrough thinking from inside the box', *Harvard Business Review*, December.

15 Mike Marquardt (2005), *Leading with Questions: How leaders find the right solutions by knowing what to ask*, Jossey Bass: San Francisco.

16 Tim Harford (2011), 'Trial, error and the God complex', TED talk, 15 July, www.ted.com/talks/tim_harford.html.

17 John Hagel III and John Seely Brown (2013), *Institutional Innovation*, Deloitte University Press.

18 Philip E. Tetlock (2005), *Expert Political Judgement*, Princeton University Press: New York.

19 Paul Ormerod (2005), *Why Most Things Fail: And how to avoid it*, Faber and Faber: London.

20 Stuart Kauffman (1996), *At Home in the Universe: the search for the laws of self-organisation and complexity*, Oxford University Press: Oxford.

21 Lu Hong and Scott E. Page (2004), 'Groups of diverse problem solvers can outperform groups of high ability problem solvers', *Proceedings of the National Academy of Sciences*, volume 101, number 46, pp. 16385–16389.

22 Tim Harford (2012), *Adapt: why success always starts with failure*, Abacus: London.

23 D. Kahneman and A. Tversky (1979), 'Prospect theory: an analysis of decision making under risk', *Econometrica*, volume 47, pp. 263–291.

SECTION 3: ENGAGEMENT

1 Clay Shirky (2010), 'Cognitive surplus: creativity and generosity in a connected age', Penguin Press: New York.

CHAPTER 7

1 John Kay (2011), *Obliquity: Why our goals are best achieved indirectly*, Profile Books: London.

2 D. G. Myers and E. Diener (1996), 'The pursuit of happiness: new research uncovers some anti-intuitive insights into how many people are happy – and why', *Scientific American*, May, pp. 54-56.

3 Tim Kasser (2002), *The High Price of Materialism*, MIT Press: Cambridge, MA.

4 This quotation is from Tim Kasser (see above) who in turn quotes it from Kurt Anderson's article in the *New York Times Review of Books* (1999) about *The New York Thing* by Michael Lewis. Clark's actual statements can be found in Lewis M. (2000), *The New Thing: A Silicon Valley Story*, Norton: New York, pp. 259–261

5 Thorstein Veblen (1899), *Theory of the Leisure Class: An economic study in the evolution of institutions*, Macmillan: New York.

6 T. Kasser and R. M. Ryan (2001), 'Be careful what you wish for: optimal functioning and the relative attainment of intrinsic and extrinsic goals', in P. Schmuck and K. M. Sheldon (eds), *Life Goals and Well-Being: Towards a positive psychology of human striving* , Hogrefe and Huber: Goettingen, Germany, pp. 116–131.

7 K. M. Sheldon and T. Kasser (1998), 'Pursuing personal goals: skills enable progress but not all progress is beneficial', *Personality and Social Psychology Bulletin*, volume 24, pp. 1319–1331.

8 C. S. Dweck (1986), 'Motivational processes affecting learning', *American Psychologist*, volume 41, pp. 1040–1048.

9 Daniel Gilbert (2007), *Stumbling On Happiness*, Vintage Books: New York.

10 Daniel Gilbert (2004), 'The surprising science of happiness', TED talk, posted September 2006, www.ted.com/talks/dan_gilbert_asks_why_are_we_happy.html.

11 Pew Research Center (2008), 'Free time: middle america's top priority', report posted 9 July 2008 on www.pewresearch.org.

12 Joseph Campbell (1988), *The Power of Myth*, Broadway Books.

13 James March (1994), *A Primer on Decision Making: How decisions happen*, Free Press: New York.

14 Chip Heath and Dan Heath (2010), *Switch: How to change things when change is hard*, Random House Business: London.

15 Jens Förster, Ronald S. Friedman and Nira Liberman (2004), 'Temporal construal effects on abstract and concrete thinking: consequences for insight and creative cognition', *Journal of Personality and Social Psychology*, volume 87, number 2, pp. 177–189.

CHAPTER 8

1 Daniel Kahneman (2010), 'The riddle of experience over memory', TED talk, 1 March 2010, www.ted.com/talks/daniel_kahneman_the_riddle_of_experience_vs_memory.html.

2 E. M. Hallowell and J. J. Ratey (2006), *Delivered from Distraction: Getting the most out of life with attention deficit disorder*, Ballantine Books: New York.

3 B. K. Alexander (2008), *The Globalization of Addiction: A study in poverty of the spirit*, Oxford University Press: Oxford.

4 Kent C. Berridge quote from Emily Yoffe (2009), 'Seeking', on www.slate.com, 12 August.

5 Kent C. Berridge and Terry E. Robinson (1995), 'The mind of an addicted brain: neural sensitization of wanting versus liking', *Current Directions in Psychological Science*, volume 4, number 3, pp. 71–76.

6 Mihalyi Csikszentmihalyi (2002), *Flow: The classic work on how to achieve happiness*, Rider: London.

7 Daniel Gilbert (2004), 'The surprising science of happiness', TED talk, posted September 2006, www.ted.com/talks/dan_gilbert_asks_why_are_we_happy.html.

8 George Leonard (1991), *Mastery: The key to success and long-term fulfilment*, Plume: USA.

9 Fred B. Bryant and Joseph Veroff (2006), *Savoring: A new model of positive experience*, Psychology Press: Sussex.

CHAPTER 9

1 Lisa F. Berkman (1995), 'The role of social relations in health promotion', *Psychosomatic Medicine*, volume 57, pp. 245–254.

2 Lisa F. Berkman and S. Leonard Syme (1979), 'Social networks, host resistance, and mortality: a nine year follow-up study of Alameda County residents', *American Journal of Epidemiology*, volume 109, number 2, pp. 186–204.

3 Jonathan Haidt (2007), *The Happiness Hypothesis: Finding modern truth in ancient wisdom*, Arrow: London.

4 W. Fleeson, A. B. Malanos, N. M. Achille (2002), 'An intraindividual process approach to the relationship between extraversion and positive affect: is acting extraverted as "good" as being extraverted?', *Journal of Personality and Social Psychology*, volume 83, pp. 1409–1422.

5 S. Cohen and T. B. Herbert (1996), 'Health psychology: psychological factors and physical disease from the perspective of psychoneuroimmunology', *Annual Reviews of Psychology*, volume 47, pp. 113-142.

6 S. L. Brown, R. M. Nesse, A. D. Vinokur and D. M. Smith (2003), 'Providing social support may be more beneficial than receiving it: results from a prospective study of mortality', *Psychological Science*, volume 14, pp. 320–327.

7 E. Diener and M. E. P. Seligman (2002), 'Very happy people', *Psychological Science*, volume 13, pp. 80–83.

8 Sherry Turkle (2013), *Alone Together: Why we expect more from technology and less from each other*, Basic Books: New York.

9 'Phubbing' – Tom Chatfield actually attributes the term to Alex Haigh, a 23-year-old Melbourne resident, but it has been 'popularised' by Chatfield. Phubbing describes 'the act of snubbing someone in a social setting by looking at your phone instead of paying attention'. Tom Chatfield, in 'The rise of phubbing – aka phone snubbing', *Independent*, 5 August 2013.

10 Sherry Turkle (2013), *Alone Together: Why we expect more from technology and less from each other*, Basic Books: New York.

11 danah boyd study in Maggie Jackson (2008), *Distracted: The erosion of attention and the coming of the dark age*, Prometheus Books: New York.

12 R. I. M. Dunbar (1992), 'Neocortex size as a constraint on group size in primates', *Journal of Human Evolution*, volume 22, number 6, pp. 469–984.

13 Jorge Moll, Frank Krueger, Roland Zahn, Matteo Pardini, Ricardo de Oliveira-Souza and Jordan Grafman (2006), 'Human fronto-mesolimbic networks guide decisions about charitable donation', *Proceedings of the National Academy of Sciences*, 17 October, volume 103, number 42, pp. 15623–15628.

14 Carolyn E. Schwartz, Janice Bell Meisenhelder, Yunsheng Ma and George W. Reed (2003), 'Altruistic social interest behaviors are associated with better mental health', *Psychosomatic Medicine*, volume 65, number 5, pp. 778–785.

15 Kelly McGonigal (2013), 'How to make stress your friend', TED talk, September 2013, www.ted.com/talks/kelly_mcgonigal_how_to_make_stress_your_friend.html.

16 In Jonathan Haidt (2007), *The Happiness Hypothesis: Finding modern truth in ancient wisdom*, Arrow: London.

17 W. Cutler, C. Garcia, G. Higgins and G. Prett (1986), 'Sexual behaviour and steroid levels among gynecologically mature premenopausal women', *Fertility and Sterility*, volume 45, pp. 496–502.

18 Eckhart Tolle gives a nice talk on being present in relationships, without past. Find it on YouTube, 'Eckhart Tolle – being present in relationships', uploaded 4 February 2008, www.youtube.com/watch?v=vshBnR4Z9x8.

19 Barbara L. Fredrickson (1998), 'What good are positive emotions?', *Review of General Psychology*, volume 2, number 3, pp. 300–319

20 I. Altman and D. Taylor (1973), *Social Penetration: The development of interpersonal relationships*, Holt: New York.

21 M. Losada and E. Heaphy (2004), 'The role of positivity and connectivity in the performance of business teams: a nonlinear dynamics model', *American Behavioral Scientist*, volume 47, pp. 740–765. (Note: there has been some questioning of the accuracy of some of the complicated mathematics behind this ratio. It's not worth worrying about the specific number, but the principle of the ratio of positive to negative still holds)

22 John Gottman (1994), *What Predicts Divorce?: The relationship between marital processes and marital outcomes*, Erlbaum: Hillsdale, NJ.

23 S. L. Gable, H. T. Reis, E. A. Impett and E. R. Asher (2004), 'What do you do when things go right? The intrapersonal and interpersonal benefits of sharing good events', *Journal of Personality and Social Psychology*, volume 87, pp. 228–245.

24 M. E. P. Seligman, T. A. Steen, N. Park and C. Peterson (2005), 'Positive psychology progress: empirical validation of interventions', *American Psychologist*, volume 60, pp. 410–421.

CHAPTER 10

1   Richard P. Feynman (1985), *Surely You're Joking Mr Feynman: Adventures of a curious character*, W.W. Norton and Company: New York.

2   Edward Tory Higgins (1997), 'Beyond pleasure and pain', *American Psychologist*, volume 52, number 12, pp. 1280–1300.

3   Klodiana Lanaj, Chu-Hsiang 'Daisy' Chang and Russell E. Johnson (2012), 'Regulatory focus and work-related outcomes: a review and meta-analysis', *Psychological Bulletin*, volume 138, number 5, pp. 998–1034.

4   Steve Peters (2011), *The Chimp Paradox: The mind management programme to help you achieve, confidence and happiness*, Vermilion: London.

5   Ronald S. Friedman and Jens Förster (2001), 'The effects of promotion and prevention cues on creativity', *Journal of Personality and Social Psychology*, volume 81, number 6, pp. 1001–1013.

6   A. F. Arnsten (2009), 'Stress signalling pathways that impair prefrontal cortex structure and function', *Nature Reviews Neuroscience*, volume 10, pp. 410–422.

7   B. L. Frederickson and C. Branigan (2005), 'Positive emotions broaden the scope of attention and thought-action repertoires', *Cognition & Emotion*, volume 19, number 3, pp. 313–332.

8   American Psychological Association (2010), 'Stress in America 2010 findings', www.apa.org/news/press/releases/stress/2010/national-report.pdf.

9   James Gross (2002), 'Emotion regulation: affective, cognitive, and social consequences', *Psychophysiology*, volume 39, pp. 281–291.

10 P. R. Goldin, K. McRae, W. Ramel and J. J. Gross (2008), 'The neural basis of emotion regulation: reappraisal and suppression of negative emotions', *Biological Psychiatry*, volume 63, pp. 577–586.

11 K. N. Ochsner, R. D. Ray, J. C. Cooper, S. Robertson, J. D. Chopra, J. D. Gabrieli and J. J. Gross (2004), 'For better for worse: neural systems supporting the cognitive down and up-regulation of negative emotion', *Neuroimage*, volume 23, number 2, pp. 483–499.

12 T. A. Judge, E. A Locke, C. C. Durham (1997), 'The dispositional causes of job satisfaction: a core evaluations approach', *Research in Organisational Behavior*, volume 19, pp. 151–188.

13 Brené Brown (2010), 'The power of vulnerability', TED talk, December 2010, www.ted.com/talks/brene_brown_on_vulnerability.html; Brené Brown (2012), 'Listening to shame', TED talk, March 2012, www.ted.com/talks/brene_brown_listening_to_shame.html.

14 This exercise is based on James Pennebaker's writing exercise, described, along with the robust supporting evidence of its effectiveness, in Timothy D. Wilson (2011), *Redirect: The surprising new science of psychological change*, Little, Brown and Company: New York.

15 J. E. Maddux and R. W. Rogers (1983), 'Protection motivation and self-efficacy: a revised theory of fear appeals and attitude change', *Journal of Experimental Social Psychology*, volume 19, pp. 469–479.

16 M. Csikszentmihalyi (1998), *Finding Flow*, Basic Books: New York.

17 D. H. Schunk (1991), 'Self-efficacy and academic motivation', *Educational Psychologist*, volume 26, number 3–4, pp. 207–231.

18 The Liverpool story comes from an article by Ian Herbert in the *Independent*, 'Dr Steve Peters: the psychiatrist charged with ridding Anfield of the fear factor', 28 March 2013.

19 Vilayanur Ramachandran (2012), *The Tell-Tale Brain: A neuroscientist's quest for what makes us human*, W.W. Norton and Company: New York.

20 Peter Drucker (1954), *The Practice of Management*, Harper Business: New York.

CHAPTER 11

1 Leroy Watson Jr (2009), 'Forgotten stories of courage and inspiration: Glenn Cunningham', 12 June, www.bleacherreport.com.

2 K. Patterson, J. Grenny, D. Maxfield, R. McMillan and A. Switzler (2011), *Change Anything: The new science of personal success*, Piatkus: London.

3 S. Booth-Butterfield and B. Reger (2004), 'The message changes belief and the rest is theory: the "1% milk or less" campaign and reasoned action', *Preventive Medicine*, volume 39, pp. 581–588.

4 R. B. Cialdini and D. A. Schroeder (1976), 'Increasing compliance by legitimizing paltry contributions: when even a penny helps', *Journal of Personality and Social Psychology*, volume 34, pp. 599–604.

5 Howard Leventhal, Robert Singer and Susan Jones (1965), 'Effects of fear and specificity of recommendation upon attitudes and behavior', *Journal of Personality and Social Psychology*, volume 2, number 1, pp. 20–29.

6 W. Hofmann, R. F. Baumeister, G. Forster and K. D. Vohs (2012), 'Everyday temptations: an experience sampling study of desire, conflict, and self-control', *Journal of Personality and Social Psychology*, volume 102, number 6, pp. 1318–1335.

7 Roy E. Baumeister, Ellen Bratslavsky, Mark Muraven and Dianne M. Tice (1998), 'Ego depletion: is the active self a limited resource?', *Journal of Personality and Social Psychology*, volume 74, number 5, pp. 1252–1265.

8 M. Oaten and K. Cheng (2006), 'Longitudinal gains in self-regulation from regular physical exercise', *British Journal of Health Psychology*, volume 11, pp. 713–733.

9 M. Oaten and K. Cheng (2006), 'Improved self-control: the benefits of a regular program of academic study', *Basic and Applied Social Psychology*, volume 28, pp. 1–16.

10 M. Oaten and K. Cheng (2006), 'Improvements in self-control from financial monitoring', *Journal of Economic Psychology*, volume 28, pp. 487–501.

11 M. Bateson, D. Nettle and G. Roberts (2006), 'Cues of being watched enhance cooperation in a real world setting', *Biology Letters*, volume 2, pp. 412–414.

12 B. Wansink (2006), *Mindless Eating: Why we eat more than we think*, Bantam Books: New York.

13 D. T. D. de Ridder, G. Lensvelt-Mulders, C. Finkenauer, F. M. Marijn Stok and R. F. Baumeister (2012), 'Taking stock of self-control: a meta-analysis of how trait self-control relates to a wide range of behaviors', *Personality and Social Psychology Review*, volume 16, number 1, pp. 76 –99.

14 For more on StickK.com see Ian Ayres (2010), *Carrots and Sticks: Unlock the power of incentives to get things done*, Bantam: New York.

15 In R. F. Baumeister and J. Tierney (2011), *Willpower: Rediscovering the greatest human strength*, Penguin: New York.

16 Ronald Heifetz (1994), *Leadership Without Easy Answers*, Harvard University Press: Cambridge, MA.

17 R. Kegan and L. Lahey (2009), *Immunity to Change: How to overcome it and unlock the potential in yourself and your organisation*, Harvard Business School Press: Cambridge, MA.

Index